Training and Supervision in Sport and Exercise Psychology

Training and Supervision in Sport and Exercise Psychology presents a labyrinth of choices and challenges for trainees and supervisors, such as training and supervision mixing the science of doing sport and exercise psychology with the art of judgement and decision-making to deliver services to athletes. With a multitude of skills to master and competencies to gain, trainees and supervisors need assurances about best practice in their field and the assessments they can trust.

Including cases, trainee autobiographical cases, and examples of good practice drawn from current and ex-trainees who have become sport psychology consultants, this book aims to educate trainees how to deal competently with professional and ethical guidelines. We aim to educate trainees to get started in service delivery, set up placement, work with clients, use supervision effectively, conduct academic research, and write sound assessments before preparing for a viva voce and beginning the transition to the workplace. This book shall serve trainees and their supervisors on their journey through to qualified status.

Training and supervision to become a sport and exercise psychologist is of the utmost importance in the growing profession of sport and exercise psychology. This book aims to bring clarity, guidance, and support to learning and mastering professional skills in applied sport psychology service delivery. This book is key reading for undergraduates and postgraduates studying sport and exercise psychology and those studying for taught and professional doctorates in sport and exercise psychology.

Paul McCarthy, PhD, leads the taught doctorate in sport and exercise psychology at Glasgow Caledonian University, UK. He is a BPS chartered psychologist, HCPC registered sport and exercise psychologist, and Senior Teaching Fellow. He developed the first taught doctorate in sport and exercise psychology in Scotland and the UK.

Sahen Gupta, PhD, is a lecturer and practitioner in sport and exercise psychology at the University of Portsmouth, UK. He has published peer-reviewed papers in psychology and sport and exercise psychology in SCOPUS indexed journals, including in Frontiers in Psychology. He specialises in resilience, positive environments, integrative psychotherapy, and youth sport environments.

Lindsey Burns, PhD, is a senior lecturer in psychology at Glasgow Caledonian University, UK. Lindsey is a chartered psychologist with the British Psychological Society and an HCPC practitioner health psychologist. She is a Senior Fellow with AdvanceHE, a member of the BPS Division of Coaching Psychology and holds qualifications in coaching.

Bryan McCann, PhD, is a BPS chartered sport and exercise psychologist and HCPC practitioner psychologist. Bryan provides psychological support to a range of national, international, and Olympic level athletes and teams in different sports, including football, golf, swimming, table tennis, and skiing and provides consultancy for organisations such as the Scottish FA, The Camanachd Association, Scottish Swimming, and Sport Scotland.

Training and Supervision in Sport and Exercise Psychology

Paul McCarthy, Sahen Gupta, Lindsey Burns, and Bryan McCann

Routledge
Taylor & Francis Group
NEW YORK AND LONDON

Designed cover image: Dr Sahen Gupta

First published 2024
by Routledge
605 Third Avenue, New York, NY 10158

and by Routledge
4 Park Square, Milton Park, Abingdon, Oxon, OX14 4RN

Routledge is an imprint of the Taylor & Francis Group, an informa business

ISBN: 978-1-032-43418-6 (hbk)
ISBN: 978-1-032-43417-9 (pbk)
ISBN: 978-1-003-36720-8 (ebk)

DOI: 10.4324/9781003367208

Typeset in Times New Roman
by KnowledgeWorks Global Ltd.

To Lesley, Liam, Euan, and Niamh, for all time.
—Dr Paul McCarthy

To Sudhesh Sir, Santhosh Sir, Sreenath Sir, Piyali Ma'am, and Subhra Sir, gurus who taught me how to learn.
—Dr Sahen Gupta

Contents

Acknowledgements

Thank you to David Varley and Megan Smith from Routledge for their encouragement, support, and guidance. Thank you also to the students and staff we work alongside for their vision, engagement, and compassion.

Thank you to all our teachers, past, present, and future.

Section I

Getting Started

1 Being a Trainee Psychology Consultant

Introduction

If you have just picked this book and are flipping through it (or scrolling), you may be wondering how it might help you. You may already be on your training journey, considering beginning your training journey or even be close to its completion. The intention of this chapter is to summarise the lived experience of being a trainee, so that you can find resonance in the journey that you are on, with others who have been on this journey. With the increased professionalisation of sport psychology, there are many qualifications, numerous routes or pathways of training, many styles of working, and many areas of development (see Chapter 2). More often than not, trainees feel overwhelmed by the newness and the sheer volume of it all. In this chapter, we unpick the essentials and provide you with a blueprint of how to navigate this journey from reflections of a trainee's journey.

Let's explore, reflect, discover or even stumble upon *your* normal for this journey.

Preparing for a career as a sport psychology consultant

There are many careers in the world. There are various careers in sport and exercise. You could be a coach, a physiotherapist, a performance analyst, a Strength & Conditioning Coach (S&C), physiologist, manager, logistics division, and so on. Why choose to be a sport psychology consultant?

Similarly, there are many careers in the field of psychology. You could be a psychologist working in clinical, health, counselling, cognitive, forensic, legal, education, research, neuropsychology, or other settings to name a few. Why choose to be a sport psychology consultant?

Answering this question is an important starting point. What were some of the thought processes and personal/professional needs that informed this decision to be a sport psychology consultant? Likewise, if you are reviewing multiple paths and this is one of them, it is an important question to consider. We will use the transtheoretical model of behaviour change (Sutton, 1997), to guide this self-reflective process:

1 Precontemplation (oh, this seems interesting/is a good option)
2 Contemplation (I need to do some research and uncover more about this field and how it may look like as a career)
3 Preparation (what plans or actions do I need to take to embark on this career path?)
4 Action (I am starting my higher education in psychology/sport science/sport and exercise psychology, is there anything I need to do beyond it?)
5 Maintenance (I need to look at development opportunities, what are some postgraduate routes? What will the finances look like? What about this do I enjoy? What are the next steps in my development?)

DOI: 10.4324/9781003367208-2

This five-stage model originated from health behaviour change research, but is often helpful to review any behavioural decisions. If you are preparing or starting your journey, try to take a pause here and ask yourself these questions. If you have already begun your journey, then try to reflectively trace the stages that have informed you and your journey so far. The purpose of this exercise is twofold: (a) to provide you with an understanding of the motives, intentions, and motivations driving your decision; (b) to start the process of reflective awareness. Let's see how this looks in the 'Life Lived' box below.

Life Lived

My journey to be a sport psychology consultant was an unconventional one. But as I keep reminding myself, my clients, and trainees, 'one simply cannot decide whether they want to watch the movie, after they have watched the movie'. I did my Bachelor's in Psychology, Sociology, and English (Triple Major) from India and worked as a Project Coordinator for a life skills-based intervention which had components of sport (see Sudhesh et al., 2021). This started my pre-contemplation around a potential career in sports as a subfield of psychology. Drawing upon my experience playing competitive sport, I then looked at avenues for opportunities within the field. Not being too sure, I did my undergraduate project with athletes (Gupta & Sudhesh, 2019), and this began my initial foray in sport psychology, (i.e., contemplation). I armed myself with this certainty because I had done clinical psychology and rehabilitation psychology internships – they were not my cup of tea. My preparation stage was linked to action – trying to find out educational institutions where I can pursue higher education and become a sport psychology consultant. I found there were limited opportunities in India and also in the Global South. A long-drawn visa affair, scholarship applications, and frustrations later, the action of going across three continents to study because a reality. Maintenance was a challenging state for me because I also had part-time work in a new country to cover the non-tuition costs of living. I also had to secure a placement in a city and country I had lived in all of 98 days. I started early, putting myself through the contemplation (what sport? What club?), preparation (reaching out, sending my CVs, asking my supervisor), and action (going for visits to cubs, giving interviews). Maintenance was also made challenging by the fact that COVID happened. I had to re-train myself in digital psychotherapy and interventions – here the model came in handy again.

Career development and understanding of all factors

Career development has been defined as a lifelong process of managing learning and work in order to live and work with purpose and create a quality life (Bezanson, 2003, p. 9). In preparing to be a sport psychology consultant, this is a helpful definition to guide our understanding of career development. In sport, athletes change, coaches change, playing patterns change, and sport changes. The person we are changes and develops through stages and time as well.

First, career development is a lifelong process. An athlete's career lasts between 5 and 20 years, with the average being 10 years. The sport psychology consultant will typically have a career span of 20–35 years. Therefore, we view career development as a process that unfolds. By having this approach, we can recognise that aims, priorities, and the nature of work will probably change. For example, a trainee might start off thinking that they want to work in elite pro football but may find meaningful working in developmental tennis and community sport and therefore shift career path. Second, we need to consider the person behind the professional (i.e., the values, interests, personal goals, personal demands and the different roles in our lives). Third, we can view career development as a 'managing' task that we have an active choice and role in. This allows us as sport psychology consultants to seek developmental training, continue learning, adapt to complex environments, and keep a continuous reflection cycle rather than think of a career as a static entity. Remember – humans change. Generational changes and challenges appear too. For example, in 2023, when I work with a 28-year-old athlete compared to a 16-year-old athlete, I have to rely on different reference points, cultural and linguistic references, and even technological elements.

It is therefore helpful to trace the different levels within which our career development takes place. Preparing to be a sport psychology consultant means we can chart this out at the following levels:

1. **Individual level** (our personal beliefs, values, life stage, career stage, personal needs, and motives)
2. **Sport level** (the specific factors of sport, demands of the sport you are working with, and contextual sport factors)
3. **Organisational level** (nature of organisation of work, licensing, professional development, job-specific organisational level, job role, and organisational environment)
4. **Global level** (multicultural factors, diversity, advances in knowledge, and nature of sport)

We consider each of these levels and with reflective examples in the 'Life Lived' box below.

Life Lived

I write this sitting on a veranda surrounded by plants of many kinds, several of whom I cannot name. It is raining, a proper tropical downpour in the middle of August. I sit here in the familiar thoughts of thunder lashing through the sky. The red soil that interspaces the grass and trees smells rusty and earthy at the same time. This is familiar. I have had many a cricket game and quite a few tennis matches rained out for this growing up. But I also think of the icy-cold breath, the crisp wind that leaves a cold embrace on your face and the pinpricks of smattering rain that usually characterise Glasgow in November. They are both part of my habitus and our experiences of how things are, our expectations of how things should be. My habitus also includes being stuck in traffic and not being able to do anything about it. It includes seeing talented individuals sacrificing aspirations to circumstantial realities. It includes a constant battle between orthodoxy and liberal. It includes 'working hard will get you everything you want' and 'working smart will get you everything you need'. I work hard because I have seen everyone around me at it as a basic part of life – there was no other option; it is now a core belief. I am a male single child, but ever since I was 17, I had deep interpersonal relationships with females, allowing me to understand that experiences of this world are often gendered. I wanted to work in sport because it is an arena where people work together to achieve a target. Perhaps that motive had Maslow's belongingness need somewhere in there too. These are all my 'default settings' – what are yours?

The individual level: Who am I? Who do I want to be?

An essential starting point for career planning is to understand the *person* behind the professional. This is even more relevant to the career as a sport psychology consultant since the sport psychology consultant is a psychologist, and with it, they have to consider their motivations, limitations, strengths, interests, life goals, age-stage needs, and biases.

An occupation differs from a profession since (a) there is an element of interactive practice with humans; and (b) practising members are expected to develop professional identities (cf. Costello, 2005, p. 17; Poczwardowski et al., 2004). Our identity of who we are as people are our constructed habitats. Habitus constitutes 'cognitive and corporeal schemata of perception, appreciation and action that agents engage in their practice' (Bourdieu, 1990, p. 401). It sets a defined and stable pattern of how we perceive things, what we value, and what behaviours we engage in. Habitus has three elements:

1 The individuals' **unconscious assumptions** of how the world works.
2 The **'tastes' and preferences** we have as individuals which are formed because of the individual's upbringing and constitute a core part of identity. Some key elements are cultural micro-interactions such as the meaning behind actions, gestures, and other social information that we use to make snap assessments, lived experience, and other 'default settings'.
3 The **emotional identity** referring to the different emotional orientations which to a degree are shaped by characteristics such as gender, race, socio-economic status, national heritage, and others (Costello, 2005). This is then further shaped by the training received which moulds, shapes, and, at times, re-shapes it.

As we can see, the different areas of habitus allow us to get an initial understanding of who we are as people. It is also important to consider our habitus in line with our different roles (e.g. parent, psychologist, student, partner, individual, friend, researcher, etc.).

Schein (1980) proposed that across the development of a career, we engage in a gradual clarification of our own self-image around our professional lives, needs, talents, skills, values, and motives. He proposed this process is like finding a 'career anchor' where the anchor is a set of needs, skills, and values that the person will give up only if forced to make a choice. We outline the anchors below. Reflect on these to identify a list that you think is essential for a psychologist.

1 **Technical/functional competence:** learning, refining, and continuously developing your core skillset for applied practice. You derive your sense of identity from being 'technically good' (e.g., 'My CBT formulation skills are excellent because I have 200 hours of training in it'). You typically find meaning and joy when your job role allows you to apply these skills.
2 **Managerial competence:** looking for vertical growth within an organisation to engage in managerial tasks to integrate multiple individual's efforts and be responsible for a particular unit. Example: being the head sport psychology consultant in an academy pathway responsible for a team of three sport psychology consultants. You typically enjoy the responsibility, collaboration, and power associated with it.
3 **Security/stability:** financial, contractual, and other forms of professional stability in professional life. Examples include a permanent contract, a clear process of planning and career progression within contractual parameters, and others. You typically want to have the feeling of security as a person and a professional.
4 **Autonomy/independence:** the need to have a high degree of autonomy in the job role that allows you to set tasks, decide timelines, and choose areas of application to provide you with

flexibility regarding how and when you work. You typically enjoy that sense of autonomy and do not enjoy rigid structural parameters in professional and personal life.

5 **Service/cause dedication:** seeking larger causes of professional goals that signify the achievement of something of value, to win over difficult circumstances and to overcome obstacles for a larger achievement. An example could be 'I want to work with this squad to achieve Premiership qualification over the next two seasons' or 'I want to work with this team for the next Olympic cycle and target a medal winning programme development'. This typically involves a need for a sense of accomplishment from these tasks.
6 **Lifestyle integration:** when you value a situation that permits you to balance personal with professional (i.e., the personal needs, family needs, and career requirements are placed on an equal importance). You typically strive to achieve this 'balance' and over time seek opportunities and prioritise this integration.
7 **Pure challenge:** the continuous striving to work on seemingly unsolvable problems, win over tough situations, and make the jump to solve big issues despite obstacles and pragmatic barriers, or when others would discourage you. You typically feel a sense of purpose and a need to prove that it can be done.

Life Lived

Reflecting upon my trainee journey, I realised that there was often a shift from one thing to the other – like going on a trek. I am a person who likes to have goals. I am also a person who takes structured action towards those goals. Through the three years of my training, I had different milestones. These were decided upon based on my existing competencies and skills at that point, as well as areas I thought needed improvement. For example, I had extensive 'Managerial Competence' because I had previously held leadership positions coordinating projects with a team of 40 people. So, I knew what the fundamentals of working with a large team were. However, I did not have any prior experience with that in sport. Therefore, I set developing Managerial Competency in sport as a priority and sought experiences during placement which would allow me to do that.

A different pattern happened for Autonomy/Independence. I am a person who values autonomy and can function independently without extensive micromanagement – in fact; I prefer it. I set processes with my supervisor to agree to bi-weekly meetings where I would ask questions, get suggestions, critical inputs and make plans which I would autonomously target and follow up. By contrast, a friend of mine on the course struggled with autonomously hitting all targets and decided that she would also opt for extensive peer supervision in research.

Identify your anchor, how it helps you get the best learning experience and plan accordingly.

Some reflective questions to help you understand your habitus and priority process are as follows:

- If I had to put three core values I have across all scenarios of life, what would they currently be?
- What are the various work and life roles I occupy? Which has the highest psychological demands, which has the highest psychological satisfaction.

- What professional experience have I had that has allowed me to be me? (express my values, my skills, fit into the environment, etc.).
- When have I felt most fulfilled at work? What can this tell me about my professional anchors.
- What is my long-term vision about how I want to live my personal life and professional life.
- Do I have a deep understanding of my values/priorities/interests at this points of time? What are my strengths and limitations.

The sport level: What sport? Why? Why now?

As a sport psychology consultant, your applied practice will be in sport at any level or in several roles or in exercise. An obvious example is working as a sport psychology consultant for an Olympic team, a professional club, or a pro athlete in golf. Other examples include working as an organisational psychologist in sport, leisure management, player development pathway, researcher, coach development roles, and similar educational roles. There are many factors to consider while choosing which sport to work with or in. While all sport shares some common factors, each sport has its own unique traits that play a role in the job of a sport psychology consultant. For example, tennis players travel every 10 days for competitions; their staff-support travels with them. Some leagues have home and away formats. Endurance sports like a rallying have five-day blocks in extreme weather (e.g. Dakkar Rally or the Ouninpohja Rally in Finland). Some factors to consider while you plan and prepare for a career are:

- **Familiarity with sport:** we are familiar with certain sports and we are not familiar with others. There are 40 sport categories in the Paris 2024 Olympics, and it is estimated that there are 3000+ competitive sports in the world (World Sport Encyclopaedia). It is unlikely that we will be familiar with the rules, regulations, and demands of every sport. Often, trainee sport psychology consultants choose this career path because they have been involved in a sport to a certain extent or are ex-athletes themselves. This is an important point to consider since being a sport psychology consultant in a sport differs from being a coach/player/logistics manager in that sport. This brings in considerations of the dual role which we detail later on (see Chapter 2). Two key questions to ask are: Do I feel comfortable in my ability to learn about this sport during my role as a sport psychology consultant?; and Does this sport environment allow me to learn and develop?
- **Level of sport and specialisation:** there are different levels of sport ranging from community, development, performance pathways, and, of course, the professional level elite sport. Each level has different demands and job roles. Each of the levels and the job roles within also has their own distinct professional ladders. Placement and supervised experience during your trainee days help to figure this dilemma out. Another element to reflect upon is the idea of how your personal needs or desires are influencing this choice. For example, is your abandoned playing career in football a driver behind the intention to be a sport psychology consultant in elite football? A final consideration is also the choice between specialisations at the level of a single sport or multi-sport.

The organisational level: What organisational context?

As individuals, we often work within organisational contexts. This is more apparent when we work for a professional team, club, or sports institute. But this also holds true if we run a small practice or work individually with athletes as a sport psychology consultant. Therefore, we operate within a social network in the organisation. These networks, at times, determine career opportunities, progression and may act as obstacles. For example, elite sport has time challenges, organisational constraints, multiple stakeholders, constant changes in personnel, power politics, interpersonal conflict, external pressure, financial outcomes, and other challenges stemming from the organisation which are external to the performance challenges on field of play (see Eubank et al., 2014; McDougall et al., 2015).

So, what might certain considerations be?

- **Conceptualisation of organisational role:** what role do I have in the organisation and what are the key functions of the role? Is the role clearly outlined? For example, applied sport psychology consultants often have the role of a sport psychology consultant or mental training coach within the academy set-up. At other times, they may work as player performance coordinator or player lifestyle manager or player development guide. At other times, they may work with hospitals and universities for community sport and exercise interventions. It is important to know what the conceptualisation of the role is.
- **Responsibilities:** what are the key responsibilities that I have to fulfil as a part of my job role? Do I have the skills to fulfil these responsibilities? Is there support should I need it? Are these responsibilities clearly outlined in my role? This process typically involves reviewing the essential and desirable skills needed for the job role and mapping it against one's training, professional experience, and career goals.
- **Demands-facilitators:** what are the demands this career will place on me? What are some facilitators or 'selling points' that will aid me? This may include considerations of personal goals such as considerations of where to live, financial compensation aspired for, and others.
- **Organisational culture:** what is the larger collection of expectations, values, and practices that guides and informs actions of everyone in the organisation? For example, a sporting organisation may offer a very lucrative role and salary but have a high turnover, with a very rigid culture unamenable to change. Another role might be within a flexible organisation, with new management looking to change and develop, but does not offer as high a financial compensation.
- **Professional development:** will this role (a) allow me to implement and develop the skills I have received during my training? (b) allow me the opportunity to continue my professional and personal development?
- **Time commitment and periods:** what time does the job role require of me? Organisational roles in sport typically operate around sport season cycles (World Cup, World Championships, Leagues, Olympic cycles, and others). Typically, these require a greater commitment of time (and travel) during major events. Some other sports (e.g. leagues that follow home-away format) require travel every other weekend. It is important to consider the impact this has on the person and their capacity to fulfil their job role.

These organisational factors are a key determinant of how the sport psychology consultant applies their skills to the context for effective practice. Person-specific decisions also allow the individual to continue development. Let's look at the 'Life Lived (Three Lives)' box for a couple of examples.

Life Lived (Three Lives)

An experienced practitioner today started out in the 1990s after his training, when sport psychology was a field often discussed in hushed tones and very much about to grow. He told me how there were few sport psychology consultants, even fewer women in the field, and how there was always an uphill battle to 'smuggle' psychology into the sport context. He noted how in those initial days (in his late 20s), he said yes to everything and tried to grab every opportunity he could. He honestly noted that 'everything was professional development' and that factors such as organisational culture barely factored in his decision-making.

In the mid-2000s and 2010s, things started changing a lot more with the increased inclusion of sport science provisions into professional sport. Money became an important factor, with sport being funded better, and therefore becoming an area where support provisions opened up. Throughout this time, there was a massive push towards the commercialisation of sport, which organisations being run similar to corporations. As he also looked to start a family, he looked at 'demands-facilitators' quite a lot more in terms of fiscal stability, time away from family, and job stressors. This coincided with a successful Olympic game for the squad he was working with, giving him 'social capital' and seniority in the field. In the late 2010s to present, he is an experienced practitioner who balances private practice and university research. This choice was driven by his 'Conceptualisation of Organisational Role' which for him was signalled by the importance of taking the field forward through improved research and train the next generation of sport psychology consultant. It was also motivated by the desire to cut down on travel time because of other life responsibilities.

The global level: Culture, geopolitics, socio-economic

In the 1940s, Alan Barth said, 'News is the first rough draft of history'. The saying was made popular by Philip Graham, co-owner of the *Washington Post* newspaper. Fast forward to August 2013, Bill Gates says, 'the internet is becoming the town square for the global village of tomorrow'. In the 70 years between the sayings, humans went from newspapers to space, back down on earth for high-speed internet. The common theme: global connectivity and human connection. In a decade since 2013, artificial intelligence can now write and edit drafts (this book is not written by it, I assure you) and has been compared to the discovery and popular use of electricity.

Considerations of being a psychologist come with inherent considerations of global factors that affect human beings. This is because the individual does not live in a cultural vacuum. With the interconnectivity of technology, this is even more important to consider. Take, for example, an athlete I worked with. He was an Indian swimmer. He loves Tom Daley, because he is one of the 3 million Instagram followers Tom Daley has. He considers him a role model, although there is little in common between them. The increasing nature of global interconnectivity also opens up considerations of geopolitics. For example, you may have all the qualifications and grades needed to study in a country, only to be denied a study visa because there is a trade dispute. We look at elements of how the global level influences the individual. The goal is to reflect on these considerations while preparing your career.

- **Personal knowledge:** who we are as individuals can be traced to the personal knowledge we hold about how the world operates. This personal knowledge has been shaped within the cultural environment that we grow up in. This is what we consider 'normal'. This also extends to language, food, eat-sleep patterns, meaning of sport, ideas on what a career should be, what personal life should be and others. This affects both us and our clients. For example, I (SG) was invited to a colleague's home for dinner in Glasgow. I was at the supermarket picking a wine around 6 pm, with a travel time of approximately 40 minutes. I got a phone call from him asking if I was coming or not. It was my first introduction to the cultural reality that people in the UK have dinner around 6 pm.

- **Intersectionality:** this refers to the interconnected and overlapping nature of social identities and categories that any individual holds. Examples include race, culture, gender, sexual orientation, caste, religion, and others. Your identity may have one or more levels of intersectionality which may act as a facilitator (i.e., privilege) or roadblock (i.e., hindrance) to your career. For example, research has indicated it is more difficult for women to gain access to and work in male professional sport teams with several instances of sexism (Goldman & Gervis, 2021). Existing accounts also highlight the difficulty non-western, non-white ethnicity/race individuals have in securing training and gaining entry in professional sport (Gupta, 2022).
- **Global trends:** these refer to the larger influence of culture, geopolitics, economic systems, financial stability, intercontinental mobility, and other factors that are common to sport. For example, in the 1990s, basketball became a global phenomenon, with Michael Jordan and the Chicago Bulls coinciding with the rise of the internet. Three decades later, basketball is a well-funded sport where sport psychology consultants are actively at play. Cricket is another example of an increase in popularity and funding with the launch of the IPL in 2008. On a geopolitical and financial basis, global economic trends also affect sport. For example, in 2009, post the financial crisis and recession, sport witnessed a drop in sponsorships which had a knock-on effect on sport funding and therefore limited job opportunities.
- **Technology:** it is a rapidly evolving scene, and it has already affected the work of a sport psychology consultant. In the last decade, sport has actively incorporated technologies within biomechanics, virtual reality, performance analysis, and in sport and exercise psychology as well. These may include simple wearable technologies, such as heart rate trackers, to gauge the level of pre-competitive anxiety.

Some reflective questions to guide you at the global level as you prepare are as follows:

- What are the national and global trends that are currently taking place in sport and how do they affect the profession of sport and exercise psychology?
- What opportunities/constrains are present in the current global scenario?
- How do I trace the impact of global, national, and cultural factors that shape my clients experiences and expectations?
- What do I offer that is 'unique'?
- How do I manage tension and friction that may arise from global factors at the systemic level that impacts my individual clients and team?

Being a trainee: Stitching an identity, not printing it

A quote I read early in my training journey talked about skills as 'the essential element of any skill is the ability to implement a sequence of choices to achieve objectives' (Nelson-Jones, 2005). By its very definition, this implies that the development of skill will also require the individual to go through a sequence of choices. Therefore, throughout this book, we refer to the process of learning and being a trainee.

As psychologists, we know from research that there are variables and variances in people: historical, current, biological, personality, cultural, cognitive, and others. Such variances exist in trainees too and make comparisons extremely difficult. All training journeys are *differently experienced* even though the institutional step-by-step process may be shared. Therefore, we say it's stitching together an identity. Stitching gives the process an innately personalised and unique outcome, compared to it being printed off a big, depersonalised central machine. Let's begin your journey now!

2 Setting the Scene

Guidelines for Ethical Professional Practice

Introduction

Most people who read this book are somewhere on their journey to become a sport psychology consultant. Perhaps you are thinking about training in sport and exercise psychology once you complete your postgraduate degree or perhaps you are picking your way through the necessities of a taught programme (e.g., at a university) or independent (e.g., British Psychological Society Stage 2) training route. Wherever you find yourself on your journey, we are glad to be travelling with you.

Most journeys through training programmes puzzle and panic trainees because, though there might be several helpful signposts along the way, one rarely feels convinced they are going the right way. One reason some trainees feel perplexed about the training routes lies with choice. Not only do trainees have multiple training routes (e.g., British Psychological Society (BPS) and British Association of Sport & Exercise Sciences (BASES) within the UK), different therapeutic approaches (e.g., cognitive behaviour therapy (CBT), rational emotive behaviour therapy (REBT), person-centred therapy, (PCT)), and academic qualifications (e.g., taught doctorate or a professional doctorate) to choose from, but also, they need to select the most accessible and economic option for their circumstances (Eubank & Tod, 2018). For instance, you might wish to train independently, but you value the company of other trainees to share learning experiences and gain a doctoral qualification along the way. Or you feel passionate about training in a person-centred approach, but this approach does not feature on your chosen university's curriculum.

With all these choices, where is best to begin? We suggest you begin with you. What are your values, motives, and interests? Where does your passion lie in sport and exercise psychology? How would you like to contribute to the field? Your unique mix of these foundations shapes your approach to training, how much you invest in it, and how much you reap from it. Though you may not have answers to all these questions now, many of these answers reveal themselves throughout the training programme and grow with your adventures. Training to become a sport psychology consultant means you are joining and shaping the professionalisation of our industry. You will meet people who agree with your views and those who disagree with your views. What matters most, however, is to take your opportunity to shape our profession for the good of the people within it and those who choose to use our services. The field of service delivery in sport and exercise psychology is overflowing with energy, opportunity, and challenge!

Why do you need this book?

As the field of sport and exercise psychology grows, we are witnessing more students undertaking education, training, and supervision. Leading standards for education, training, and supervision are crucial to ensure trainees are professional, competent, ethically secure, and innovative

DOI: 10.4324/9781003367208-3

scientist-practitioners fully suited to service delivery in sport. But trainees seeking work in the dynamic and unique nature of sport still have to revert to more traditional resources from counselling and clinical psychology to navigate the shifting tides of education, training, and supervision to contribute to their professional development. This book shows trainees how to use their education, training, practicum placement, supervision, and research opportunities to develop into holistic scientist-practitioners.

Briefly, the aim of this book includes educating trainees how to deal competently with professional and ethical guidelines to get started in service delivery. Next, the trainee learns to establish practicum placement, work with clients, use supervision effectively, conduct academic research, and write comprehensive assessments before preparing for a viva voce and beginning the transition to the workplace. This book will also include cases, trainee autobiographical cases, and examples of good practice drawn from current and ex-trainees who have become sport psychology practitioners.

This book offers trainees a map to navigate the education, training, and supervision typical in a doctoral programme (e.g., taught doctorate, professional doctorate) or independent training route (e.g., BPS or BASES within the UK). We, as educators, practitioners, and supervisors, amassed much experience over the past 20 years and witness consistent gaps for trainees wishing to become sport psychology consultants. The key gaps we see fall into five categories. First, trainees need a sound grounding in guidelines for professional practice (including ethics), philosophy of practice, and the centrality of reflective practice to drive their learning and experience in the training field. Second, with this foundation, trainees are fit to practise and work with clients, but we encourage confidence and reassurance when guided through their usual worries (e.g., getting started with a client, preparing a formulation). Third, awarding bodies assess trainees' progress mostly through their written work, so trainees need guidance about how to write case studies and process reports which can they can submit for peer review at publishing journals. Fourth, supervision runs throughout education and training for trainees, but trainees are usually unsure about launching supervision, supervisory models, troubleshooting with supervision and getting the most from the supervisory process. Finally, trainees are eager to pass their viva voce and so begin the transition to the workplace in an organisation or in private practice.

We intend this book to be wholly practical to you, the trainee, written in a conversational style with sufficient references to guide you towards further reading and learning. In short, this book offers you more 'how to' rather than 'why' in education, training, and supervision to become a sport psychology practitioner.

What do we need to consider for professional guidance?

A sport psychology practitioner has several responsibilities to their clients: safety, confidentiality, respect for their autonomy, avoiding exploitation, safe record keeping, and appraising their competence and seeking supervision. In the cycle of professional practice, we typically combine key ethical values of respect, competence, responsibility, and integrity with five core skills of assessment, formulation, intervention, evaluation, and communication. Combining these five core skills, we assess and establish an agreement to work with a client, formulate their needs and problems, implement an intervention, evaluate the outcomes, and communicate through reporting and reflecting on outcomes (BPS Practice Guidelines, 2017). How, where, and with whom sport psychology practitioners work means safeguarding, making and maintaining agreements, requesting informed consent, managing data and confidentiality, responding when things go wrong (e.g., managing conflict and complaints) within the legal and professional obligations are necessary.

Ethics and professional practice

One might wonder why the second chapter of this book begins by exploring ethics and professional practice in sport and exercise psychology when helping athletes, coaches, and teams perform to the best of their ability defines our work as sport psychology practitioners. It is precisely this point that challenges us most because we ought to know where we stand as trainee and qualified sport psychology practitioners in the balance of performance and well-being and the consequences of our helping work. To protect our clients, our professional bodies commit us to ethical standards, which we might ordinarily lose sight of, such as discussing boundaries, not exploiting our clients and the struggle, for example, between shielding clients and allowing them to define their own lives. Also, sport psychology practitioners operate in loose or informal environments (e.g., training arena, locker room, courtside) compared with some (e.g., counselling psychologist) but not all health and care practitioners (e.g., physiotherapist). In these informal settings, the connected constructs of privacy, confidentiality, and privilege need more of our attention, not less. Andersen (2005) suggested this looseness might be in part because of the myriad of educational and training pathways to assume the role of psychological caring for athletes and coaches.

The crossover between a psychological perspective on sport and a moral or ethical one arises endlessly. From a psychological perspective, one might explore how endurance runners maximise performance in an ultramarathon. From an ethical standpoint, we might wonder whether our support jeopardises the health and well-being of the athlete. In practising psychological therapy, we offer support to the client using our expert knowledge and skills, but this wholesome focus on theory and practice leaves little room for understanding and integrating ethical practice.

What we suggest here widens the space to discuss values and principles to guide our practice. To think critically about ethics in sport and our ethical decision-making from the point we enter the profession as a trainee we might discuss how one should distribute the resources of a sport psychology practitioner among coaches and athletes within an Olympic sport, and what should the process be for deciding? One sport psychology practitioner might philosophise on such matters while another, seeing oneself as a doer, gets on with helping everyone, all the time. Some might argue there is no time for metaphysical debate because the everyday practical needs of athletes ought to be addressed. Sport psychology practitioners get caught up in the lives of athletes and ethical tensions ensue. For instance, two Olympic athletes wish for on-site support, yet their training bases lie thousands of miles apart. Should the sport psychology practitioner spend time with the most likely medal winner or the least likely medal winner? The performance manager and coaching team cannot agree. In these contexts, we need reasoning and reasonableness (Hope, 2004) or sense and sensibility. We present reasons for our view, based on theory, research, and practice, while remaining open to change our view based on reasons. But reasoning remains insufficient; we also need the sensibilities to keep our humanity before us.

The professionals

When sport psychology practitioners claim to be professionals, we assume they possess specialised knowledge and technical skills to help athletes manage psychological problems, enhance athletic performance, and contribute to the athlete's well-being. If we scrape the surface of these terms (e.g., knowledge, skills, problems, athletic performance, well-being), we witness the absence of sharp boundaries and definitions. What precisely do we mean by these terms (e.g., knowledge, skills) and who exactly decides who possesses expertise? This woolliness drives controversy and power struggles, which we witness every day (e.g., in print and social media) and in the process of professionalisation monopolises forms of expertise and constructs social boundaries to judge who enters the profession (Strawbridge, 2017). For instance, to enter and practise as a sport psychology practitioner, one has to accept extensive training and qualifications. Yet, without extensive training and qualifications, do we benevolently serve the public? In upholding the ideals of public service, selflessness, and genuinely working to prevent abuse of power, we engage interrelated systems of regulation (e.g., ethical, legal, political) and the statutory regulation of psychology by, for example, the Health and Care Professions' Council (HCPC) in the UK.

Our claim to professional status as a sport psychology practitioner, therefore, we claim specialised knowledge and skills broadly in psychological therapy bound by sound, ethical practice. Rest (1982) and Rest and Narvaez (1994) presented a model of ethical conduct that helps us to understand ethical competence in education and training (BPS, 2015). In Rest's model, ethical thinking grows through four stages: sensitivity, reasoning, motivation, and implementation.

- **Ethical sensitivity** means noticing which ethical issues arise through a course of action. By extension, not noticing ethical issues posts an obvious threat to ethical practice. If we, as instructors and supervisors, were to present a vignette, it is likely that the number of issues identified by each student or trainee would vary. Through training and supervision, however, the instruction and experiences of experienced staff allied with the trainees' experiences, reflections, and learning enhance their capacity for ethical sensitivity.
- **Ethical reasoning** reflects one's capacity to articulate one's rationale for taking a course of action. New trainees within the field possess fewer experiences of ethical reasoning in applied sport psychology practice, so we need to match their learning with their level of training and experience.
- **Ethical motivation** means acting (or not acting) once we identify (are sensitive to it) and articulate (reason for a course of action) for an ethical problem. Our ethical motivation might be clear and consistent or lacking depending upon a mix of social, cultural, and psychological factors. For instance, working as a member of a multidisciplinary team in a professional football with whom you identify strongly might mean siding with the multidisciplinary team rather than reporting unethical behaviour which might cost you personally.
- **Ethical implementation** means planning a course of action and putting it into action. To plan and implement a course of action, however, requires sensitivity to which course of action best addresses the ethical issue at hand, which bumps against another ethical challenge. For instance, keeping records is a requirement of trainees and practitioners, which has implications for their work time, especially if they are attending a training camp and reason between more clinical time with the squad or keeping detailed notes of their practice.

This model of ethical competence, which grows through sensitivity, reasoning, motivation, and implementation, represents the stages a trainee learns through lectures and seminars before it occurs experientially in practice with clients. But before the trainee gets started, it is incumbent on training programme staff to work with trainees to ensure client safety, professional competence and fitness to practise, respect for differences among clients, respect for client autonomy, non-exploitation of clients, confidentiality, contracting, and upholding the profession's reputation (Reeves & Bond, 2021). We shall explore responsibilities to the client in the next section.

Client safety

We, as sport psychology practitioners, are not responsible for the client; however, we are responsible to the client. This responsibility to the client means we protect the client from harm while undertaking service delivery with us. We can minimise the chances of causing harm to the client by considering the risks in advance. As an example, we might consider physical safety, psychological safety, online safety, and insurance. In sport and physical activity settings, the risk of physical injury relates to the activity (e.g., cycling, rugby) and these injuries are commonplace. One might not expect to be injured while attending service delivery, but it does not mean someone might not slip (e.g., on a wet surface), trip (e.g., on a mat or electric cable), or bump their head (e.g., on a bookshelf). To avoid such legal liability and perhaps paying damages to a client, it seems prudent to think about physical safety first. We, as sport psychology practitioners, need to ensure physical safety for the client and if something untoward were to happen, we have insurance (e.g., public liability insurance) to handle the aftermath. Setting up a safe and predictable meeting space is our responsibility as sport psychology practitioners, so we need to consider any hazards or unprofessional behaviours (e.g., leaving other clients' confidential notes open in your meeting room).

When we work with a client, we might focus upon psychological sources of harm to their psychological safety. We might assume that the methods, models, theories, and practice will address the client's needs and achieve their goals with minor challenge; however, service delivery brings issues at each stage of assessment, formulation, intervention, evaluation, and communication. As an example, it takes time to develop trust in a working alliance and we need to honour this trust by working as well as we can at each of these stages listed, ensuring we work with respect, responsibility, integrity, and competence. We need to work with our supervisor to discuss issues from our case load and ensure we are working safely and safeguarding our clients. For instance, more sport psychology practitioners now offer online (or remote) services (e.g., via e-mail, video platforms) especially since the COVID-19 pandemic (see Price et al., 2021 for digital working guidance). Though there is much ease working remotely (e.g., no travel), the practitioner and client still seek safety and a space conducive to service delivery. Working from a home environment often means unintended intrusions (e.g., a family member walks in) for each party so minimising these self-disclosures, especially by the practitioner, is critical because of the stress created for the client. At a general level, security settings using online platforms need to be set to safeguard the integrity of the session. Similarly, e-mails, text messages, and mobile phone calls ought to offer the security and privacy one might experience in a face-to-face session in a clinical setting.

All the issues listed above might lead to the risk of legal action against a sport psychology practitioner; however, the risk is relatively small, which is why the premiums are relatively low per annum. Regardless, it is a requirement for all practitioners (i.e., trainee and qualified) to have adequate indemnity insurance in a personal capacity or through an employer. Professional indemnity insurance to cover professional liability (e.g., malpractice) and public liability insurance (e.g., a client injuring herself) is essential for the practitioner and the client.

Life Lived

Keeping client notes or progress notes from your work with clients fulfils a basic competency. We must keep and manage full and accurate records under relevant legislation, protocols, and guidelines (e.g., HCPC, 2016). The gravity of this requirement emerged for a trainee on practicum placement when a client sustained a personal injury and required immediate medical treatment and a brief stay in a hospital in a foreign country. The client raised potential issues and the possibility of injury regarding accommodation and travel for an upcoming tournament abroad at a site he attended previously with accessibility issues for his wheelchair. To support her client, the trainee noted the issues and raised these concerns on behalf of the client in two separate multidisciplinary team meetings. She asked for her concerns to be taken as minutes in the meeting. She also kept notes from these team meetings. Following an independent inquiry following the event, the independent committee commended the trainee for her care, support, and advocacy on behalf of her client and especially for the progress notes regarding the client's wishes from their work together.

Professional competence

Working within one's competence is a professional and ethical requirement for sport psychology practitioners within a professionally regulated body. Sport psychology practitioners need to know what lies within and outside their boundaries of competence to avoid additional emotional distress and psychological harm to the client. To know what lies within one's area of competence depends on one's training and qualifications, so each practitioner will probably have commonalities and differences. To work ethically, safely, and professionally lies in the hands of the practitioner; however, the goal of the practitioner ought to be to surround oneself with professional support systems (e.g., supervision, peers, mentors) and learn from feedback from clients. Together, these systems lean on evidence-based practice within the field to continue learning and practising effectively within the field. Competence establishes a minimum standard to practise and many trainees, once qualified, seek further training and development towards excellence for personal endeavour or to gain employment in a competitive workplace (e.g., in an Olympic sport).

A taught doctoral training programme, for example, seeks to establish a minimum standard of competence to allow trainees to start and continue practising as trainee sport psychology practitioners. Within this doctoral programme, a systemic infrastructure of personal and professional development leans on members of the faculty to instruct and set assessments for the trainee to show their specific competencies. For instance, writing a process report to show therapeutic competence working with a client. Also, trainees will have supervisors guiding their development through a training programme. At a broad level, there will be a baseline of minimum: teaching hours (i.e., face-to-face or online), client contact hours, supervision hours, and various placements. This continuous assessment model and professional guidance brings the trainee to qualified status when they graduate with qualifications and gain their registration or accreditation. Following accreditation, we continue our professional development, so the learning journey never ends because organisations' needs change, clients' needs change, and society (e.g., social justice) and technology (e.g., remote working) changes.

On an everyday level, because we usually work privately with clients, we need to judge our standards of competence adequately to continue practising competently. One way of doing so would be through peer mentorship or supervision. Regular and ongoing supervision, especially when one is qualified, offers a conduit within which one can share successes, failures, doubts, worries, and strengths. Through peer mentorship and supervision, the likelihood of professional development grows because of recommendations to attend courses, conferences, and workshops, reading journals, and contributing to applied practice to these journals.

These close networks (i.e., societies, supervision, mentoring, peer groups) allow us to seek help when, through the course of our work, we run into personal or emotional difficulties, illness, disability, and so on. We might not always recognise how we are coping (e.g., exercise dependence, alcohol, drugs) with personal or emotional difficulties, for example, so supervision could offer us support when life difficulties impair our functioning. A recent loss (e.g., bereavement), excessive workload, personal illness, illness in a family member could impair one's functioning and a temporary hiatus might seem appropriate. The sporting milieu and its extreme mantras (e.g., winners are workers) might also impair one's ability to function and one needs to make choices about what to do (e.g., take a break, seek support) because our fitness to practise reflects our ability to function effectively as a practitioner.

Respect for difference

Social diversity and cultural differences run through every facet of sport and exercise activities and communities. Acknowledging diversity, difference, anti-oppression, anti-discrimination, tolerance, acceptance, and cultural competence brings us closer to safe, ethical, and effective professional practice in our communities. The client-athlete sitting in front of you confronted with issues of deselection might bring us to points about performance impairment or performance enhancement but not necessarily to social background, community, or culture. With this narrow overreliance on the characteristics of the client-athlete, we might mis-attribute to the individual something that lies outside the individual, and this stereotyping or scapegoating disrespects and misunderstands the client-athlete (Cousins, 2019; Reeves, & Bond, 2021).

Legal protection against discrimination for specified human characteristics (e.g., age, disability, race, sexual orientation) means the law works to protect people over and above what might happen in one's practice in the UK, for example. Different people from different cultures mean the cultural characteristics from past and present influence our identity, faith, moral stance, moral purpose, and work in ways we do not always acknowledge. Over the past few hundred years, some agrarian societies gave way to the industrial revolution and to the present-day sitting at our desks working and communicating with athletes across the globe.

Respect for client autonomy

Clients possess the right to self-governance. As practitioners, we respect this ethical right of the client's autonomy. Yet, in sport settings, ethical challenges in professional practice mean an organisation's goals and personnel might compromise a client's autonomy. For example, a client-athlete forced to receive support to manage his anger before being allowed to re-join the squad. Although service delivery usually means a client choosing to engage with a sport psychology practitioner to meet the client's needs, wants, and wishes, issues of power, identity, and control unwittingly drain the autonomy from the client. A sport psychology practitioner might have an agenda regarding preparation and performance of all athletes in which the client feels compelled to adhere because of the practitioner's close relationship with the team manager. Or perhaps, the board of directors' demands 'outcomes' from the psychology department within the organisation that anyone can see in games won across a season.

This balance between what the client needs and wants and what the practitioner might feel is appropriate also forms a tug-o-war in different therapeutic approaches. The expertise of the practitioner gathered through years of experience, research evidence, and professional reflection plays different roles in a psychodynamic approach compared with rational-emotive-behaviour therapy. There might be good reasons for giving advice in one therapeutic modality (e.g., REBT) but less so in another (e.g., PCT). A client's autonomy, for example, might differ between one's workplace and one's home or between a relationship with a boss and a relationship with a spouse. It remains the client's choice ultimately what the client does. In vulnerable situations, however, a sport psychology practitioner might believe they know the correct course of action for the client, so all the client needs to do is follow their remedy. Hidden within this process are the practitioner's needs for power and control over others and their ways of working (e.g., using a preferred therapeutic approach).

In sport settings, power brokers (e.g., managers, coaches, directors) reward athletes for their compliance. Some client-athletes see this power in action and make sense of it; others are so used to their feelings being invalidated that they cannot see what is happening and if the same were to happen in the working alliance with the practitioner, it would go unnoticed. The responsibility, therefore, lies with the practitioner, to self-assess their practices, share them with their supervisor, and act to address those tendencies when they turn client autonomy into client dependency. Together, the sport psychology practitioner and client strive for choice by the client to take part in service delivery or not. In sport organisations, their 'outcomes' might not align with the client and tensions arise when the goals of the organisation mean a change in the client's behaviour. Though the organisation might wish for the best outcomes for the client, it might not transpire in that way. Of course, an athlete might wish to transfer to another club, so turns up late for training or remains absent at different times, to engineer a move away. Not understanding the cause of this behaviour and assuming problems in living at home, the manager sends the athlete for support from the sport psychology practitioner. Engaging with psychological services might allow the athlete enough time to secure a transfer to another club.

Differentiating between a disciplinary issue and a need for support places the sport psychology practitioner in a quandary. At the heart of all this work lie one's boundaries of responsibility. Sometimes the practitioner takes on the responsibilities of the client. Only by reflecting upon one's actions does one realise how far they have slipped outside their boundaries and the need to re-route back within them. The client's responsibilities are the client's responsibilities. The good intentions of the practitioner might still pickpocket the client of their capacity to act in their own self-interest as an independent person. By helping clients to know themselves better, they can act in their own best interests by choosing what is best for them.

Non-exploitation of clients

Related to some examples in the last section, sport psychology practitioners get themselves trapped ethically and professionally for several reasons while working with clients and organisations if perhaps they gain fame (e.g., work for a professional team) and/or fortune (e.g., a well-paid contract) through their association with a successful professional team or professional athlete (e.g., issues of privacy and confidentiality). One might erroneously assume that the sport psychology practitioner orchestrated the success of the professional tennis player, for example. In reality, however, the practitioner can only take responsibility for the process of service delivery while the client takes responsibility for the outcomes of service delivery in their lives. The good conditions created in service delivery may have made these outcomes possible (e.g., win an Olympic gold medal) but these are things (i.e., Olympic gold medal) the client achieves, not the sport psychology practitioner. These and other challenges ranging from dual or multiple relationships to conflicts of interest to acting on behalf of a client (e.g., to protect the client) when the client ought to act on their own behalf. There are exceptions to acting on the client's behalf when the practitioner acts to protect the client or others from harm. One issue that might arise with dual or multiple relationships concerns power or authority over others, for instance, if a sport psychology practitioner were involved in the selection of players and distribution of professional contracts to youth athletes while also serving as a sport psychology practitioner.

Confidentiality

Twenty-four centuries ago, Hippocrates, the Father of Medicine, who was born on the Greek island of Cos around 460BCE and gives his name to the Hippocratic Oath (i.e., the Hippocratic Oath is an oath of ethics), knew about the centrality of confidentiality. Twenty-four centuries later, similar to helping professions like medicine, when we examine our professional guidelines for psychologists today, how relevant does the following sound about confidentiality? 'Whatever, in connection with my professional service, I see or hear, in the life of men, which ought not to be spoken of abroad, I will not divulge, as reckoning that all such should be kept secret'.

A viable and healthy working alliance matures upon the foundations of the ethical principle of confidentiality. To confide in someone means to trust wholly or have faith that what one shares remains with that person, and with that person alone. If a client discloses anything to a sport psychology practitioner, the client does so in the belief that what one reveals remains between them. If, however, the client does not feel safe to disclose to the sport psychology practitioner, then the next phase in the working relationship cannot develop – trust, respect, and rapport. Without these relational features, critical information might not materialise, rendering the therapeutic support relatively fruitless. Knowing the substance of confidentiality in the therapeutic relationship signals to the sport psychology practitioner that confidentiality intertwines with the threads of respect, genuineness, unconditional positive regard to form the fabric of effective professional and ethical practice (Rogers, 1957).

Though personal truthfulness lays a foundation for an effective therapeutic alliance, achieving it presents more than a few hurdles. One's anxiety about confidentiality seems wholly reasonable when one considers normal social encounters; however, working with a sport psychology practitioner suspends those normal rules to offer safety and security to share thoughts and feelings one might be struggling to acknowledge even to oneself. The regularity of one's everyday working life as a sport psychology practitioner means that what the sport psychology practitioner feels is usual (e.g., a client sharing personal thoughts and feelings with a trusted professional), a client feels unsettling, scary, or terrifying. We can easily skip the feelings of the client about confidentiality in our efforts to help the client based on what they share within the relationship. These feelings, however, might mean the client cannot talk freely if they do not feel safe to do so. We, as practitioners, increase a client's feelings of safety when we address confidentiality immediately because confidentiality acts as a bulwark to protect the client (e.g., against stigma) by putting them in charge of how they use service delivery.

Equally, while confidentiality is a priority, protecting others from serious harm means an ethical dilemma arises and one might be required to breach a client's confidence. A general right to privacy also means limits to these rights because of the wider social context and protecting people within that society.

Contracting and consent

A contract establishes the plans and procedures of service delivery. This contract involves informed consent, meaning that all parties have agreed to participate with a full understanding of the methods, potential risks and benefits, and alternative courses of action. Informed consent also means to choose freely to participate rather than being manipulated or coerced. A contract establishes respect for the client's autonomy and we, as practitioners, work with clients to account for each person's needs in the working alliance. We usually draw up contracts at the outset of service delivery, outlining privacy and confidentiality for the client and their data and circumstances in which the practitioner needs to break this agreement. The client also receives a copy of the contract and an updated copy if the practitioner and client make and agree changes. Contracts usually include venue, address, fees, frequency of sessions, number of sessions, missed or cancelled appointments, process of referral, responsibilities of each party (e.g., homework; data storage), ethical guidance, ending service delivery, practitioner's supervision, accreditation, and signatures of each party. Practically, however, asking a client to establish a contract when their need for support is obvious (i.e., the client is in distress) seems insensitive and disrespectful. One way to overcome this circumstance is to present this information (e.g., contract) to the client before the client attends for the first session. In this way, you can ask whether the client has read the guidance and will proceed based on what they read. Once beyond this point of immediate distress, you can explore the contract further with the client. It is likely that you will revisit the contract periodically depending on the progress or lack of it in the therapeutic process. You will find much more about contracting, an example contract with a client, an example contract for supervision, and all the elements of doing sport psychology in *Counselling Skills in Applied Sport Psychology: Learning How to Counsel* by McCarthy and Moffat (2024).

Summary

There are tensions within the bedrock of respect for autonomy, fidelity, justice, beneficence, non-maleficence, and self-interest (Thompson, 1990) which bump up against each other and the overall sense that these principles emerge from a westernised culture that are too individualistic rather than inclusive of family, tribe, and community. Returning to the time of Aristotle, virtue ethics expressed in personal qualities, for example, offer support to multicultural contexts and feminist perspectives (Bond, 2017). Our challenges in sport and exercise psychology are many; yet, beginning with our standards and ethics for sport and exercise psychology in action seems judicious.

3 Practice Philosophy and Style

Introduction

Applied sport psychology practitioners harness sport psychology knowledge, skills, research, and practice to help athletes, coaches, parents, and teams to achieve their goals. These goals might be to enhance sport performance, gain more vitality from competing in their sport, or manage issues like a performance slump or a low mood. The consuming public (e.g., athletes) need to know whether the knowledge and skills presented by applied sport psychology practitioners help them achieve their goals, so professional organisations (e.g., the Health and Care Professions Council in the UK) register people as sport and exercise psychologists who meet the competencies to achieve registration or accreditation. Those qualified to practise applied sport psychology, however, do so with different motives, practice philosophies, and styles emerging from personal, social, cultural, academic, and supervisory experiences. Similar to their clients, they may share a different culture, ethnicity, gender, sexual orientation, religion, and so on from their clients, but to practise well, they need to be competent and accepting of those who share different cultural backgrounds, sexual preferences, and so forth. Beyond the narrow lens of performance enhancement, athletes' mental health and well-being come into sharp focus. Not only are athletes and coaches facing the same challenges as all people, perhaps they are at greater risk of psychological health issues. For instance, compared with the general population, eating disorders are more prevalent among athletes. Considering these manifold challenges, one's practice philosophy and style need a firm foundation upon which to develop and withstand the vicissitudes of working as a sport psychology practitioner. In this chapter, we shall introduce trainees to a brief yet critical foundation of practice philosophy and style in training routes, with particular attention paid to dominant philosophies of practice in sport and exercise psychology service delivery.

Philosophy of practice

Trainees occasionally query why they cannot just 'get on with doing sport psychology' rather than needing to hold or practise a philosophy. It seems a reasonable query, particularly when clients want support, not a philosophy of practice. But it is precisely because others need our aid that we need to understand and build from a coherent philosophy of practice, so neither the client nor the sport psychology practitioner falter unnecessarily in their work (Eubank & Hudson, 2013). For example, a practitioner with a need to rescue clients sets about 'fixing' the client's presenting issue (e.g., eating disorder) because the practitioner feels they can manage and help the client. But according to our Practice Guidelines, for instance, sport psychology practitioners need to develop and maintain high standards of competence in their practice and work within the recognised limits of their knowledge, skill, training, experience, and ethics (BPS Practice

DOI: 10.4324/9781003367208-4

Guidelines, 2017). We can achieve these goals through a dependable philosophy of practice. A dependable philosophy of practice presents at least three benefits to practitioners. First, it allows them to work within professional guidelines, standards, and ethical boundaries. Second, it supports them when undertaking applied practice using a theoretically grounded framework. Finally, it guides them when they defend and explain service delivery to others (e.g., client-athletes) while reflecting on their actions to increase their effectiveness in service delivery.

Poczwardowski, Sherman, and Ravizza (2004) presented a hierarchical structure of professional philosophy in five layers, from internal and stable to external and dynamic components. These layers included the practitioner's core beliefs and values, theoretical paradigm (e.g., humanism), model of practice and relationships (e.g., person-centred), intervention goals (e.g., performance enhancement), and intervention techniques or methods (e.g., person-centred therapy, PCT; cognitive behaviour therapy, CBT). These layers rank from conceptual on one end to technical at the other. At the conceptual end, one's personal core beliefs and values reflect one's innermost beliefs and values about the world and human behaviour that form the foundation for that individual's professional philosophy. We might consider respect for human life, truth, privacy, freedom, autonomy, commitments, and concern for weak, vulnerable, helpless, human dignity and equality and orient towards growth and development. Grounding one's professional philosophy in one (or more) theoretical and philosophical paradigms of psychology helps us to describe and explain human behaviour, leading us to predict and control behaviour change. Some examples of these theoretical paradigms include the psychoanalytic, cognitive-behavioural, and humanistic. One's model of practice and consultant role emerges from the deeper layers of professional philosophy (i.e., personal core beliefs and theoretical paradigm). Some of these include models of practice and consultant role include (a) psychological skills training (PST) model, (b) counselling model, (c) medical model, (d) interdisciplinary sport science model, and (e) supervisory consulting model with integrative approach. The intervention goals (e.g., performance enhancement; personal growth and development) emerge from the model of practice (e.g., PST model), the theoretical paradigm, and personal core beliefs and values (e.g., concern for the vulnerable). Finally, the intervention techniques and models emerge from the layers below it (i.e., personal core beliefs, theoretical paradigm, model of practice, and intervention goals). Poczwardowski, Sherman, and Ravizza (2004) suggested that this conceptualisation supports teaching, applied practice, and guides research to explore the relationships among professional philosophy, content, process, and effectiveness of sport psychology services.

Applied sport psychology textbooks and journals favour intervention techniques and methods over models of practice and theoretical paradigms, so it seems reasonable to assume that practitioners use interventions and methods, though perhaps without being able to explain or justify their actions. Although such technique-focused work might help some athletes (e.g., learn a psychological skill such as self-talk), complicated issues leave practitioners unable to proceed or if they proceed, deliver unhelpful or damaging services (Tod & Eubank, 2020). To offer safe, reputable, and sustainable services to a community, we need to know not only what we are doing but also why we are doing what we are doing (Figure 3.1).

So where should we begin? If the theoretical orientation fits with the service delivery techniques, practitioners can effectively help athletes through their working alliance. A theoretical orientation (i.e., cognitive map) supplies a mental plan of the influences, expressions, and outcomes of behaviour and likewise gives guidance on how practitioners can assist clients. For instance, using a cognitive behavioural map, we might consider how thoughts, feelings, physical reactions, and behaviour interact and influence each other in a chosen environment. Then, through a process of assessment, formulation, intervention, evaluation, and communication, we learn more about what works when working with client-athletes and why it works. Equally, we

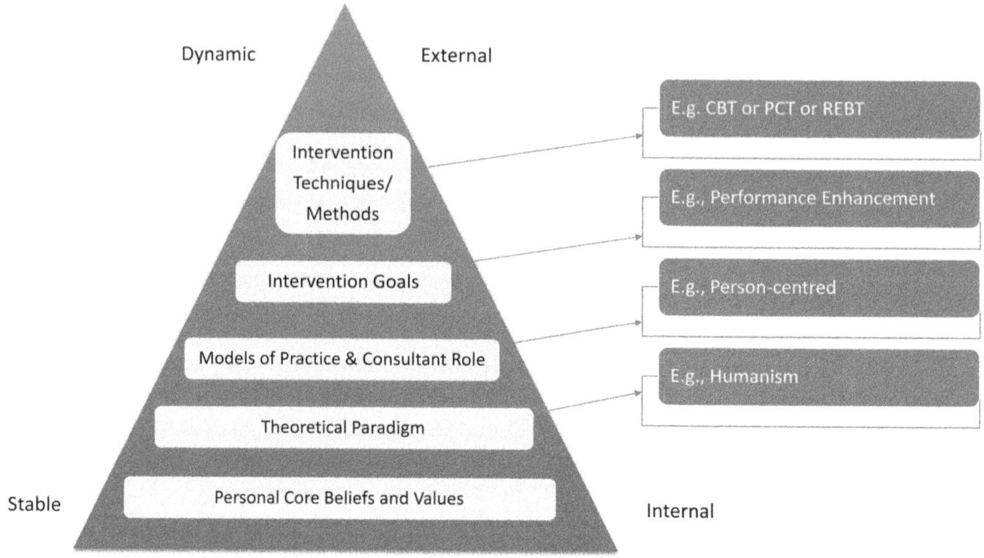

Figure 3.1 Philosophy of practice structure. Adapted from Poczwardowski et al. (2004)

might use a psychodynamic map or a humanistic map to guide our work. During your education and training, it is likely you will learn about various theoretical orientations, for instance, about behavioural, cognitive, existential, gestalt, person-centred, or psychodynamic orientations and about several leaders in the history of psychotherapy (Aaron Beck, Albert Ellis, Sigmund Freud, Fritz Perls, Carl Rogers, and Irvin Yalom, to name a few). Sometimes these theoretical orientations presented during your education and training reflect those of the original curriculum, teaching staff, or supervisors guiding service delivery. Regardless, it is your choice to know more about these influential leaders and their related theoretical orientations (e.g., similarities and differences) so you broaden and deepen your knowledge, understanding, creativity, and application of skills to meet clients' needs and wants.

In summary, a theoretical orientation represents a way of working with clients to help them address their problems in living, problems in performance, or aspirational goals. The orientation you choose takes the strain off you, the trainee, because you follow the lead of the orientation or model (e.g., CBT) to help the athlete and guide you on each unfolding step in the helping process. We like to use the analogy of a carpenter's workshop where the client and the practitioner work on the presenting issue(s) together on a workbench like two craftspeople. If we do not follow a model, we are likely to blame ourselves for poor outcomes, yet this is wholly unfair because we have been trying to undertake a task (i.e., helping a client) without understanding the helping process and the knowledge and skills to use at each stage. One craftsperson assumes responsibility for managing the service delivery process (i.e., the sport psychology practitioner) and the other craftsperson (i.e., client) assumes responsibility for the outcomes of service delivery in their lives.

Theoretical orientations

Theoretical orientations help us understand why people behave the way they do alongside the causes and consequences of human behaviours and how therapy might help them change. A theoretical orientation builds from a theory-based framework to collate a client's experience and behaviour, generate a working hypothesis to make sense of what the client presents, generate a treatment approach, and evaluate the therapeutic process as it unfolds. Practically, it means that a theoretical orientation helps a practitioner to (a) enable a helping process between practitioner and client, (b) describe a client's behaviour (including thoughts, feelings, and situations) (c) explain (form a working hypothesis of) the causes and consequences of the client's behaviour, (d) acknowledge individual difference, (e) yield a treatment to address presenting issues, and (f) evaluate outcome success and process success.

As an example, Laura, an athlete, begins working with Zoe, a sport psychology practitioner. Zoe practises CBT and Laura feels comfortable working with this therapeutic modality. Laura shares her story and together with Zoe, they make sense of what Laura shares (i.e., thoughts, feelings, physical reactions, and behaviours). Zoe helps Laura to understand what might explain her current circumstances (causes and consequences) from what she shared while acknowledging what it means specifically for Laura in her unique situation. Together, they plan a treatment and evaluate progress, or lack of it, each week when they meet. Finally, they judge the outcome of treatment (i.e., were the goals of treatment achieved) and the process of treatment (e.g., did Laura learn skills for her future). This last point seems critical in sport, exercise, and performance settings because many client-athletes might not be successful objectively (e.g., win the race, win the championship); however, they might have learned skills successfully to be deployed in future scenarios.

Theoretical orientations are frameworks. Frameworks do nothing. It is the practitioner and the client working effectively together that drive success in service delivery. On that scale, the emphasis for the practitioner and client is on the working alliance and, to a lesser extent, the treatment. The helping skills (e.g., attending, listening, and observing) of the practitioner play a substantial role in the helping process. When we add the parts together: theoretical orientations, relationships, treatments or interventions, we have a greater chance of securing successful client outcomes.

Fitting theoretical orientations into our journey

To understand the causes and consequences of a client-athlete's behaviour in a sport setting, we need to know about different processes (e.g., cognitive, developmental, emotional, and social), individual differences, theoretical underpinnings, research, and research methods. To work safely and effectively with client-athletes on the helping journey, we need to grow our competencies in ethics, communication (e.g., interpersonal, written), clinical skills and strategies and the process of service delivery before we are fit to practise in the field. But we also need to know where we are in our developmental trajectory so we can walk before we run; so, we can travel safely and confidently from one phase to the next. Rønnestad and Skovholt (2003) presented six phases to describe changes across the therapist's life course (the lay helper phase, the beginning student phase, the advanced student phase, the novice professional phase, the experienced professional phase, and the senior professional phase). This developmental model helps each trainee or practitioner to recognise where they are in a therapist's life course. If you are at the beginning student phase or the advanced student phase, what does that phase mean to you? Rønnestad and Skovholt (2003, 2013) outlined developmental tasks for each phase and for beginning and advanced students; one development task is to select theories and techniques to apply in practice (i.e., choosing an orientation) (Rønnestad et al., 2018). A key positioning for most educational establishments and training courses is to help students to understand various approaches (e.g., humanistic, existential, PCT) and to specify one or two approaches where they offer specific teaching, training, and supervision (Hutter & Pijpers, 2020). Training and supervision are critical in this phase of development because trainees are eager to apply theory and practise (e.g., Hutter et al., 2015) but often do not thoroughly understand what the approach means, why it is effective, and how it works in practice.

Each trainee arrives at this point with a unique experience of personal history, education, and training. Alongside these influencing factors are personalities, which also influence one's choice of theoretical orientation; however, the client remains the primary focus in the therapeutic process. For example, a practitioner might prefer a person-centred approach to work with client-athletes, yet the needs of the client come first so might choose a more directive approach (e.g., cognitive behaviour therapy (CBT) and rational emotive behaviour therapy (REBT)) to meet these needs and circumstance. The population receiving services from sport psychology practitioners has increased, as have the locations they perform these services, the motives for the services, and how they provide them. For example, beyond sport and exercise contexts, practitioners work in business, healthcare, and the military and focus on mental health, youth development, and counselling support (Sly et al., 2020). With an increasingly diverse practice, not only do we need to gain cultural competence as practitioners but also recognise that clients wish to choose culturally sensitive psychology support that meets their needs (Norcross & Wampold, 2019). Clients need and want to be involved in their treatment decisions.

Over ten years ago, Aoyagi and colleagues (2012) postulated that the future of the applied profession would depend on successfully gaining key competencies in (a) the psychology of performance, (b) mental health counselling, (c) consulting psychology, and (d) a performance specialty domain (e.g., sport, performing arts, business, high-risk occupations, p. 36). To accommodate these competencies, we need to recognise the landscape of theoretical orientations and begin.

Turning towards an integrated approach

With so many theoretical approaches available to us to choose from, how do we choose which approach or approaches fit best? As a field, sport and exercise psychology does not have the tangled debates we see in various schools in counselling, psychotherapy, and clinical psychology, though perhaps we have not developed our knowledge, awareness, and needs of service delivery because of this limited debate. Although we might have heard of orientations as elective or integrative, we need to know what these terms mean and how they influence how and why we practise as we do. Integration means joining different theoretical approaches and strategies to improve the efficacy, effectiveness, efficiency, and ethics of services offered to clients (Castonguay et al., 2015; Fernández-Álvarez et al., 2016; Tod & Lafferty, 2020; Zarbo et al., 2016). Practitioners integrate several systems to meet their needs and those of their clients with a sound justification for their actions. We often ask trainees to justify integrating theoretical orientations so that they build sound justifications for their services based on client preferences, client needs, cultural diversity, and so on. Because there is no integrative model, rather, practitioners choose to present their integrative models based on preferences, influences, and context. For example, most trainees, through personal and professional development, taught modules and assessments, learn about their values, preferred philosophies, and theories. Teaching staff, practitioners in the field, peers, and supervisors also influence trainees regarding values, preferred philosophises, and theories. Practicum placement presents the experiential training that challenges trainees about how they work with individuals and teams presenting with various issues across the short-, medium-, and long-term. Sometimes, these collective experiences through university degrees and independent training programmes satisfy the needs of trainees, but it is more likely that through personal and professional development, trainees seek different ways of working with different methods to meet personal preferences, clients' needs, and clients' preferences (McEwan et al., 2019).

With so many ways to travel towards integrated practice, do we all end at different destinations? Norcross (2016) presented four paths: technical eclecticism, theoretical integration, assimilation, the common factors approach, or some blend of these four. Technical eclecticism means choosing interventions for clients based on their presenting issue(s). Their presenting issue(s) are the data guiding the practitioner. Rather than leaning on theory, and coherence between theory and application, the practitioner fits their services to the clients' needs. Theoretical integration, however, integrates theoretical orientations at conceptual and intervention levels. This creativity brings new methods and applications to the practitioner. One can imagine many years in a professional practice capacity, working with clients in various contexts, blended with a smorgasbord of personal and professional experiences, leading to theoretical integration that reflects such diversity. In assimilative integration, practitioners begin with one theoretical orientation (e.g., PCT) and are open to other practices from other schemes (e.g., CBT). This compact foundation means one can integrate other interventions as one develops professionally (Rønnestad & Skovholt, 2013). The common factors pathway means locating commonalities from different theoretical orientations and engineering them into a service delivery model. Sieving theoretical orientations for the best ways of working with clients often means finding similarities and nuance.

In summary, although the routes differ, it is likely that this network of routes means we are travelling along any of the four routes at different points on our professional life journey. Sport and exercise as a service delivery process remains in its infancy and there is much to explore about integration in these contexts (Tod, Hardy, Lavallee, Eubank, & Ronkainen, 2019). Appreciating the richness of theoretical approaches, methods, interventions, and clinical skills means a lifetime of learning unfolds before us and we, as sport psychology practitioners, alongside our clients, will benefit.

Life Lived

Over the past 15 years, lecturing and supervising on our doctoral framework, I (Paul) have encouraged students to read widely about humanity – the quality or state of being human. Compassion, generosity, and empathy, for example, and their opposites help us know people in all their semblances. The universal themes of human experience such as time, memory, love, loss, fear, anger, joy, uncertainty, pain, and death are everywhere around us, yet perhaps most vivid in poetry, literature, plays, music, and sport. The more we listen and read, the more our unimaginable futures echo in the pages of poetry and literature of those past and present. We are privileged as sport psychology practitioners to join with clients for a few moments on their life journey. Many of the poems, stories, and plays we read about come to life before us in the stories of our clients and we can reflect upon them, learn from them, and enrich our lives personally and professionally. One example concerns the sadness of loss and the choice we have to endure the pain or, in our folly, choose a senseless solution. At a professional football club, Martin, a coach whose career was cut short because of injury at 21 years of age, refused to mourn the loss of his career and cultivated grievance instead. He lived with frustration and anger. He coached with contempt and indifference for years. His story reminded me of Miss Havisham in Charles

Dickens's *Great Expectations*. Miss Havisham refused to mourn when she was jilted on her wedding day and fostered grievance instead. She locked herself away, emptying love and compassion from her life. I shared the parallels of this story with Martin. The following week, the film, Great Expectations, was shown one morning on his day off over the Christmas holidays. To his great surprise, he watched the film. The following day, he came to see me and said, 'I don't want to end up like Miss Havisham. I'm just as bad as her, I reckon. I stopped the clocks the day I got injured. And I'm trying to make the boys into Estella – that's not right. Is there any hope for me?'. I asked if he had watched to the end. He said he had. 'Did you feel that there was hope for Pip and Estella?' I asked. 'Definitely. I'd rather model myself on Pip. You know, that's the sort of fellow I used to be before I got injured'.

Promoting an integrative stance – A case example

In our taught doctoral training programme, we provide education, training, and supervision for trainees, promoting an integrative stance among trainees as they mature across the phases of their professional development. To reach this integrative juncture, trainees need education, training, practicum placement, and supervision beforehand. In our three-year programme, trainees learn theory and methods of various systems specialising in a person-centred approach and a cognitive behavioural approach across the first two years. With a rich diversity of educators, trainers, and supervisors, cross-fertilisation of ideas, methods, and practices ensues. The sport and exercise psychology taught doctoral training programme runs alongside health psychology and counselling psychology, creating a framework for learning and teaching, staffed by practitioners from at least four fields of practice (i.e., sport and exercise psychology, health psychology, clinical psychology, and counselling psychology) with many years of experience practising in private practice, teaching and researching at university, and supervising trainees and qualified practitioners. We do not force integration; rather, it is an encouraged standpoint for the future. Though our starting point is a person-centred approach (non-directive), we follow with a cognitive-behavioural approach (directive) and expose trainees to as many other approaches and systems (e.g., existential, psychodynamic, family systems) as the curriculum allows in weekly taught content over three years. Trainees receive at least one year of counselling skills training before immersing themselves in practicum placement; however, they need to pass their fitness to practise examination before beginning practicum placement. The intention with a diversity of approaches, professionals (e.g., sport and exercise, counselling, health), and experiences is to generate diversity among graduates who can think, feel, practise, and reflect as independently as possible.

Across the three years, students receive practice-based instruction and reflection for personal and professional development. All assessments reflect their profession (i.e., sport and exercise) with a range of client-case studies, process reports, logbooks, reflective essays, individual and group interventions, and basic and applied research. The assimilative path towards integration emerges in client-case studies in the final year of their study, presented through a logbook illustrating theories and techniques from other schools applied to the written case and especially in the viva voce. Personal and professional development classes across the three years of study continue with the emphasis on establishing, developing, maintaining, and repairing therapeutic relationships. These modules emphasise case-based approaches, role plays, use of props, scene setting, and other creative methods and skills-based assessments.

Besides group supervision, trainees also receive one supervision hour for at least each 8 hours of client practice. We offer one supervision hour for each 6 hours of client practice for the first 50 hours as a new trainee on placement. This supervision ratio means there is a scaffolding within supervision to allow the trainee to explore personal integrative journeys with the support of an experienced supervisor. There are several ways to support this integrative journey that match the developmental needs of the supervisee. Supervision in sport and exercise contexts is in an embryonic stage and beginning to grow; however, it remains at a sluggish pace. Supervisors will be at different points on their professional development journey as practitioners and supervisors with several challenges to support trainees through their training. To promote an integrative stance as a supervisor means understanding where the integrative foundation fits within the professional training journey of the trainee.

Summary

In this chapter, we opened with an exploration of one's philosophy of practice and the theoretical orientations, which help us understand why people behave the way they do together with the causes and consequences of human behaviours and how therapy might help them change. We fit theoretical orientations into our learning and experiential journey as trainees and arrive at an integrated approach when we get to grips with all the moving parts of working with clients. Our practice philosophy and style are ours – our signature – to work with clients in a mutually beneficial and sustaining way. Doing what we do, and doing it well, for its own sake, is joyous.

4 Being a Reflective Practitioner

Introduction

What is reflective practice? By definition, reflective practice is the development of insight and practice through critical attention to practical values, theories, principles, assumptions, and the relationship between theory and practice which inform everyday actions (Bolton & Delderfield, 2018, p. xxiii). To most trainees and qualified professionals, this definition encompasses the actions of a reflective practitioner engaging in reflective practice, but what lies behind reflective practice? Reflective practice expresses an attitude towards work, life, and how to learn from experience. This experience for a trainee might include study, work, supervision, others, and the wider social and cultural structures (e.g., university, professional football club) especially how these institutions are constructed, maintained, and mould those within them. If we take professional football as a working context, we might draw different conclusions about applied sport psychology in the English Premier League (Gilmore et al., 2018). Gilmore et al. (2018) presented a rare account of the working life of a sport psychology practitioner in the English Premier League (the elite division of professional football in England). As a new profession in professional sport, applied sport psychology practitioners lie in a precarious position because their job security might depend on their ability to steer through unpredictable managerial change. This example illustrates the complex and volatile workplace of professionals who need intricate and assorted reflective and reflexive processes to manage them. We aim to keep the realities of training in the words, feelings, and actions of the trainees as they experience them. Although one trainee might find working in professional sport unpredictable, confusing, and threatening, another might find it exciting, challenging, and liberating. Equally, we all need to continue travelling on our learning journey, so we need a mechanism to assess and change our thinking about ourselves, others, and the world alongside our actions. If we are all trying to make sense of our world, change it where necessary and possible, then it seems worthwhile to bring what is inside out. We can achieve this goal through writing, for instance. In this chapter, we shall explore reflection and, keeping a practical focus, offer methods for you to choose which suits you and your needs best.

Why should reflection matter to trainees?

Hawkins and McMahon (2020) presented seven key capacities at the heart of good practice in the helping professions: learning and unlearning, reflecting, embodying learning, relating, collaborating, sustaining resilience, and understanding one's deeper motivations. It is close to impossible to come by a textbook about training and supervision of trainees in various professional domains that does not put 'reflection' as a critical component of professional practice. Professional

DOI: 10.4324/9781003367208-5

education and training programmes aim to engender safe, ethical, and independent learners to lead their own education in the short- and long-term because our learning journey never ends.

One facet of learning common to training programmes in applied sport psychology is experiential learning. Experiential learning rests on the individual's experience upon their learning; yet can we truly grasp our learning opportunities if we do not reflect upon them?

One example of an experiential learning cycle comes from Kolb (1984). Kolb proposed an experiential learning cycle in which a person moves from experiencing something concrete, to reflective observation (i.e., watching) of that experience, to forming generalisations and developing abstract concepts (i.e., thinking) connected to the experience, and then to actively experimenting, before beginning the cycle again and reflecting on the concrete results of the experimentation. The reflective observation of the person relates intimately to the person because it captures one's innermost beliefs, values, attitudes, opinions, knowledge, assumptions, and personal experiences in the world. The view or views we hold about ourselves, others, and the world percolate through these layers (e.g., beliefs, knowledge). If we are to truly open ourselves to change our perspective on an issue (e.g., learning, teaching, psychotherapeutic work), we need to know where we stand now (i.e., what we believe, value, assume) and where we wish to stand. We need a mechanism to comprehend, experience, reflect on the experience, and experience again before beginning the cycle once more to allow us to reflect, question, challenge, and change.

When we reflect, we make sense of our experience through layers of assumptions, attitudes, values, beliefs, and so on (Figure 4.1). But does our reflective practice lead us to feel entrenched? Or do we feel emancipated? Do we keep on justifying our actions or seek new ways of thinking, feeling, and acting? What does it mean to hold a belief about human performance or well-being? If there is one goal in this chapter, it relates to a choice. We, as trainees and professionals, choose to explore our thoughts, feelings, actions, values, and beliefs, or we do not. When a trainee reflects, the trainee tells us their first-hand account of their experience, for instance, working with a client to create a contract or a formulation. Often, however, the trainee does not realise how 'personal' this story is in their learning journey. What we mean here

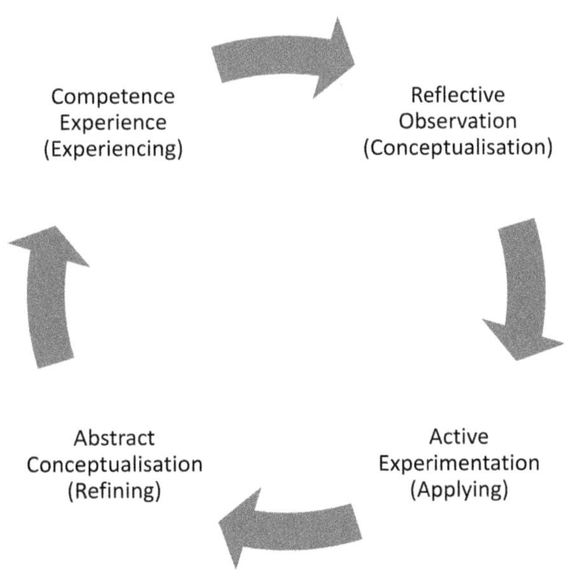

Figure 4.1 Kolb's learning cycle

is that the trainee chooses when to write, what to write, how to write, what to include, what to exclude, and, with hope, a justification for their actions. This agency, in flow in the reflection process, ought to alert the trainee to how deeply personal learning is to all of us and how much we hold the reins of what we wish to think, feel, and do in our unfolding professional journey. It also means that the people within professional bodies who establish our standards to allow us to work ethically, legally, and professionally within our competency framework, allow us to develop our distinctive identity, leaning on our strengths, undertaking tasks for the sheer joy of doing it, to the best of one's ability. In a wider sphere, doing our best benefits the welfare of all people we serve in sport, exercise, and performance psychology. Reflection and the reflective practice process place the reins of our learning and development in our hands.

Reflecting, learning, changing

The engine of sport, exercise, and performance steams along at pace and all those involved within it tether themselves in ways they see (e.g., training hours) and do not see (e.g., entrapment). Whether as a player, coach, backroom staff, or parent, the quest for faster, higher, and stronger knows no bounds. In this unbounded territory, and the 'hurry-up mentality' (Cropley et al., 2023) of professional applied practice, means acting now leaves critical reflective thought far behind in the starting blocks. But this critical reflective thought allows us to transform experiencing into learning and, by extension, changing. Cropley et al. (2023) highlighted how reflective practice is a purposeful yet complex process that requires good questions to generate deep, critical thought, recognising the self as an agent of change, leading to change as an outcome. This last point about change as an outcome means that we actively witness the change in values, beliefs, and behaviour – a change in the self. When we consider this movement from what was, to what is, to what will be, we probably do not grasp the enormity of what change means to a person, their personal and professional development and practice. Perhaps our opinions and attitudes are open to exploration, but digging further into one's values and beliefs might be quite an undertaking. These behavioural predispositions (i.e., opinions, attitudes, values, beliefs) we gain in our ever-changing social, cultural, political, and economic environment ought to be explored to understand where we stand in relation to critical concepts (e.g., education, sport) (Campbell, 1963).

From this stance, we can move in whichever direction takes our fancy, but without knowing where we are, it is difficult to know where we wish to go. We believe that regular reflective practice offers mental hygiene, like flossing offers dental hygiene, to get into those thoughts, feelings, and behaviours that tell us more about ourselves than we might wish to know yet clarify our position and widen our space for reasoning and intuition. Too often, our reasoning and rationality dominate our thinking, squashing creativity, feeling, intuition, relationships, and context into the corners of our experience. We rather consider these two parts (reason vs intuition) cooperating and competing to bring the best out of each other – a superlative performance – no one ever imagined. When we fine tune all parts of ourselves, we do not change all immediately, but gradually; to change everything immediately would feel foolish and unmanageable. Perhaps the greatest joy emerges from those parts of ourselves we discard, dismiss, and neglect because one context dominates over others. Our 'self-configurations' or 'self-states' (Mearns & Cooper, 2005) show us we think, feel, and act differently depending on the context and with whom we share that context. Consider the differences in thoughts, feelings, and actions between (a) sitting with a board of directors at a football club explaining your use of resources to support the senior team and (b) sitting with a trusted colleague, reflecting on the bounty of mutual relationships sustaining the lifeblood of the club. Each of these habitats (e.g., conversations, relationships) with their own ecology allows us to learn from life when it waxes and when it wanes (Faris & van Ooijen, 2012; van Ooijen, 2013).

As with all professional journeys, there are points of growth, maintenance, stagnation, and decline, and each juncture has much to teach us about ourselves. We might need creative ways to reflect, learn, and grow. We might need ways to reflect on the 'here and now' through our imagination without knowing where we shall arrive, just trusting ourselves to have an experience. A world of activities is open to us, like writing a letter, an adventure story, or poetry. Digital advancements allow us to record reflections and create a transcript of our recording. Or perhaps we might wish to use props like cards, or objects to tell a story to ourselves, another, or a group. We might paint, draw, listen to music, or role play as a creative process to reflect on client work or work with myth, metaphor, and imagery (van Ooijen, 2013). Though written reflection (e.g., diaries, case reports, self-reflections) is the most reported format in the literature, many post-graduate programmes or professional training routes use professional development seminars or group supervision workshops to offer a natural habitat for reflective conversations.

Critical to all these forms of reflection, however, are *time and place*. What we mean here is that although 'time' is a frequently reported barrier (e.g., Cropley et al., 2012) to reflective practice, time dedicated to critical reflection ought to be built into all processes in training and supervision as a priority for learning and change – reflective practice deserves its place. We hold this position for several reasons, but critically we see the ideology of individualism (in a neoliberal socio-political climate) pervades all levels of sport (and other domains like business and education) where the individual represents a set of assets to be managed and maintained and the performativity monologue dominates. This performativity sermon outlines skills, goals, productivity, and effectiveness of the individual, which is so common in sport and performance settings, we probably cannot see it (Uphill & Hemmings, 2017). As practitioners within these systems, we need to ask ourselves if we are acting ethically preserving the neoliberal staus quo (Sugarman, 2015)? As practitioners, we have many critical questions to ponder on our personal and professional development relating to, for example, gender, sexuality, and power in sport (Douglas & Carless, 2009).

Life Lived

'And another thing, I just don't get it – I just don't get why I need to do reflective practice?' This account was part of a frustrated diatribe from a trainee early in his training journey. And when I (Paul) asked him what he enjoyed reading, he said 'I'm too busy to read anything'. Empathising with his worry and overwhelm, and with the Christmas break around the corner, a holiday seemed more than welcome. A little later, after we had talked things through, with his hand on the door about to leave the room, he enquired, You know, if I were to read a book, maybe over the holidays, which one would you recommend?'. 'You know, I think you'd enjoy Grapes of Wrath by John Steinbeck'. A week into the new semester, there was a knock on my door. The same student asked if I had a few minutes. 'Sure, how can I help?' 'I need to apologise for my behaviour before Christmas. And I think I know why you recommended that book too. Do you think I am Al Joad? That's not so important; what's important is that I could not put it down, and I learned so much, especially about myself – felt like I was right there with them too. Reflective practice makes sense now, so much sense. Thinking and writing about our experiences, like Steinbeck did, helps us to learn from them for the future. We're in the humanity business, aren't we? And you wanted me to see realise it for myself. I get it. And it's not all about me'.

Reflective practice in supervision

If supervision is characteristically a reflective and self-reflective process (Barney & Andersen, 2014), the practice of reflection (and self-reflection) forms a substantial part of our training. But rather than looking at reflective practice as a process for a specific outcome (i.e., pass the training programme), perhaps it is better to consider a reflective life (Barney & Andersen, 2014) where we reflect on all aspects of our lives (e.g., family, friends, work) working towards congruence and authenticity. Perhaps we do not consider reflective practice so much outside training and supervision; however, when we are looking deeply at the self as the instrument of service, much also changes (often imperceptibly) in our personal lives.

Keeping these points in mind, we are ostensibly better practitioners following supervision; however, supervision needs to be effective. By effective, we mean supervision meets the trainee's needs (e.g., skill development, supportive feedback) especially developing the ability to self-reflect and raise one's confidence in therapeutic practice (Watson, Lubker, & Van Raalte, 2011; Wheeler & Richards, 2007). With the aid of effective supervision, one's self-reflection as a trainee (written in logbooks; shared in supervision) brings another practitioner's ear to the story, offering insight, challenge, and opportunities to explore those hidden or blind spots we miss on our own. A trainee's professional efficacy, though perhaps shallow at the outset of training, grows with this broad (e.g., integrative practice) and narrow (e.g., use of summaries as a counselling skill) focus as the supervision journey unfolds.

One's caseload consumes most of the supervision time in each supervision meeting. And because most supervision deals with what has happened, reflecting on those experiences means the trainee has a story to tell about content (i.e., what the client presents) and process (i.e., the nature of the relationship between the trainee and client). Depending on one's chosen therapeutic modality (e.g., cognitive behaviour therapy (CBT) and psychodynamic), a supervisee and supervisor might reflect deeply on cognition in CBT and emotional states in psychodynamic supervision. Supervision for different modalities differs and so the content of reflection differs as well. To illustrate, a supervisor would likely explore eight competence domains as an assessment of core CBT skills to deliver formative and summative feedback about a trainee's performance within an observed or recorded treatment session (Muse & McManus, 2013). These domains would include (1) agenda setting, (2) formulation, (3) CBT interventions, (4) homework, (5) assessing change, (6) effective use of time, (7) fostering therapeutic relationship, and (8) effective two-way communication. In short, the content of supervision ought to reflect the detail of the dominant therapeutic modality.

In supervision sessions, case reflections exploring the what, how, and why of a trainee's decisions mean supervisors ought to be competent in theoretical frameworks, offer sufficient supervision time, work collaboratively and cooperatively, adhere to robust professional and ethical boundaries in all aspects of supervision, show interest in the trainee, the trainee's supervisory journey, and the supervisor process (Barney & Andersen, 2014). Similar to common factors that improve the quality of psychotherapy and client change in clinical and counselling psychology, a trainee and supervisor ought to explore whether the supervisory relationship works for each of them. Feeling safe and understood, working in a supportive relationship with a logical structure, co-created direction, clear and achievable roles, and boundaries means the trainee and supervisor are likely to work well together and achieve the goals of supervision.

In summary, reflection in supervision runs throughout the supervisory process. Part of the trainee's reflection ought to explore how and why supervision works for the trainee or does not. Supervision ought to be a space to learn, explore, and fail often. The safety offered in an empathic, non-judgmental supervisory relationship means the supervisee shares achievements, worries, and perceived failings, with care, compassion, and curiosity about one's self and one's professional self as it unfolds. A helpful interrogation of your supervision relates to how well your supervisor tunes in to you as supervisee, rather than how much insight and information they have for you. Supervisors make mistakes too, but what makes them skilled and deepens their supervisor relationships is their ability to reflect on their supervision, remain accountable, and make amends when they get things wrong.

Ways and models of reflecting

We have several methods available to us to reflect. Various trainees enquire about the reflection process, what it means, and how it is done best. There are several ways to respond to these questions; however, it seems fitting to begin with a pedagogical model that supports reflective practice.

Schon (1983, 1987) recommended reflective practice to explore one's assumptions, personal theories, and behaviours as practitioners, but to do so requires an ability to reflect in action (i.e., during an activity) and on action (i.e., after an activity). And for several reasons, we might take every opportunity to protect ourselves (e.g., like a narcissist protecting oneself from core shame) in our self-reflection, never lifting the veil to see what lies beneath. But because the concept of self-reflection is atheoretical, though perhaps built on some general models of reflective practice (e.g., Dewey, 1938), it is unsettling to know how it all works (Watson et al., 2011). Our cognitive biases (e.g., blaming, self-serving bias) mean we need to tell our story so we can reflect on it. The tendency towards bias and irrationality seems reasonable as we tell our story, so we also need to hold ourselves to account using other forms of support, like supervision, group supervision, and peer sharing.

The first step, however, is to grab something we understand as a structure to guide us through reflective practice. One possibility is the storytelling arm of the narrative inquiry literature. But we also have several reflective practice models or frameworks to underpin our reflections. These models evolved from singular to mixed paradigms, offering a structure for deep reflections. Reflective practice models are cyclical, reflecting the choice of definition and model paradigm depends on the person and what seems fashionable (Finlayson, 2015). It is this choice and personal process that means individuals can choose a reflective model that works for them and the goals (e.g., informal, formal) for which they strive. Self-questioning is used in informal reflection, whereas formal reflection needs to be supported by theory and research to build the frameworks used in practice.

We wrote about Kolb's (1984) learning theory earlier. Later in that decade, Gibbs (1988) proposed a six-stage model that included: (1) description, (2) feelings, (3) evaluation, (4) analysis, (5) conclusions, and (6) action plan. Within this model, the individual needs to capture experiences to learn from them (i.e., autobiographical self) and this private learning occurs within the socio-cultural space of the individual. A trainee, for example, creates a narrative (e.g., evaluates, analyses) at each stage of the model to draw a conclusion and an action plan. The reflective cycle would need to continue to understand what happens with the action plan. In 1995, Johns presented a five-stage model: (1) description of the experience, (2) reflection, (3) influencing factors, (4) could I have dealt with it better? and (5) learning. This five-stage model brings the narrative of the autobiographical self in each stage of the model to interact and discuss with a mentor. In a change of direction, Brookfield (1998) presented a model in which individuals view events through four lenses: (1) autobiography, (2) learner's eyes, (3) our colleagues' eyes, and (4) theoretical literature. There is a mix of the autobiographical self and contextualising reflections from the observations of others.

The model that follows presents a simple format of a reflective framework. Driscoll's reflective cycle (Driscoll, 1994, 2007) is an approach to reflection or problem solving that comprises three elements:

1 What? (returning to the situation)
2 So what? (understanding the context)
3 Now what? (modifying future outcomes)

In the first element, we present a scenario from the field of clinical practice, and we select certain elements of it for deeper analysis. What did I see or do? In the second element, we evaluate the event and identify any lessons we can take from it. How did I feel at the time? What was positive? What remains challenging? In the final element, we explore: What have I learned? How might I act differently next time? Do I need to act now? If so, what shall I do?

These models offer ways of reflecting for personal and professional development. The stories you share ought to be an 'archaeological dig' through all your experiences rather than those 'things that seemed to work' or those 'things that look and sound good'. Learning in professional practice means learning from 'successful' and 'unsuccessful' experiences. Although our tendency is to learn from those who are successful, as Smith (2014) described, we are likely to witness 'survivor bias', which is the tendency to focus on the characteristics of 'survivors' and attribute their characteristics as reasons for their survivorship (Uphill & Hemmings, 2017). Smith (2014) referenced an example of World War 2 aircraft coming back from battle. The aircraft that experienced combat often had bullet or shrapnel damage to the wings and tail of the plane and the military initially intended to strengthen these areas. By turning their attention to those planes that did not return home, they reinforced the cockpit, engines, and fuel tank, a choice that saved countless lives.

Summary

From its pivotal beginnings (Dewey, 1938) to present day (Finlayson, 2015), reflective practice is not only fashionable but also a source of learning and a tool of competency in fields of professional practice like sport and exercise psychology. Though reflective practice is one of the most popular theories of professional knowledge, much remains to be understood by the term 'reflective practice' (Kinsella, 2009). For our purposes, learning about the values and principles of reflective practice, its theories, and contexts means the power of the story can offer ourselves and others a perspective we might not have known unless we wrote about it to uncover what we know. In the words of Sartre, 'A man is always a teller of tales, he lives surrounded by his stories and the stories of others (Sartre, [1938] 1963, p. 61). So, let us set off with an open mind, not fixed points on a map, but to the open dynamic territory (Bolton & Delderfield, 2018), which at the same time is 'to arrive where we started/And to know the place for the first time' (Eliot, [1936] 1974, p. 222).

5 Working with Equality, Diversity, Inclusion

Introduction

In our working lives, I (Sahen) can attest to the fact that I have met people from every continent except from Antarctica, every religion, every race, every gender, and a vast age range. I actively work across multiple countries, automatically working with multiple ethnicities, languages, and cultural backgrounds. Sport reflects society itself in its diversity and difference, but sometimes also its structural inequalities. As a sport psychology trainee, it is important to understand and be cognisant of these conceptualisations starting out. This chapter has the twin aims of clarifying what equality, diversity, inclusion (EDI) means, and how it can be addressed through several areas of focus. We also provide 'Life Lived' boxes and applied practice directions to improve by showcasing the 'T-R-E-E-S' model for EDI practice.

What is equality, diversity, inclusion (EDI)?

EDI refers to the active set of strategies that ensure fair treatment and opportunity for people, regardless of any personal characteristics that may cause prejudice and discrimination. But you must be wondering, how is that possible in sport? After all, the stopwatch actively discriminates between a runner who is fast and who is slow. EDI is not about the outcome alone, but it is about the opportunity provided to (a) have access to sport; (b) continue in sport; (c) compete in sport; and (d) have a chance for success in and through sport. EDI is not about getting people to the stadium so that the stopwatch can decide who is fast and slow, rather than their ingrained personal characteristics such as race, religion, socio-economic status, and others. Now that we have a rudimentary understanding of where EDI sits in sport, let us clarify its elements:

1 **Equality** means fairness. In applied work, equality means the active behaviours adopted to ensure that individuals or groups are not treated any less favourably because of their protected characteristic (see below). Equality also includes equality of opportunity (i.e., where affirmative strategies are adopted so that disadvantaged individuals and groups get access to fair opportunities to provide them with the best chance of success).
2 **Diversity** refers to the recognition, respect, and celebration of differences across language, culture, race, gender, sex, religion, and other protected characteristics. In diversity, individuals who are representative across these categories have a different lived experience which must be accounted for.
3 **Inclusion** refers to the process of creating an environment, policies, and practices that allow individuals from diverse backgrounds and perspectives to feel welcome and valued. An inclusive environment does not reject the fact that there may be unconscious and structural

DOI: 10.4324/9781003367208-6

biases, but adopts strategies to manage them. Inclusive environments promote equality and diversity. For example, in sport teams, inclusion is achieved by ensuring an inclusive team environment regardless of age and experience to ensure that younger players/new players/players from different backgrounds have the freedom to express themselves, develop and are not treated differently. At a structural level, an example could be UK Sport's dedicated female coaches' leadership programme, which brought together 28 experienced female coaches across 16 sports to improve representation of female coaches in Olympic and Paralympic high-performance community by Paris 2024.

Note: Protected Characteristics (protected under the Equality Act 2010 in the UK, Civil Rights Equality Act 1964 in the United States and national Constitutions in other countries) are legally protected categories preventing discrimination on these grounds to be illegal. Discrimination (direct/indirect), harassment, victimisation, and bullying under the grounds of age, disability, marriage/civil partnership, pregnancy/maternity, race, religion/belief, sex, sexual orientation, and gender reassignment are illegal.

EDI and ethics

As a sport psychology consultant, we adhere to ethical codes of conduct. Depending on your geographical location of practice, this will be mandated by a legislative body such as the Health Care Practitioners Council (HCPC) or organisational bodies such as the American Psychological Society (APA), British Psychological Society (BPS), British Association of Sport & Exercise Sciences (BASES), Canadian Psychological Society (CPA), and others.

To conduct our applied practice in an ethical and socially responsive manner, it is imperative that we are inherently grounded in a range of competencies aligned to EDI. This includes socially responsive ethical decision-making, where dilemmas and actions are considered through an EDI lens. Ethical codes did not always have EDI considerations. For example, the APA code of ethics, which is the most widely adopted one from 1953, did not have any consideration of culture and diversity as a part of ethical decision-making (Golann, 1969). The latest version approved by the APA Council of Representatives in 2016 (APA, 2017) has included an emphasis on culturally responsive practice and EDI but is still considered as being underdeveloped (O'Donohue, 2016). In contrast, more recent versions of the BPS and CPA code of ethics focus on the personal protected characteristics and cultural context on ethical decision-making. For example, CPA explicitly states that ethical issues should involve the consideration of 'the cultural, social, historical, economic, institutional, legal or political context, or other circumstances in which the ethical problem arose' (CPA, 2017, p. 5).

Let us look at Welfel's (2016) 10-step model of ethical decision-making:

1. Develop ethical sensitivity and awareness.
2. Consider facts and stakeholders in the context prior to defining the issue.
3. Examine ethical standards.
4. Examine laws and regulations.
5. Examine the professional ethics literature.
6. Apply principles and virtues.
7. Seek consultation (with supervisors).
8. Independently deliberate on dilemma.
9. Make and implement decision and document each step.
10. Reflect on the process and decision made.

Welfel's (2016) model of ethical decision-making focuses on the initial development of ethical awareness and consultation with resources before moving on to the consideration of facts, the stakeholders and the sociocultural contexts to define the ethical issue. This is important in aligning ethics to EDI, since what is unethical when viewed from an EDI lens may be completely normal when viewed without an EDI awareness. Once these fundamental standards are specified the application of fundamental ethical principles such as respect for autonomy, beneficence, justice, non-maleficence, and fidelity are considered. You will cover the full outline of what these ethical principles are in your training programme and supervision. We signpost you to an excellent primer by Nagy (2011) for further reading on mastering the core essential ethics for psychologists.

More recently, Juntunen et al. (2023) proposed a socially responsive ethical decision-making model that comprises the following seven steps:

1 Identify the issue with a wide and diverse lens (including EDI).
2 Engage in self-reflection that includes own biases and judgements (including unconscious biases and beliefs).
3 Consult with ethical standards, laws, ethnic/cultural minority guidelines, and commentaries.
4 Consult with diverse peers and colleagues.
5 Develop multiple options or pathways.
6 Develop and implement an action plan.
7 Reflect on both process and outcome, involving diverse colleagues.

Juntunen et al.'s (2023) model incorporates greater consideration of stakeholder identities aligned with EDI principles and the ways those identities apply to the operation and understanding of individual and groups. It also accounts for understanding structural or personal unconscious biases within an EDI perspective that allows looking at the dilemma holistically. We recommend drawing from the multicultural orientation framework (see David et al., 2018) and the T-R-E-E-S model (see below) to absorb cultural comfort, cultural curiosity, cultural humility, and self-reflection to the development of EDI underpinned ethical professional identity. This allows the decision-making to be grounded in the sociocultural context of the dilemma and the lived experience of stakeholders being involved in the courses of action being considered. We refer you to Juntunen et al.'s (2023) article which includes applied case examples where this model has been applied.

Anti-discriminatory practice (ADP) while working with EDI

ADP is the ethical basis related to protecting people's dignity. ADP is how EDI-related equal treatment regardless of demographic characteristics is translated into applied practice. Typically, ADI within training and licensing programmes are classified as 'social justice competencies' and include a broad range of responses, such as affirmative action in practitioner training, critical reflective skills, and multicultural psychotherapy skills (see Brown et al., 2019; Gupta, 2022). ADP, as an approach to applied work, is important when we look at the nuances of EDI in work. As we have clarified above, discrimination sometimes arises from enforced exclusion of desirable opportunities and experiences. For example, I have often worked with athletes who felt 'forced' to work with a sport psychology consultant in English, which was their third language, just because the sport psychology consultant did not speak their native tongue. Athletes have also fed back how sometimes when a sport psychology consultant who does not know their culture and lived experience works with them, the work is often superficial and without context.

Therefore, the essence of anti-discrimination or ADP in action is the inclusion of equality and diversity. One way where ADP and EDI work together to promote individuals is through a process called 'Integration'. Integration refers to a situation where there is an inclusion of different individuals and groups through equal opportunities, but also an active recognition and action that facilitates contacts and good relationships between different groups. For example, you are the sport psychology consultant at a football club in the UK, and a 'wonderkid' from Chile is moving over. Integration actions in this sense would be something like developing your cultural understanding of the player's culture, particular background, and lived experience. Integration would take it a step further to work with the club and the team to ensure that the player is involved within the social identity of the team and feels a part of it via group level interventions and activities. A real-life example of this is teams not spraying alcoholic champagne or beer over their teammates in order to respect their religious beliefs (e.g., Bayern Munich with Ribery, Australian Cricket Team with Khawaja are some examples).

Working and understanding how 'Privilege' leads to discrimination and structural inequality is another area where ADP assists EDI. Privilege refers to the inherent advantages of particular social identities and groups which are typically automatically helpful. At a broader level, psychology and psychologist training is a white, middle-class profession (Spalding et al., 2019). This is also the case in sport psychology as a field (Gupta, 2022; Gupta & Divekar, 2022; Quartiroli et al., 2022; Schinke et al., 2009). Research into the line of privilege was initially conducted by Peggy McIntosh in the United States (McIntosh, 1988, 1990). She compared her circumstances as a female to African-American female colleagues and listed an autobiographical account of unearned racial advantage. Although societal change has happened in the three decades since, I highlight some pertinent reflections below with some adaptation to larger culture and sport:

- I can if I wish arrange to be in the company of people of my race, ethnicity, and culture most of the time.
- I can see people of my social identity group widely and appropriately represented in media.
- I can worry about discrimination without being worried that I am self-seeking or self-interested.
- If my day or week or year is going badly, I need to ask if each negative episode or situation had racial, religious, or other discriminatory overtones.
- I do not actively have to change my behaviours in day-to-day life at the fear of potential discrimination and lack of opportunity.

While some may consider that sport, an arena where things are gauged by the stopwatch, does not have any place for privilege, there are indeed elements of privilege in sport. The simplest one is financial backing and socio-economic status (SES) which gives greater exposure, access to infrastructure, and better access to coaching. This is the reason some of the more 'expensive' sports, notably golf and motor racing, are severely underrepresented by minorities and low SES individuals, not just as players, but also as support staff. Another example shows how structural racism combined with privilege leads to institutional subtle backstage racism. For example, minority underrepresentation of BME in football leadership positions across Europe is an 'open secret' (Bradbury, 2013, p. 300). This underrepresentation reflects wider inequalities such as limited social mobility, which has a knock-on effect through territorial and infrastructural isolation. An example of this intersectionality is how 'White-collar' jobs in football clubs are based in 'white' locales (Bradbury, 2013). Such clandestine backstage racism in sport occurs privately, untouched by public activism (Hylton & Lawrence, 2016).

Life Lived

Working within professional sport, especially franchise type leagues, often includes the necessity to adapt to a new player coming in through a transfer. The player was a 17-year-old centre back from Moroccan-French origin who had moved to the UK with his mother and brother from Nantes a few years before he got picked up by the club. I had a very little understanding of French-Moroccan culture and other markers of diversity. However, working to integrate the player within a predominantly white, UK, middle-class demographic within the performance pathway was a primary goal for me.

Several key cultural factors emerged. Some were familiar to me (from my personal experience of having been brought up outside the UK, and being from the Global South myself), others were unfamiliar territory. Some key factors which were diversity markers within the environment were his religion (practicing Muslim), language (spoke English, Arabic and French fluently), and attachment pattern with his immediate family. There was also a high degree of importance attributed to education, since his mother perceived sport as an unstable and 'risky' career. In times of low performance and on one instance an injury, this acted up as a major stressor and perpetuating factor. A big focus was on cultural awareness to understand what parts of his cultural identity he treasured, what were elements he found difficult to adjust to, and how open he was to the assimilation process to the team and to UK culture after the first couple of years there. A key part of this was to acknowledge differences in culture; to give him the space and support to understand that his identity was being valued; and to understand and engage in a knowledge-sharing process to know the things that were unknown instead of keeping them unacknowledged. This culminated in the team joining into Eid celebrations, and the player leading a Moroccan tea brewing morning where everyone took part. Conversely, during Christmas and Easter, he was an active part of the dressing room decorations and the celebrations. This was an example of building togetherness and inclusivity within the team's social identity itself.

ADP and EDI work requires training and a model of reflective practice. Before we delve into the T-R-E-E-S model, let us clarify certain terms and phenomena below:

1 **Culture** is the total of traditions, beliefs, patterns of behaviour and creative productions of a particular identity group that are important to that group. In sport, there is a sub-culture of a sport. For example, golf and track-field will have a different subsets of traditions and patterns of behaviour which will be distinct from one another. 'Culture' as a concept can be developed for any identity group and is not just linked to protected characteristics alone. The beliefs, behaviours, and the co-created action over a period allow us to gain an insight within that culture.
2 **Cultural competence** refers to the ability of an individual (at times a larger sport organisation, see Wagstaff & Burton-Wylie, 2018) to acquire sufficient knowledge of the diversity within a culture. This promotes tolerance, reduces stereotypes, prejudice and improves acceptance (Pope-Davis et al., 2003). In applied psychology, the aim goes beyond knowing and developing patterns of action to ensure support provided is culturally sensitive and

respected within the context. An over simplistic example would be understanding how to dress in a sporting event, or when invited to a wedding of a different culture where you are not sure.

3 **Microaggressions** are commonplace verbal, environmental, or behavioural messages that may be intentional or unintentional communications of hostile, derogatory, and negative attitudes towards stigmatised and/or culturally marginalised groups (see more Sue, 2010; Sue et al., 2007). Microaggressions are not single instance incidents. Rather, they reflect an ignored, overlooked, constant, and cumulative hostility that subtlety communicates prejudice and discrimination. Microaggressions can be microinsults (e.g., rudeness or insensitivity to EDI), microinsults which exploit protective characteristic derogations (e.g., overt insults, avoidance behaviour, active discrimination), and microinvalidation which are communications that invalidate diverse experiences.

4 **Social devaluation** is the process where an individual is cast into negative social roles, typically in association with some aspect of their social identity. This is a process of stigmatisation that occurs as discrimination. Some examples may include denial or restriction of opportunity for participation, functioning, or development (e.g., refusing entry of women to cricket club Pavilions); systematic rejection by social agencies or from social networks (e.g., exclusion of opportunity or deselection due to race, ethnicity, religion, or other); 'Symbolic marking', i.e., surrounding identity with negative, degrading and/or damaging labels that lead to stereotypes (e.g., senior men's England football players Saka, Rashford and Sancho received racist 'monkey' labelling's after their Euro defeat), or an assumption of higher manipulative power.

ADP and reflective learning: The T-R-E-E-S model

Literature has pointed out that a key part of ADP is to mitigate the conspiracy of silence (Sue, 2005) and critically reflect on EDI elements and discuss them during training and education (Carter & Davila, 2017; Gupta, 2022). By reflecting on the action, we can better implement EDI-based practice for applied practice in the future to accelerate ADP (Gupta, 2022). This is important in the dynamic and multicultural context of a sport, where the EDI elements of practice such as multidimensionality, cultural awareness, cultural humility, and contextual understanding cognisant of protective characteristics are essential (see Gupta & Divekar, 2022). Therefore, we outline the T-R-E-E-S model (Gupta, 2022) that provides a framework to develop a fluid reflective ability grounded in ethics and EDI values to understand what we *wanted* to do, what we *did, how* we did it, and *why*.

The T-R-E-E-S model echoes the need to be an effective scientist practitioner within a how-to framework to develop ADP skills. We outline it below with examples to explain it further.

- **T** = Theory. This element refers to the theory, literature, and evidence that underpin all applied practice at all levels (Harwood, 2016; Moran, 2013). This theory and literature form the roots of ADP training. On a practical level, growing the theoretical roots as a trainee will refer to developing a familiarity with ADP literature base. Some suggestions for further reading are Amari (2021); Appuhamilage (2012); Blodgett et al. (2015); Brown et al. (2003); Caudwell (2017); Jarvie (2003); Lago and Smith (2010); and Sarantakis (2017).
- **R** = Research. Research is the process of investigation that every trainee engages in formally or informally to explore new avenues, evaluate our interventions, change

elements and components, and actively look to generate knowledge you may not be familiar with. This forms the trunk of the tree. This is how we actively engage in the research process to upskill and develop. For example, during these initial years of training, I did not find any literature on reflections and multicultural practice in sport psychology during my doctoral training on critical inquiry in psychology. I then worked to convert this training into reflection papers (see Gupta & Divekar, 2022), intervention research in new cultural consequences (Chungath et al., 2023), and emotional intelligence in an Indian sport context (Aravind et al., 2022). We are not saying that every trainee must engage in new research to upskill themselves in ADP and EDI: however, every trainee should actively engage in some formal or informal research within their practice per guidelines.

- **E** = Ethics. Ethics are the branches that determine the course of our actions. We have provided a model of how ethics can be implemented in an ADP context above. The situation and context-specific reflection of ethics is important in ADP practice to ensure EDI. For example, when working with an interpreter or a translator, it is important to conduct client contracting to get an understanding of that. As the branch of the tree, ethics is the combined application of theory (roots) and research (trunk) in context-specific situations.
- **E** = Experience. Experience refers to the lived experience that we as individuals possess. This is an essential part of reflective practice, since our experience directly influences our interaction with EDI. Applied work often requires an embedded practitioner, and applied work too is not contained within a microcosm. Rather, our personal experience is influenced by social construction (Cameron, 2020). There is an active transfer of our unique identities and experience into the sporting experience, which should be considered and reflected upon (see Gill & Kamphoff, 2010; Schinke & McGannon, 2015). A key component of education is to improve the self-recognition of our lived experience of how our culture, race, gender, sexual orientation, and other elements have shaped our beliefs. This reflective process is a continuous process in the training environment that can allow the individual to constantly revitalise their skills by learning from their life experience and new diversity exposure (see Bolton, 2010; Quartiroli et al., 2020). These experiences are the leaves of the tree which are present but often shed and alter as the seasons of our experience comes through (see 'Life Lived' box below).
- **S** = Specificity. Specificity refers to the context-specific combination of the different elements of the T-R-E-E to bear the fruits of ADP for EDI during our applied work with our clients. Specificity allows us to be grounded in work. This may include considerations of culture, language, religion, sport context, competitive environment, or our own biases. For example, ADP looks different when we switch geographical locations with their cultural differences, causing a difference in the dominant hegemony. For example, think of an ethnically white practitioner born and brought up in the UK, who then secures a contract to go work in Saudi Arabia where he is the religious and racial minority (the same can be reserved). They would have to understand the T-R-E-E in the culture they are in, rather than view this with the cultural lens from the UK.

We recommend using the T-R-E-E-S model as a metaphorical reflection map. When we continuously focus on building a reflective capacity, we can develop it via training, supervision, and refine it through a willing effort. These T-R-E-E-S forms the foundation to make meaning from diverse experience by engaging in ADP to achieve EDI, especially when working with clients with diverse experiences. This is achieved via an introspective exploration within our 'self' and different sociocultural identities within who we are. Some strategies to develop practices to develop our T-R-E-E-S are listed in the section below. For now, let us look at T-R-E-E-S in action in the 'Life Lived' box below.

Life Lived

T-R-E-E-S distilled within an applied practice of ethical reflective learning will be the focus of this life-lived box. We will look at the case of an athlete who grew up in a household with two refugee parents who travelled to the UK from Afghanistan for political asylum. Supporting this athlete through a cricketing transition while he was managing wider adjustment concerns was a challenge for me.

I adopted the T-R-E-E-S model to understand how to negotiate this.

- **T** – Theory, I sourced literature from social psychology around assimilation, immigrant communities, wartime immigration, resilience post catastrophe and political persecution, and the mental health of refugees.
- **R** – Research was guided by investigating IOC documentations on refugee athletes, and community sport as a way of assimilating refugees into a new culture. Beyond this, my research also included documentaries and films to understand lived experience so that I would have a reference point to start from and be culturally aware.
- **E** – Ethics was an important pause point here since it would be unethical to start any interventions without understanding the cultural legacy and context which the athlete holds to be a big part of them. However, there was very little ethical documentation on multicultural practice. I reflected with the Anderson et al. (2004) model to apply situational ethics and constantly checked in with my supervisor.
- **E** – The experience of being multilingual and having orthodox Asian origin parents is something I have grown up around and have seen in other people. I drew upon this experience as a starting point and checked in with the client, which allowed us to build trust, rapport, and get him to share his experiential viewpoints. Some existing qualitative literature from general psychology also helped.
- **S** – Specificity in work was important. The adjustment issues the client was facing were because of the discrepancy between cultural orientation at home and in their external life. There was also a pressure of adapting sport to fit around everything his family demanded of him. Specificity was also important in interventions. For example, his self-talk interventions were in English, but his emotional regulation-related self-talk was in Arabic, which was the language he defaulted to under emotional stress.

Strategies to engage in ADP for EDI during trainee days

Quartiroli et al. (2020) report that greater exposure to ADP training workshops, diverse clients, and research improves the perceived cultural competence of sports psychology consultants. Literature also indicates that trainees and sport psychology consultants who abstained from critical reflection and debate around EDI/multicultural concerns were the most likely to show greater lack of awareness about privilege, cultural issues and be blinded in practice. This is a problem, since it actively inhibits the ability to develop culturally appropriate interventions (Chao et al., 2011). But the fact is, it is not an automatic process. Therefore, trainees need to adopt certain strategies to progressively develop these skills. We have listed them below. It is helpful to keep in mind that all these strategies are not the be all and end all. There is also not a mandated requirement to do them all in one go.

- Reflecting via individual and professional development process groups (read more at Yalom & Leszcz, 2020) is one avenue. Process groups study the behaviour of individuals through a learning process where interpersonal communications across situations are used to navigate through applied practice behaviours through experiential learning (see more at Swiller, 2011).
- Checking our assumptions, particularly in relation to what is visible and/or invisible (this may be our own privileges and surroundings of personal constructs and work).
- Understanding Complex Discrimination concepts – this might be breaking constructs down into social components, historical and cultural components to understand something (for example of race, we can understand the history of structural racism, how it permeates intergenerationally and how it impacts sport in modern times).
- How and when do we use our 'voice'? How is it best to 'be'? This relates to the particular context and knowing ourselves so that if areas of practice arise where EDI and ethics are being violated, we are cognisant and supportive of corrective action. For example, this may be an interview that you are giving as the sport psych and a sexist comment being made. You could either ignore it or call it out and correct it. Something as simple as microaggressions such as name mispronunciation or abbreviation of names without consent are also anti-EDI behaviours.
- Pressure to 'be' and how to act are informed by how we are who we are. This is relevant if you are a part of a minority group yourself.
- Behaviour is best understood in context – when making adaptations to a service/intervention, listen to the voices of the people whose needs we are trying to meet! On this note, especially when working with multicultural elements of groups that you may not be familiar with, dialogue is important to understand the needs of the 'other'.
- A desire to help others should be balanced with an individual perspective, there should be an inclination to help, to not want to offend, or be too quick or eager. We must remember to pause, listen and not assume that we 'know'.
- One minority group does not hold the monopoly on discrimination. All forms of discrimination are violations of EDI. Aligned with the concept of intersectionality, we should recognise that diversity exists within minority groups.

Working with and supporting EDI: Concluding comments

It is hard to keep an open mind, respecting the individual experience of clients from diverse backgrounds. Be an ally of EDI as well. You do not have to agree with everyone or everything. I have found it difficult to agree with every perspective that every client has brought into the sessions. But that is not my job. Remember that you do not have to agree to learn how people think, feel, and experience life. You do not have to share their cultural background or identity to be curious about what shaped them to be who they are today.

Acknowledge who you are. Appreciate and respect the identity of who others are. Reflect on the connection of both to inform your practice.

Section II

Getting Started with Service Delivery

6 Establishing a Placement

Introduction

Regardless of where you are on your professional journey, the excitement of 'doing' sport and exercise psychology is most likely the reason you are where you are. Placements are a crucial part of your development as a sport psychology consultant and form the core component of all training and development routes. It is important to find placements which stimulate, challenge, reward, and develop you as a practitioner, but identifying and securing suitable placements can be daunting. There is a lot to consider when seeking the perfect placement, and spending some time planning your approach can help you get the most from the experience.

There can be a temptation to dive straight in at the beginning of your training and start contacting sport clubs, gyms, and other organisations hoping to secure an exciting placement. Often there is a temptation to head straight for the top, and you would not be the first trainee to email a professional sport club promising to transform their fortunes before you even start your training. That enthusiasm and energy will be important and so keep it to hand, but it's helpful to take a step back and consider the role your placements have within the context of your training and your future career.

Which kind of placement?

Which settings excite you? Which sports can you see yourself work in and contributing to? Which skills and experiences are you desperate to learn and apply? Before starting to frantically search local clubs and organisations, take a moment to consider which placements might be most beneficial for you and your career development. Pragmatically, the ideal placement might simply be the one that you can start immediately and which guarantees your client hours within the time limits of your programme, but having one eye on where you want to be in the future might inform your decisions and direction. Placements which provide you with depth and breadth of experiences working in different applied contexts will enhance your CV, and if these align with the type of career or context you want to work in post-qualification, then all the better.

As a starting point, you might map out a five-year plan to help you understand your ambitions in terms of a future role, the type of organisation you see yourself working in, and the clients you see yourself supporting. There are lots of resources available online that can help with this horizon scanning and future planning, and it can be an important and fruitful activity. Once you identify the type of career, you might like to have (sport and exercise psychology is a profession which is growing with increasingly diverse roles and contexts where you might work), then it becomes easier to determine the type of placement that might be suitable. Some decisions here can be easy: if you really see yourself working in an elite or professional sport, then it is likely

DOI: 10.4324/9781003367208-8

helpful to gain experience within that space. If the picture of your future is a little fuzzier, then consider more variety in your placement and client experience to keep your options open and bring that picture into focus whilst you show competency in various contexts. Sometimes placement experiences can be just as useful in confirming the settings we definitely *do not* want to work in as they can in confirming the contexts we do …

One last thing to consider is what kind of placement and role are likely to motivate you. Deci and Ryan's (2000) self-determination theory has reached a point where applying it here can almost sound clichéd, but in the context of placement the Basic Needs Theory (Deci & Ryan, 2000) might offer some guiding principles for determining the suitability of suitable placements (and jobs in the future). If you can find placements which offer you the opportunity to fulfil your basic psychological needs of competence (i.e., you can apply your skills and develop new ones), autonomy (i.e., you have some control over the way your placement is set up, and the way you work with clients), and relatedness (i.e., you get to work with interesting colleagues and develop meaningful professional relationships within your placement), then the experience is more likely to be a positive and rewarding one. Applying psychological theory and knowledge to yourself is also a significant step in being a practitioner who practices what they preach!

Knowing me

Before contacting prospective placement organisations, it can also be helpful to take time to reflect on your existing skill set and experience. Some placement opportunities can be competitive, requiring you to set yourself apart from other applicants within applications and interviews. When contacting organisations directly for a placement, you will want to clearly emphasise your strengths and ability to contribute positively to their activities. You can also consider securing a placement as a practice for securing jobs in the future. You may need to submit CVs and cover letters for placement roles along with application forms, and then be invited to interviews, and preparing for these activities will enhance your chances of securing the ideal placements (as well as provide practice for future employability opportunities).

If you do not already have one, or it is not up to date, then crafting or revising your CV will always be a valuable use of your time to support securing placements. A CV should be a live document in the sense that you update it as you gain valuable experiences, but also in the sense that it should be adapted where possible for each role you are applying for. The university where you completed your undergraduate or postgraduate studies may offer careers support for alumni, including access to resources, advising, and checking on CV and cover letter content, and conducting mock interviews. Not enough students or graduates take advantage of the career's services offered by their institutions, but they can be invaluable in helping you demonstrate just how fantastic a candidate you are! There are other sources of support for developing CVs and cover letters offered by professional bodies and engaging with these resources will not be wasted effort. When pulling together your CV be sure to emphasise the education, training, skills, and experiences that most closely align with the role of a sport psychology consultant and consider the transferable skills that you can bring to any placement role.

During the process of mapping out your skills and experience within a CV, you might also want to consider the connections you have and networks you are part of, as these might also be helpful in securing appropriate placement experiences. The world of sport and exercise can be small, and we can achieve a lot by generating and managing your networks. Consider who you know within the professional landscape you see yourself in. Who might open some doors, put in a good word, make introductions, or find out the best contact within an organisation for you to communicate with? We should absolutely secure placements on merit, but maximising the connections you have might bring about some exciting opportunities.

The last step before seeking placements is to be quite clear about who a sport psychology consultant is and what they do. Our profession is still relatively young and there will be various clubs and organisations with limited or no experience of working with a sport psychology consultant. You will need to sell the profession and the difference it can make within an organisation if you want them to take you on placement. You will also need to be clear about the skills and competencies you have as a trainee, what you can and cannot provide, who you can and cannot support, and what the requirements are of the placement from a training perspective (e.g., skills, experiences, client hours, paperwork). As you will see below, being as clear, informative, and direct in your communication and in detailing both what you can offer during a placement and need from it is crucial, and so put the work in first to craft that message.

Finding suitable placements

As previously mentioned, consider finding suitable placements similar to that of finding a job in the future. The process can be exciting but also time consuming and disheartening when progress is not being made. You may have some quick wins but also some frustrations, disappointments, and dead ends. Hopefully, having done some of the above steps, you will be in a better position to have a positive experience, but do be prepared to have to persevere as the right placements are out there. There are different ways of searching for and securing placements:

- **Advertised placements.** These are not yet too common within our profession, but some exist. If completing your training via a university, you may have a placement coordinator who makes links with organisations and posts opportunities when they become available. You may also see advertised placements shared via your professional body or practitioner networks (which is why it helps to join these) or on social media. Where placements are advertised there is normally an application form and/or the need to submit a CV and cover letter, followed by an interview, and so do engage with the employability services and resources outlined above. Also, be prepared for applied demonstrations (e.g., demonstrating how you might engage with a client, or being ask to conduct a session with limited preparation time) and presentations to form part of professional interviews, even for placements, and consider these wonderful (if stressful!) opportunities to gain experience of this process as it will be invaluable when applying for jobs in the future.
- **'Cold-calling' organisations.** This approach is likely how most placements are secured by trainee sport psychology consultants. Although the number is increasing, few placement opportunities are advertised by organisations and so you are likely going to have to generate placement opportunities by contacting organisations directly. You might start initially by considering any existing personal and professional networks you have that might facilitate placements. Do also be sure to make use of the support offered by a placement coordinator and/or supervisor (depending on training route) who might make connections for you with suitable organisations. Some decisions might need to be made at this stage about the nature and context of the type of placement you are looking for, especially if you are struggling to generate opportunities. For instance, if you already have experience within a context (e.g., within a specific sport as an athlete or coach, or as staff or user within a leisure/gym setting), then you will want to balance the pros and cons of continuing to work in that space. Pros might include easier access to placement opportunities through your existing networks and gaining experiences working within a context and environment that you are familiar with.

Cons might include possible conflicts of interests (e.g., working with athletes with a dual coach/sport psychology consultant role, or even needing to work with athletes you compete against!). Cons might be not adding breadth to your CV and showing that you have experience in a range of settings.

- **Existing placements.** Some trainees will already work within organisations that can provide a placement experience, such as within a football academy or academic institution. Training might be part of a programme of professional development agreed as part of that trainee's role, and the organisation might provide the trainee with access to clients to fulfil all their placement hours. Trainees in this position are incredibly fortunate, but will also want to consider whether their existing role/employer provides the opportunity to work with the variety of clients and using a range of approaches that most professional training pathways require.

Whether applying for an advertised placement or seeking to create your own opportunities, a common task will be to do your research about the organisation(s) you are hoping to undertake a placement with. Knowing the context (e.g., sport), organisation, set-up, and activities well will mean that you can make your approach to them, whether application or via email, as specific to the organisation's needs and aims as possible. Some key things to consider when approaching and communicating with placement organisations:

- **Advertised placements**
    - As mentioned already, make sure you have an up-to-date CV to send to prospective placement organisations.
    - Be prepared to draft a cover letter explaining why you are interested in the role and how you meet the person specification.
    - Both the CV and cover letter should be made specific to the placement opportunity. Your CV might not change dramatically but you may wish to reorganise content to emphasise your experience in relation to key requirements within a person specification.
    - Make sure applications are submitted in time and to the correct place.
    - If possible, it is always a good idea to contact the named person for an advertised opportunity to discuss the opportunity further and answer questions. Doing so makes sure you can make your application as specific and focused on the role as possible, but also puts you on the recruiter's radar (hopefully because they are looking forward to reading your application!).

- **Approaching organisations directly**
    - Make sure that you clearly communicate in an introductory email what you are looking for from a placement and the value you can bring.
    - An up-to-date CV should be attached to an email.
    - Always try to identify a named individual within an organisation that you can direct your initial email to. If you are not sure who that might be, call or email the general email address for the organisation and ask who you should direct your correspondence with.
    - Avoid emailing seeking a placement directly to the general enquiries email address for an organisation as there is no guarantee the email will be passed on.
    - Do not expect to convince an organisation to agree to take you on placement after just one email. Summarise the opportunity and suggest a meeting to discuss the next steps.
    - Consider offering to complete a brief consultancy project to kick off your placement where you map out the opportunity and develop a process that will facilitate you gaining the client hours you need whilst also making the biggest difference within the organisation.

Agreeing a placement

You've done the hard work and convinced an organisation that they should take you on placement and that you can contribute positively to their operation whilst meeting your course requirements. The next step in the process is to agree on what a placement will look like and to map out expectations on both sides. There will be different requirements at this step depending on your training route. For instance, you and your placement organisation may need to complete paperwork to register the placement and show that you will gain a suitable experience that meets your learning needs. They may also ask you to complete paperwork or checks depending on the organisation and the clients you will work with. During this process of working out what the placement will look like, you might gain clarity and confirmation of some of the following:

- **Payment.** Whether trainees should be paid for placements is always a tricky topic with no simple solution. If you can find a placement that pays you as a trainee, then you are on to a good thing, but do not expect that to be the norm. In an ideal world, all sport and exercise psychology placements would be paid, but unfortunately, the profession is not at the point where that is the case. Many of the organisations that trainees complete placements are run by volunteers and do not have funding to pay for psychological support. There is work to be done as a profession to demonstrate the value that we bring and to create a culture where that value is recognised in appropriate payment, but that might be a little way off. In the meantime, you need to balance the opportunity a placement provides you. Regardless of your training route, you will need access to clients via placements to meet and demonstrate your competencies, and so a placement offers you vital experiential learning and development. In return, you offer psychological support to clients within that placement organisation. There is a win-win element within that arrangement in that you are both gaining from it, and when in that space you can promote the profession of sport and exercise psychology and demonstrate first-hand the value that a sport psychology consultant can add. Try to make yourself as indispensable as possible, hopefully leading to paid employment in the future within the organisation.
- **Expenses.** Whilst you might not expect payment from some or any placements, you should not be expected to be significantly out of pocket because of a placement experience. If you feel appropriate, request that reasonable expenses be provided to cover some of the logistical costs involved in your offering support to the organisation. These costs are most likely associated with travel, and whilst you might not feel it is appropriate to, for instance, request travel expenses to attend training, if you need to travel to games or outside of your local area to support clients, then you should push for the placement organisation to cover any additional costs to you. Your placement coordinator and/or supervisor should be able to offer additional support and guidance about how to manage such conversations with your placement organisation.
- **Shape of placement.** Although you will have outlined what you can and cannot offer as a trainee sport psychology consultant, it might only be through discussion and placement with the placement organisation that you get a sense of what the 'day-to-day' activity of your role during placement might look like. It is vital that as part of discussions and any agreement, you are happy that the placement will provide you with the experiences needed to demonstrate competencies within your training programme, which normally means guaranteed access to clients. Where placement organisations have never had sport and exercise psychology input, it might be challenging for them to be able to conceptualise what such a placement might look like, and you will need to be confident in your approach to structuring

a placement to meet your needs. Again, some consultancy at the start of the placement might help you scope out what the placement experience might look like and how you maximise the opportunity it offers.

- **Expectations for placement activity.** It will be important to have clarity and agreement about what the organisation expects from you as a member of the support team supporting clients. Some organisations may prefer you to be arms-length from the day-to-day activity and accept referrals as and when needed, but more rewarding placement experiences are those where you are integrated into the wider team within an applied context. It can help to consider a placement as being like a job, with similar expectations of the placement organisation to treat you like a staff member. You will therefore also need to determine expectations about how often you should be at training or competitions (within sport contexts) or available on site, whether you should provide support online or in-person (or both), whether you should wear certain kit (which should then be provided), and whether you should participate in team meetings and your role within them. It is important to once again stress that you need to be forthright in explaining your own educational and experiential needs and balance these as best as possible with the needs of the organisation.
- **Expectations of a placement organisation.** Depending on your training route there may be guidance in place which outlines the expectations of all stakeholders within a placement environment (e.g., trainee, placement organisation, placement supervisor, clients). In most cases, you will need to have an identified manager within the organisation, normally referred to as a placement educator, who handles the day-to-day support for your placement within the organisation. The placement educator will be your main point of contact and is normally expected to be the named individual within the organisation responsible for ensuring that you are given appropriate access to experiences which support your learning and development. The placement educator will also likely be required to complete paperwork as part of the placement set-up as well as part of the ongoing evaluation of your work during the placement. Knowing the placement processes and deadlines well will help you to support your placement educator in completing these in a timely fashion.

Establishing a placement: Concluding comments

Placements are a vital part of your training route and development as a practitioner. Navigating securing suitable placements can be tricky, especially when you need to convince organisations of the value a sport psychology consultant can bring before they will even consider taking you on board. Identifying the unique skills and experiences you can bring to a placement, as well as considering the placement that might help you meet your long-term ambitions, will lead to more meaningful and rewarding experiences. Be confident about the contribution you can make in supporting organisations and clients, and be a passionate advocate for the role that sport and exercise psychology can have in making.

7 Getting Started with a Client

Introduction

Getting started with a client means an equally exciting and daunting challenge for most trainees. Following on from basic counselling skills classes (e.g., triads) with fellow trainees to attain one's fitness to begin practice still means meeting a new client for the first time, which funnels trainees in one of two directions. Either they enjoy the possibility and privacy of working with a new client for the first time or they fear the calamity that might unfold over the 50-minute hour. Meeting a client for the first time happens repeatedly throughout our careers and it forms a critical starting point if the client is to engage in the therapeutic process. What matters most here, however, is that we learn to scaffold a safe space and structure for our work, learn from our experiences, and continue to improve how we undertake and deliver the first session.

The initial session with a client might be the start and end of your support (e.g., single-session therapy or crisis intervention) or, more likely, the first of several sessions. If the initial session is the only session with a client, there are several reasons for this outcome. For example, the initial session is sufficient, or perhaps the client needs to be referred elsewhere, or because of financial constraints, one session is all that is possible. The nature of the initial meeting means that some practitioners extend the 50-minute hour to 90 minutes where assessment, formulation, and an initial intervention begin. The persistent demands of sport and performance settings often mean getting a grip on the presenting issue for the upcoming performance. Regardless of which issues arise in the first session, our intentions ought to be to work ethically, safely, and professionally with difference and diversity, develop a working alliance to focus on the client's needs, self-awareness, within a coherent framework of theory, skills, and techniques finishing with a reflective dimension to learn, develop, and grow personally and professionally (e.g., competence, autonomy, skills) (Ballantyne Dykes et al., 2017). These processes interact in the helping route, so it is helpful to know the cycle.

A note about clients

Before we explore each of these elements, it seems sensible to recognise and realise some broad principles about the humans with whom we work. Cozolino and Santos (2014) argued that evolution stitched genetics, biology, and relationships with minds, communities, and cultures over time to create an astonishing social organ – our brain. But because of these interdependent complexities, things go wrong, so our brain lies at the mercy of dysregulation, dissociation, and distress. To manage these challenges, however, we also possess precious tools and resources for healing, such as relationships, language, and empathy.

DOI: 10.4324/9781003367208-9

Through evolution, the old and new systems of our brain work together and apart at varying speeds with mixed goals, which means we are vulnerable to mental distress. These interdependent and mutually reinforcing belongings crafted by human workmanship include:

1 a fast and slow information processing system,
2 critical early learning,
3 core shame,
4 an anxiety bias, and
5 illusion.

To explain each one briefly, our brains process sensory, motor, and emotional information in 10–50 milliseconds, but to register in conscious awareness, it takes 500–600 milliseconds. The fast (primitive) system means we can react without conscious awareness to catch a ball or make a save – using our implicit or somatic memory. Our slow system processes conscious experience, which means we can tell the story of the save and how it happened on the pitch after the match. With this fast system, our past is present. By the time we are consciously aware of an experience, our brain has searched and scanned our band of memories, bodies, and emotions for relevant information, which means our thoughts, feelings, and behaviours launch before we have time to make sense of it all.

Our early learning disproportionately shapes our neural systems with lifelong consequences. Our fast system stores the early sensory, motor, social, and emotional learning, while conscious learning (slow system) takes years to develop. With good enough parents doing good enough parenting, the building blocks of a healthy, helpful brain lay down; however, a child abused or neglected, for example, early in life, comes to realise symptoms (e.g., explosive anger, eating disorders, drug, and alcohol problems) in adolescence and adulthood, without a conscious awareness of early life experiences.

We possess a primitive need to survive, and to survive, we need to be part of a tribe. To be part of a tribe, rather than feeling capable, worthwhile, and lovable, some children experience the opposite and witness themselves as flawed, useless, and unlovable. With core shame, we feel a sense of worthlessness, a fear of being exposed and try frantically to be faultless in case someone uncovers us. In this predicament, the risk of being cast from the tribe seems eminent, always. We witness core shame in performance settings when the performative behaviour of the athlete continues far beyond the needs of the task or environment, such as excessive practice beyond what is necessary where chronic shaming becomes the disciplinary tool. For example, statements like 'The best athletes never stop working' or 'Why don't you work harder?' question the athletes' behaviour and the noose tightens. The athlete expecting connection receives a message of indifference or disapproval, meaning one must withdraw and try harder to remain within the tribe.

A bias towards anxiety helps our species to survive. Approaching certainty and avoiding risk makes sense, so we err on the side of caution and keep surviving. This bias, however, means that scaling risk and uncertainty often occur haphazardly. The fears we hold each day, unless addressed, render us rigid and passive and keep us in a cycle of dysfunction and reinforcement. Afraid to learn a new skill, we live with what we have. Afraid to try a new strategy, we stick with the old, unhelpful one. For someone being verbally abused consistently in a relationship, their amygdala (i.e., the brain structure judging the danger or safety of experiences in our world and encouraging us to proceed with caution) might conclude 'you're still alive'.

Finally, our illusions, misperceptions and distortion of events might help us survive, but they also harbour much suffering. Part of our brain circuitry (e.g., mirror neurons) endows us with a capacity to read the emotions and intentions of others and learn through observing and practising new skills in our minds. Though we are aware of others, we seem less aware of ourselves. Perhaps this lack of awareness twists reality in our favour, but there are costs. Our defences, such as repression, denial, splitting, idealisation, projection, control, displacement and reaction formation, support us in decreasing anxiety and shame, but our belief in our position means we repeat the behaviours that damage us. Using idealisation as an example, we elevate the ordinary to the extraordinary. We might place unrealistic expectations for a new golf coach to get our professional career back on track. At the outset, the coach can do nothing wrong, but with time, the idealisation fades and brings the relationship to an end. Or we might idealise ourselves by believing we have no faults or psychological difficulties (Burgo, 2012).

These five artefacts mean evolution hard-wired us with the ability to react quickly to events (i.e., threats); learn early in our lives how to survive coupled to a need for attachments and relationships, with a tendency towards anxiety, fear, shame, and illusions because of their survival value.

A structure for the first session

The context of sport and exercise means a first session might be at a sports arena, in a private practice clinic, or at a national championship, and the client group might range from children to adolescents, to adults as athletes, coaches, and teams. These moving parts mean trainees depend heavily on their training (e.g., triad work, therapeutic modality), developing experience, and supervision to help their clients in these first sessions. What helps most clients and trainees is a sensible framework that matches a chosen therapeutic modality (e.g., cognitive behaviour therapy, CBT; person-centred therapy, PCT) and offers clarity of purpose. We present a simple acronym, **PRIDE**, as a reminder to take pride in your work and be grateful for the privilege of working with others.

- **P**lan for the first session
  - Informing the client about the process – pre-therapy
  - Addressing expectations – education and client motivation
  - Presenting ways of working – details and duration of therapy
  - Bracketing
  - Managing our mood, and the mood in the room
- **R**elate sensitively with your client
  - Meeting, greeting, and seating
  - Supportively lead the session
  - Planning our time together
  - Building a bond – empathy and acceptance
- **I**dentify the presenting problem
  - Gathering and dealing with the data
  - Structure and guidance following your chosen therapeutic modality
  - Describe and explain the problem and its implications
  - Respect the client's view and ways of dealing with the problem
- **D**ecide on an action plan
  - Consider relationships and developmental stage
  - A proposed intervention developed together

    - Translating theory into practice
    - Instilling hope and confidence

- End with clarity and next steps

    - Routine assessment of progress and outcomes
    - Setting achievable goals for the therapy, client, and practitioner
    - The following sessions – time, regularity, fees
    - Reflections on the session

Plan for the first session

The first session with a client offers the practitioner and client an opportunity to begin a therapeutic relationship on the helping journey. Developing and strengthening the therapeutic bond increases the chances of a client receiving the support they seek. Knowing these ingredients, among others, means that the first session can begin before the first session. What we mean here is that pre-therapy or pre-service delivery and any guidance about the process of service delivery can begin before the first session. We find it helpful to write a letter or e-mail to outline the date, time, location, fees, and the process of confirmation or cancellation of the appointment. This letter or e-mail contains information about our services, approach to service delivery, and some case illustrations to show how we work. Sometimes, I (Paul) make this initial contact by telephone, limiting the call to 15 or 20 minutes so that the first session does not end up on the phone. We might ask the client to complete an information sheet that presents a stage of life (i.e., age), relationships (e.g., single, married, divorced), health (e.g., relevant medical conditions), social and cultural context (e.g., ethnicity, religion), sport and level (e.g., professional basketball player). Offering guidance about our services means we can manage the client's expectations of the service, educate the client about the process of service delivery, and create a self-determined motivation to work with a sport psychology practitioner. A frequently asked questions section on a website offers information for clients to read through to manage their concerns about the process. For example, some information might relate to ways of working with client, the typical duration of service delivery, and professional accreditation.

Whether the first session is face-to-face or remote (i.e., online), preparing for your session seems sensible. For example, trainees and experienced practitioners feel anxious about first sessions with a client. Our worries, concerns, personal values, and challenges impede the work we need to do with a client, so we need to acknowledge these distractions, set them aside for now, and return to them later or after the session. We need our professional values to be in place to offer safe, ethical, and skilled support to our clients whose opinions, attitudes, values, and beliefs differ from ours. We know this process as bracketing. Bracketing also allows us to enter the room (physically or virtually) with a sense of hope and optimism for the client and their presenting problem(s) while our personal values and concerns remain outside the room. The practitioner's job is to contain and hold the client's feelings without bias or prejudice, so the client feels safe to share what feels right at their pace of disclosure.

Life Lived

My (Paul) private practice office is on the second floor of an inner city building with a glass-fronted door and secure entrance. Clients need to press the buzzer to enter the building, travel to the second floor, and ring the doorbell to enter the waiting area. It can be a little unsettling getting through the city, finding one's way into and through the building, so I am mindful to check-in with clients when they arrive. The client arrived approximately 15 minutes late and when she reached the waiting area; she appeared distressed, so I showed her to the room. When we entered the room, the client sat down (in my usual chair) and cried. I offered her the tissue box from the table. She continued to cry for the next 20 minutes with her feet on the chair and her chin lying on her knees and her arms wrapped around her legs. When she felt able to speak, she began by apologising for having her feet on the chair, said 'Oh I'm so sorry I had my shoes on your chair … thank you so much for your understanding, I feel so much lighter now'. Then she looked at her watched and said 'Oh gosh, is that the time already? I'm sorry, with this traffic, I had better leave for training. Might this time work next week also?'. I said the time was available to her, and she bounced out the door. Sometimes, initial sessions surprise me and this was one of those times

Relate sensitively with your client

The first session, like all sessions, is set aside for the client. Their privacy and confidentiality are boundaries to be addressed and respected throughout service delivery. Interruptions, last-minute changes to arrangements, cancellations, and so forth are inevitable; however, where we can minimise these, we should take every opportunity to do so. Sport and exercise locales can mean less than favourable conditions for service delivery, but it is possible to find comfort and privacy in these informal settings and do good work. The usual meeting, seating, and greeting happens, but differently. Sometimes it means sitting in the stands of the stadium or walking around the training pitches, offering more privacy than the café, for instance. In our clinic, where we have chairs set an angle so we do not force direct eye contact, we can walk and talk and make eye contact where it fits outside. Our room outside offers us an open space without intruding furniture, which can present a physical (e.g., desk) and emotional barrier between the practitioner and client. With practice, you become familiar with sensitively leading the session. We write 'sensitively' because what we mean is that we provide a steer for the client about the unfolding process in a session. A simple opening might be:

> Hello, I'm Dr John Smith (who I am). I am a sport psychology consultant and I work closely with the other health professionals at the club (what I do), especially the club doctor, Dr Phil Betta. Today, we are meeting to explore your current difficulty in more detail and think about what actions you wish to take next (purpose of the meeting). We have 50 minutes together (our time together). I usually make a few notes during our conversation and any choices we come to. You're welcome to check out these notes whenever (what you will see me doing)

Building rapport

Not only can we continue to build rapport by leading the opening in the session, but also, we can ask questions to open the client's story.

Practitioner: Dr Phil Betta referred you to me. How do you feel about Dr Betta referring you to me, a sport psychology practitioner?

Client: Don't know, not sure what someone like you can do about it (*spoken in a diffident and dismissive tone*).

One way of protecting ourselves from our pain is to talk generally rather than specifically about an issue. It might be a way for a new client to test whether you are willing and able to listen effectively (Tolan & Cameron, 2017). Though such a response from a client might make you feel you and your profession ought to be protected by explaining how you can help, it is best to stay with the client's frame of reference. Sensing unease and diffidence, you can explore more about how the client thinks and feels about his presenting problem.

Practitioner: It sounds as though you feel pretty uncertain about your situation and perhaps wondering if this session is worth your time?

Client: … yeah, that's it. Nobody has helped so far. I'm not sure talking will make any difference.

Again, although you might feel a pressure to defend yourself and your profession by sharing how you can help with a solution, we can stay with the client.

Practitioner: Are you wondering whether it's worth discussing your struggle?

Client: To be honest with you, I'm fed up discussing it …

Practitioner: You looked as if you were about to say something and dismissed it.

Client: It's not that important.

Practitioner: Perhaps you could share it? It might make sense spoken out loud?

Client: I suppose … I was just going to say that I just get so angry, I'm hopping mad inside when I go out on the pitch and no one seems to care as much as I do. It's almost like for most of the lads that it would be nice if we won, but I have to win – I must win. I'm fighting for the team like a cornered animal because we are cornered – we're in a relegation battle! People just don't get it … we're a huge club and we could go down [get relegated].

In the verbatim exchange above, the practitioner and client are building a bond together, leaning on empathy, empathetic understanding, congruence, unconditional positive regard to explore the client's presenting issue(s).

Identify the presenting problem

A summary of what the client has shared at different junctures helps the client and practitioner recognise what they have shared so far. Summaries help the client feel heard and the practitioner shares out loud the client's primary concerns as the practitioner understands them so any discrepancies can be highlighted. Summaries also help clients to be specific, relevant, with a sense of personal control about their struggle(s).

Practitioner: And if you were relegated …

Client: It would be a total disaster. Our future depends on us remaining in this league. I enjoy living here, my wife enjoys living here and our kids, too. I've lived nowhere else …I've been at this club since I was eleven. They'd probably sell me, you know, and I'd have to move across the country, and I can't imagine my wife wanting to move away from everything she knows. I don't know what's happened this season and I feel I left everyone down, the club, my teammates, the fans, my family. I just haven't been playing to my usual standard. And, of course, you know I've got sent off twice and you can't be doing that as captain.

Practitioner:	Let me see if I have understood you correctly. With so much invested, there is so much at stake and you're fighting for everything you know and everyone – your family, your club, your fans – you sound angry and frightened and exhausted. I also sense a powerlessness you feel and perhaps that they will blame you for things going wrong.
Client:	Yeah, that sounds about right. I'm doing all I can and it's not enough. I feel like I'm to blame and I blame myself whether I am to blame. I'm flogging myself for …
Practitioner:	Are you remembering something in particular?
Client:	It sounds bad to say it. I mean, what am I complaining about? But I suppose it matters to me. I always kind of knew something didn't feel right.

Over the next few minutes, the client tells a story about the guilt he has carried with him over the past year. His mother, as a single mother, had two children, him and his older sister. His older sister was a delightfully talented and committed dancer who appeared to quit dancing when he was 13. He never understood why. It seemed like she lost interest. About a year ago, he asked his mother why Jennifer stopped dancing. Eventually, his mother told him she couldn't afford to send him to the academy at the football club and Jennifer to the dancing academy. Jennifer, being four years older, persuaded her mother to do whatever she could to keep his dream alive. Jennifer had looked out for him all his life. He could not think of a time when she didn't put him first. She always seemed to disadvantage herself to give him an advantage. His mother and sister worked things so that he never realised he was poor. The guilt of these revelations shook him to his core.

We allow the client to develop their presenting problem. Sometimes the presenting problem hides the real problem, but it allows the client some time to judge the suitability of the practitioner. At other times, it is the most pressing need, but the client wishes to proceed slowly because the issue is emotionally destabilising and needs to feel safe, first.

Decide on an action plan

Athletes, like the social milieu, learn to follow rules, reason and solve problems, strive for success, and, in defeat, return to do better than before. You'll notice the 'activity' or 'doing' in each preceding point. Depending on your therapeutic orientation, maybe another way offers a possibility. For instance, in person-centred practice, the fundamental hypothesis is that we all have within us the momentum of the actualising tendency – a force moving us towards well-being and satisfying potential. But what does that mean in practice? It means that the quotidian activities like advising, guiding, problem-solving, directing people's behaviour, telling them what to do, are redundant (Tolan & Cameron, 2017). The fundamental problem here lies with the sender, not the receiver. The sender's needs, experience, confidence, and skills make these suggestions without truly considering the receiver's needs, experience, confidence, and skills. Advising, guiding, and telling people what to do are often done with the highest regard for the receiver and, in some settings, it is helpful. In person-centred practice, we trust each person to find their own way. We trust the client's process. If the six conditions are present, our clients can access their own natural drive (i.e., actualising tendency) and use it more efficiently (Rogers, 1957).

Regardless of your therapeutic modality (e.g., person-centred therapy (PCT) and rational emotive behaviour therapy (REBT)), deciding on an action plan unfolds best when the reins lie in the hands of the client while you are nearby. It is usual to address one's feelings first to manage one's mood before processing other practical or emotional issues. For instance, managing relating with one's self (i.e., internal dimension) first means that the relational dimension (i.e., patterns of relating to others) and how they relate to their past and present life-stage challenges (developmental dimension) can be better understood and adjusted.

The problems in living and problems in performance that criss-cross in athletes' lives mean changing the ways clients relate across three dimensions: themselves, others, and their past. This first dimension, relating differently to oneself, means providing ways of coping more effectively with the problems in living and problems in performance. The second dimension relates to changing how the client relates to others. Clients are often unaware of their habitual patterns of communicating and behaving with others (e.g., partner, children, boss) and so cannot see how difficulties relating with others arise. Hidden away are the open, healthy, and mutual relationships that bring joy. The final dimension relates to our past and our life-stage. Though clients cannot change their past, they can change the ways they relate to their past. The anger or frustration towards others about specific incidents in their past, for instance, can change by relating differently to it (Ballantine Dykes et al., 2017).

In the case example, the client's guilt about: his privilege, his mother's sacrifices during his childhood, his sister relinquishing her flourishing dancing career, his club's current predicament, and his underperforming role as captain. The client felt he needed to heal the relationship with himself first. He had been overdoing everything in the past 9 or 10 months to rid himself of his guilt – running more, lifting more weights, training harder, eating the bare minimum – anything to punish himself for his privilege. Being hungry and undernourished meant he got injured more and couldn't recover as quickly. He also related irritably to his wife and children when he returned home after training. Every attempt the client made to deal with the problem seemed to make things worse.

Sketching a case formulation towards the end of the session based on what has been shared in the session helps to corral and make some sense of it. The psychological puzzle combines the client's information, what you have observed and heard, data from outside sources (i.e., third parties), with the therapeutic technique, theory, and research you have studied in your training programme. Using this information to guide an intervention poses another challenge; however, this is a clear expectation of the client. The client will seek a coherent explanation or summary of their presenting issue(s). Formulations are a skill which practitioners polish through practice and experience but mean different things in different situations depending on context and therapeutic approach.

End with clarity, feedback, and next steps

Bringing a session to a close is a procedural skill in therapeutic work which matters as much as opening a session with a client. On a broader note, the counselling performance skills a sport psychology practitioner uses in a therapeutic session with a client-athlete includes basic and advanced helping skills (e.g., empathic responding, confrontation, immediacy), theoretical techniques (e.g., reframing, two-chair exercise), procedural skills (e.g., opening and closing a session), and issue-specific skills (e.g., performance evaluation) (Borders & Brown, 2022). Before, during and after a session, the cognitive counselling skills involve the thinking processes of the sport psychology practitioner. These skills also include the moment-to-moment thoughts and actions of the practitioner in the session, for instance, what is going on in the session, how to answer the client, and how to step in and then assess one's behaviour.

Self-awareness, by the practitioner, means corralling one's personal issues, beliefs, and motivations that might influence the in-session behaviour and case conceptualisation. Without self-awareness, it remains extremely challenging to judge whether the case conceptualisation reflects the true nature of what the client presents. A sport psychology practitioner, based on their personal background, might establish an exceedingly positive or negative view of the client or identify strongly with the presenting issue(s) and feel stuck about how to help the client.

Like case conceptualisation or formulation, ending a session well is also a skill. Leaving ten minutes towards the end seems like a reasonable rule of thumb. We try not to force this ending; however, with reflection, feedback from clients, and discussions with a supervisor, this skill develops. In short, we intend to summarise the session, reach a decision about future decisions, and leave time for feedback from the client.

Summarising the session means presenting a coherent narrative of presenting issues, strengths and resources, and a formulation if one has been reached. In this way, the client hears what sense the practitioner has made of proceedings. Attending to the language of the client brings a resonance, so the client feels heard rather than translating their words and phrases into therapeutic literacy that means much less to the client. Summaries occur during a session and, at the end and in effect, present an intervention in themselves because they reframe the presenting issue. The final summary, however, also includes the next steps. These next steps vary; however, they typically include a schedule for sessions, the next session, contact between sessions, and any communication to third parties (e.g., head coach, healthcare practitioners).

Contracts

Service delivery is a contractual agreement where the client and the practitioner agree to work together according to specific parameters. It might be a time-limited contract (six to twelve sessions, for example) or an open-ended contract (no limit on the number of sessions). Contracts recognise and respect the client's autonomy in a professional relationship. Contracts establish clear boundaries to protect and serve the client and practitioner, for example, limits of confidentiality, number and frequency of sessions, fees, late cancellations, number, frequency, and duration of calls, e-mails, and response times between sessions. These contracts mean each party in the contractual agreement knows where they stand. Clients need to be protected also because practitioners might unknowingly or deliberately blur the boundaries about roles and responsibilities, crease a dependent relationship, or harm the client emotionally, psychologically, or physically. Some examples might include accepting gifts, texting the client about matters unrelated to treatment or appointments, touching a client without permission, and failing to refer a client when one's competencies do not meet the client's needs.

When the session ends, most practitioners make notes about the session. Sometimes these notes are brief and expanded upon later when time permits because you need to prepare for the next client (see McCarthy & Moffat, 2024 for examples of case notes). Reflective notes typically comprise content (what was presented by the client) and process (the relationship between the practitioner and client) in the session. It is customary for trainees to focus on content before they become oriented towards the process. A good supervisor will bring a focus upon process in supervision sessions and especially through process reports (Moffat & McCarthy, 2023). In the UK, for instance, clients might request access to their notes, keeping to precise observations of the client and the client's verbatim quotes rather than one's opinion. Some sessions are recorded for training with the client's consent. These sessions help us make sense of the notes we take and the verbatim quotes of the client.

Third parties

We, as sport psychology practitioners and client-athletes, form part of larger units such as squads, backroom staff, and multidisciplinary teams. These wider teams also need to be apprised of future actions and the process of support for the client and whether a referral seems necessary. The client needs to consent to any communication with these third parties.

Summary

You can redraw the 'map' to guide the first session or specific elements changed to suit the needs of the client or the practitioner's reflection on the value of the session to the client. You can adjust the principles, aims, and techniques as you move through the steps of a first session. In sport settings, the session location (e.g., track, golf course, training ground) or context (e.g., day of competition) brings challenges to the first session; however, the principles, aims, and techniques in the PRIDE model mean you can plan for these types of sessions, relate sensitively with your client, identify the presenting problem, decide on an action plan, and end with clarity and next steps for the client.

8 Preparing a Formulation

Introduction

Picture this: You're with a client. They have been talking for the past five minutes, telling you everything. Their issues, their insecurities, their successes, and they end with 'but I don't know exactly what's going wrong, but I do know I want to work on it'. Three questions come to mind immediately after. (1) What should I focus on here? (2) What is going on with the client? (3) How can we change it?

What is formulation?

Formulation is coming to a provisional explanation or a working explanation of how an individual presents a certain issue. It considers life experience, beliefs, and other factors that led to the development of that issue. Formulation can, and does, include personal psychological, biological, systemic, and lifespan factors to provide an explanation. It helps us answer (in this order) – What is going on with the client? What should I focus on here, and How can we change it?

Formulation allows us to summarise the client's presentation and integrate it with theory. It is about knowing *how*, knowing *why*, and knowing *when* a certain issue has presented itself within the client's experience. There is a point to consider here: different therapeutic modalities have different theories. So, will formulation look different for each practice modality? Yes, different therapeutic traditions differ in:

- The explanatory theory they draw on (e.g., four-factor model, unconscious discourse, narratives, etc.)
- Their position on diagnosis
- Position on pragmatic utility of formulation vs. absolute objective truth
- Levels of client involvement, (i.e., expert vs. collaboration)

However, the formulations also share certain key elements despite the therapeutic tradition:

- It is summarising and conceptualising client problems.
- Show how difficulties and strengths relate to each other or form patterns.
- Incorporate psychological theory and evidence.
- Identifies and explains the issue present with causes, maintenance factors, and description of the issue.
- Informs elements of an intervention plan based on elements identified.

DOI: 10.4324/9781003367208-10

Why is formulation important?

Formulation is important because real-life applied practice does not always adhere to the books and simulation exercises that typically encompass training. In applied practice, the client is a real person and not a neat case presentation that is written and provided to us. The psychologist and client always start off as two people who know little about each other. Formulation allows the psychologist to explore what issue the client is facing and get extremely important details about it. Therefore, formulation has been consistently linked to better therapeutic outcomes (Johnstone & Dallos, 2013). Before we go into the details of the process of formulation, let's look at some key terms associated with formulation (see Table 8.1).

Table 8.1 Key terms associated with the formulation

Key terms	*Meaning*	*Case example*
Client presentation	Is the overall 'concern' or issue that the client is reporting or what they want to focus on	'I am finding it very hard to concentrate on relevant things and I am really anxious'
Assessment	Refers to the process of investigation around psychological variables and the individual's life that are key to the client presentation	Engages in the process of risk assessment to check for anxiety attacks, uses a psychometric like HAM-A to check levels of anxiety and other interview techniques to formulate when the stressor is leading to anxiety
Target area	Refers to the specific area of focus that is mutually and collaboratively decided upon by the client and the psychologist. Typically, this is based on a prioritisation process	The focus is on the experience of anxiety itself, and how it is manifesting
Predisposing factors	These factors make the individual vulnerable to experience a difficulty	In this case, the individual has the pressure of sponsors to achieve a certain ranking by the end of the season
Precipitating factors	These are events or triggers that lead to the development of the issue	In this case, whenever the client fails to achieve skill execution and loses points below his expectations
Perpetuating factors	These are involved in making the problem continue. They are also called maintenance factors	Cognitive cycle stating 'I will lose this match and then my sponsors' which maintains the anxiety process
Protective factors	Traits or resources that the individual holds that act as coping strategies and contribute to resilience	The individual has a supportive coaching structure and has the fundamental mental skills of visualisation and behavioural consistency under pressure
Systemic factors	Refers to wider factors that go beyond the individual's immediate control. Examples include culture, cultural biases, organisational structures, and others	Sponsors are actively exerting pressures via reminders of the target
Temporal factors	Refers to factors around time and the occurrence of events that are time-bound or time constraints such as match/tournament schedules, injury recovery, personal life milestones	Season is ending in three months and he is right on the cusp of making it to his desired ranking and securing funding
Triangulation	Refers to the process where multiple sources of information (typically three or more) are combined to provide an in-depth understanding of the situation at hand	Talking to his manager on how the sponsors are pressuring him, observation during training and competitions and in-session discussions

Process of formulation

Formulation is an iterative process. It is not a single onetime photograph of the client's issues. It is something to which the psychologist returns to inform their work. All formulation work follows a process of exploration to achieve these objectives (see Butler, 1998, 1999 for further reading). Some of them are summarised below. Although there are listed in order, these processes typically happen simultaneously:

- **Clarification of questions:** Psychologists need to work with a formulation in mind which gives them a rough idea of what is happening with the client. They guide questioning and assessment, providing a map which they can follow. This enables good practice and beneficial psychologist-client interaction.
- **Priority process:** Most clients state one issue but have other things going on as well. It is essential to have a mental prioritisation process since it is not possible to work on everything at once. Therefore, the formulation process is a prioritisation and selection of what to work on.
- **Planning interventions:** Formulation gives a clearer picture of what is going on with the client and therefore directly informs the process of *selection* of intervention. Formulation tells us what is going on, and what ought to be done about it (see Figure 8.1).
- **Predicting what 'success' looks like:** Different target areas and interventions have different parameters of success. Formulation outlines the issue and, therefore, can predict what a 'successful' resolution of the issue will look like. For example, if a client has pre-competitive anxiety, a successful intervention would imply that the pre-competitive anxiety has reduced to the point of manageable arousal.
- **Troubleshooting:** Sometimes the psychologist gets stuck. This is not the end of the world because we can return to the formulation, update it if necessary and identify another intervention if needed. It also allows the psychologist to reflect on temporal changes in the client's life or to come back to reflect on their own learning process as part of professional development.
- **Bias and referral:** Working with a formulation improves accountability since it is a record that others can check if there is any bias or in the case of a referral. This is common in sport where the psychologist is likely to have out-of-session information and interaction with the client.

Now that we know what a formulation is, we can look what are the key things that formulation explores. The exact steps or focus points of the formulation will look different depending on the therapeutic modality (see section below); however, there are certain focus points or aims that every formulation has, whether it be cognitive behavior therapy (CBT), person-centred

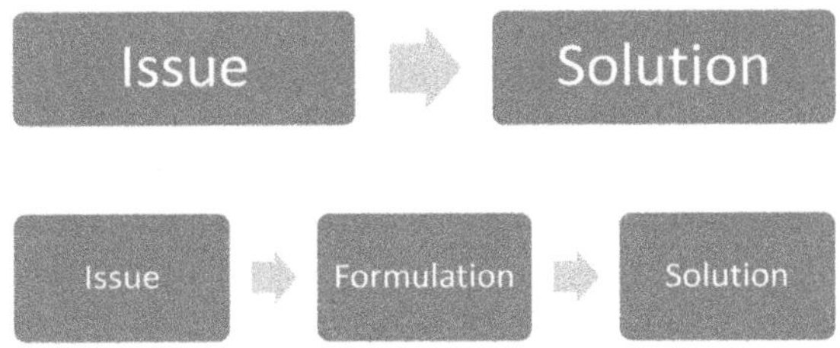

Figure 8.1 Issue, formulation, and solution

therapy (PCT), acceptance commitment therapy (ACT), or even psychodynamic formulation processes. Some of the key focus points are summarised below using the example provided in the 'Life Lived' box.

Life Lived

To this day, the most exciting and treasured moments of being a psychologist are the first sessions. The first session is the gateway to another world: the clients'. It is thrilling because you know little and are on a quest to explore what this world looks like, what are the key elements of it, and why the issue the client is facing is happening. Formulation is key for that last part. Formulation allows the psychologist to systematically go through the information that the client provides and organise them. Let me share the case of a client, 'Roger' (pseudonym) who said that they were having confidence issues. However, overtly and looking at a recent tennis performance, it seemed that the client was doing great. This was a bit of a head scratcher for me because Roger 'said all the right things'. Through assessment, it was also clear that he had fundamental mental skills of visualisation, emotional regulation, and behavioural routines that he regularly used in sport. So, we covered his mental skills, existing sporting concerns, general personal background, history in sport and started reviewing the *origin* of when he started having low confidence. The client just gave vague answers and at that point, the first session ended. The client reported that 'I'm very happy with how we have started and the progress'. I made another note in my formulation – 'client is hesitant for deep emotional processing and disclosure at this point'. We continued on and it was only in the third session that he revealed that his elder sister's boyfriend, who he initially looked up to as a role model during his teens always made fun of his career calling it a 'moving circus of bankruptcy'. This, combined with financial pressures, meant he was always doubting himself and, therefore, his 'low confidence'.

Formulation in this case was not a single time instance, but elements were added and the overall picture was refined as the work with clients progressed.

1. **What is the issue?** This is the process of clearly outlining the primary issue the client is facing in one or two sentences. This clarity is important since it summarises the many presentations related material that the client brings into the session.
2. **Origin:** After describing what is going on with the client, it is important to understand what is the origin story of the issue. Different therapeutic perspectives and modalities of work will go about this differently. Typically, when we identify the origin of the issue, we can work out what leads to the issue repeating itself.
3. **Precipitators:** This refers to the process of discovering factors that trigger or directly cause the issue which the client is struggling with. This may be a very specific situation (e.g., pre-match) or general patterns of emotion (e.g., frustration leading to loss of focus) or something else. This then allows interventions to consider the impact of these factors on the client.
4. **Maintenance patterns:** After we know what is going on, the origin, the factors that trigger it, the obvious question is what type of thinking/emotion/behaviour maintain the

issue? Is the issue being maintained over a period or only propping up in certain situations? These typically manifest as a pattern that repeats itself, causing the issue to get stronger over time.

Reflective Task: Based on the 'Life Lived' box case and these four points, try to answer what the issue is, its origin, precipitators, and maintenance patterns.

Formulation across therapeutic modalities: An overview

Formulation links the clients' issues to the wider psychological theory; however, as outlined in Chapter 3, different therapeutic modalities have different views on human functioning and development. They have sufficiently different templates and procedures of formulation as well. Note that we say *sufficiently* different, since they share many similarities. In the paragraphs below, we provide a brief overview of a few key ones in sport and exercise. These are not exhaustive, and we have provided further information and reading resources within.

CBT and REBT

Formulation is a fundamental part of CBT and (rational emotive behavior therapy) REBT (McCarthy et al., 2023) to make the client's presentations theoretically informed and meaningful to inform interventions. Both CBT and REBT use formulation to merge the client experience to the theory, knowledge, and skills taught to the client to alleviate their issue. Formulation allows CBT and REBT to link the client issues to its large evidence base to have a formulation and principle-based approach to intervention. CBT formulations allow the psychologist to get an understanding within the four-factor model of thoughts, emotion, behaviour, physiology (see McCarthy et al., 2023). For REBT, formulation is done with the A-B-C model (i.e., antecedents, beliefs, consequences). There is an antecedent event, which triggers certain beliefs, which leads to us processing information in a certain way, leading to consequences of behaviour in a certain manner (see Turner, 2022).

For CBT and REBT, this is done by collaborative empiricism (i.e., a process where both therapist and client bring experience and expertise to achieve the joint task of describing the issue). Note: CBT and REBT have different theoretical parameters and modes of guiding intervention. See Turner et al. (2023) for conceptual clarity.

PCT

Person-centred therapy developed by Rogers (1957) does not follow a structured formulation process, since one of its core tenets is non-directivity; however, it has an overarching theoretical structure which aids conceptualisation and formulation of the issues the clients are going through. In PCT theory, distress or dysfunction arise from an incongruence between the ideal self and the real self. PCT also looks at conditions of worth that are placed on the client, which blocks self-actualisation. This formulation and conceptualisation are done highly collaboratively and are client centred where the psychologist is not seen as an expert. Typically, we do not use structured templates while formulating with PCT. Instead, the psychologist and client work together to create a self-chart that is underpinned and led by the client's experience.

EFT

Emotion-focused therapy (EFT) developed by Greenberg and Elliot (2015) builds awareness of, target, and adapt unhealthy emotional processes to co-construct new, healthier emotional processes. Through EFT, the psychologist engages in an understanding of the client's emotion processing style to access, track, deepen, and, when needed, restructure emotion (see Greenberg & Elliot, 2015 for further reading). Formulation in EFT is conducted throughout and is at two levels. Level A: formulation narrative that describes the core maladaptive emotion scheme which is connecting the issue to triggering events. For example, self-critical emotions could be the underpinning of a fear response when a player commits mistakes, which triggers a core maladaptive emotion of shame. Level B: process constructive formulation (i.e., in-moment, in session information that is underpinned by the experience of emotion). We refer you to Goldman and Greenberg (2015) for further reading.

ACT

Acceptance commitment therapy (Hayes et al., 2006) is a third wave CBT approach. It is rooted in the paradigm of contextual behaviour science under the broader philosophical worldview of functional contextualism (Bennet & Oliver, 2019). Through functional contextualism, ACT attempts to understand the whole individual and their interaction with the situational and historical context of sport and life (Hayes et al., 2012). In ACT formulations, the focus is on the function of thoughts and behaviour rather than the output. What purpose the behaviour serves is the focus rather than what the behaviour is. This formulation is then used to place the behaviours and thoughts within the Hexaflex model that has six interrelated core processes of acceptance, self-as-context, diffusion, contact with present, values, and committed access. This is then used to guide interventions that are founded on the three pillars of open, aware, and engaged state to promote psychological flexibility (see Hayes et al., 2012 for further reading). The psychologist is actively involved in creating the formulation, but does not follow a highly manualised and rigid step.

SFBT

Solution-focused brief therapy (SFBT) is a short-term, time-limited therapeutic approach that adopts a nonpathological view of client issues and strives to develop a solution-based intervention to current and specific problems (Ratner et al., 2012). SFBT outlines that most issues develop and maintain themselves through human interaction, which is the prime focus of formulation. SFBT maintains that interventions need to change a part of the system to lead to change in the system-as-whole. For example, in pre-competitive anxiety, the change might be incorporation of a structured breathwork relaxation intervention to manage arousal levels, causing a changing in the pre-competitive anxiety system. Formulation in SFBT is psychologist led and is focused on problem-solution pairing.

As we can see, different therapeutic approaches lead to different patterns, styles, and goals of formulation. How we go about formulating is also linked to the practitioner's professional philosophy (see Chapter 2), style of working, and goals of work as agreed with the client. For example, if the psychologist has a very humanistic oriented formulation, they are less likely to rely heavily on standardised psychometrics to aid assessment and formulation. On the other hand, if the goals of the work are for short-term work, SFBT or CBT might be an option. For a worked example, we refer you to Turner et al. (2020) which has applied four different psychotherapeutic approaches to a single case to showcase similarities and differences.

Philosophical stances are critical to practice since we rely on them to guide our engagement with complex thinking tasks. This is linked to the fact that the psychologist relies on theory *and* a way of engaging with theory and client knowledge, to administer a psychological intervention specific to a particular form of therapy. All approaches come with theoretical viewpoints about individuals, development, maintenance, change, time, healing, and functioning. Therefore, formulation, that is, building a conceptual map of what is going on with the client is also influenced by these.

Life Lived

Let's return to the case of Roger. We know that Roger's insecurity comes from having criticism and dismissive comments from someone he used to consider as a role model. We have also looked at the different philosophies and how they impact formulation. Let us see how the same case can be formulated slightly differently with alternating philosophies of work.

Roger's formulation with CBT

From a CBT perspective, there are Cognitions, Emotions, Behaviours, and Physical reactions that interact within the CBT four-factor model (McCarthy et al., 2023). From his formulation process, Core Beliefs are formed from Assumptions and Automatic Thoughts which are shaped by life experiences in formative years. In Roger's case, his role model's comments led to automatic thoughts and assumptions which were internalised into a Core Belief of 'I am not good enough' and 'I will never be good enough'. Interventions would work on detaching the role models views from his Beliefs about his self, and engaging in cognitive restructuring to alter this core belief process.

Rogers's formulation with PCT

From a PCT| perspective, humans function to self-actualise when they are provided empathy, unconditional positive regard and active listening. Distress occurs in us when there is a high discrepancy between our ideal and real self – for Roger, his ideal self of being successful is discrepant from his real self, which makes mistakes and is learning. Roger's role model also represents a conditional punitive voice which is acting as a barrier to self-acceptance and increases the discrepancy between the ideal self and real self.

Preparing a formulation: Key steps

This section will outline certain key steps to consider while preparing a formulation. This *is not* training for applied practice formulation; all trainees need to get specialized training to engage in formulation in sport psychology. However, we list key considerations for all formulations and needs analysis which form the foundation of applied practice. This can be used as a helpful checklist during your training days and workshops.

Context: Who is the client and where is the issue located?

While 'who is the client' may seem like an odd question, it is one of the most important questions for the psychologist to consider and answer effectively. For example, take a situation where the pushy parent of a 15-year-old golfer has approached you to improve their son's performance on the course. The parent thinks he is choking and therefore needs some sport psychology intervention. Here, the client is the athlete, but the parent is the one paying the invoice. Therefore, formulation should be focused on the client, but have a sufficient acknowledgement of the pressure the athlete may experience from the parental level. This is especially important when working at the team level as well, where you have multiple individuals, interpersonal power dynamics, group cohesion, and leadership elements. Through the course of an effective formulation, one of the key things is to understand where the issue is located. Being mindful of these factors can provide a more holistic approach to the same. Asking and answering the question 'where is the issue located' also tells us if it is within the remit of the psychologist at all. For example, if an athlete is not performing because of an injury reducing their physical performance, then it is not within the remit of the sport psychology consultant.

One helpful framework to guide the asking and answering of both these questions is the Weerasekara framework (Weerasekara, 1995). This formulation framework incorporates two axes: (a) the origins of the problems (through systemic or relational levels); (b) the P-P-P-P framework (Predisposing, Precipitating, Perpetuating, and Protective). The first axis allows the psychologist to incorporate different therapeutic or intervention styles. The framework also considers four main factors to guide formulation and intervention:

1 **Dispositional factors:** The patterns that are enduring within the individual (e.g., personality).
2 **Episodic factors:** The factors that are unique to a specific situation and vary.
3 **Individual factors:** are biological, behavioural, psychosocial, or cognitive factors related to the individual across the situation.
4 **Systemic/macro:** The occupational, team, group, cultural, political, organisational, and other factors that influence the individual.

These are laid out in a grid framework so that the client and the psychologist can effectively trace issues. If there is too much focus on systemic/macro or episodic factors, then it indicates a highly externalised issue that may lie beyond the client. The grid is outlined below:

	Individual (B-B-C-P)	*Systemic (O-O-F-S)*
	Biological *Behavioural* *Cognitive* *Psychosocial*	*Organisational* *Occupational/sport* *Family/group* *Sociocultural*
Predisposing factors *Precipitating factors* *Perpetuating factors* *Protective factors*		

In the 'Life Lived' box below, we have outlined a case example with the grid framework above.

Life Lived

In this 'Life Lived' box, we return to Roger once again, but this time work to showcase the B-B-C-P and O-O-F-S Models.

	Individual (B-B-C-P)	*Systemic (O-O-F-S)*
	Biological *Behavioural* *Cognitive* *Psychosocial*	*Organisational* *Occupational/sport* *Family/group* *Sociocultural*
Predisposing factors	Punitive role model criticism	Sponsor stressor
Precipitating actors	Lack of consistency in skill execution due to normal development barriers	Sport success and ranking points
Perpetuating factors	Near qualification ranking points but not yet secured	Sponsors regularly remind him of deadlines, especially after losses in tournaments
Protective factors	Excellent coaching support network	Supportive family network who are mid-range of socio-economic status and therefore are not dependent on Roger

What are my objectives?

Every formulation has the central aim of providing a working conceptualisation or idea on how the client is and how their issue is operating. But clients are people, and rarely do we get to know everything we need to in the first session or during our first attempt at formulation. Sometimes, when we are using psychometrics, we may even need some time after the session to score them and make an interpretation. It is important to collapse the big task of formulation into smaller objectives. We list some of them in the format of a checklist that you can mentally rehearse as you are formulating. It is best practice to also reflect-on-action to realise a priority ordering system. We recommend a simple P-MP-LP model. P-Priority (action needed immediately), MP-Medium Priority (if action arrives naturally), and LP-Low Priority (action not immediately important).

Do I know the client's day-to-day patterns/lifestyle?	P / MP / LP
Do I know how the client describes the issue?	P / MP / LP
Do I know what predisposing factors may be at play?	P / MP / LP
Do I have a good understanding of the difficulties caused by the issue for the client?	P / MP / LP
Do I have a good idea at which level the issue lies?	P / MP / LP
Do I know what strategies (if any) the client has already tried to address the issue? How have they worked?	P / MP / LP
Do I know the insecurities that the client has posed about their issue / other elements of their life?	P / MP / LP
Do I feel comfortable with the areas of the client's life? If no, what do I need to know in the short and medium term?	P / MP / LP

Testing formulation

Being a scientist-practitioner who engaged in evidence-based practice, the psychologist cannot assume that it will hold true. In fact, formulations change as events change in the client's life or interventions have success. There are often debates whether formulations should be perfect or should they be useful? Messer (1991) argued that it is hard to arrive at a singular truth because individuals do not construct realities from one singular experience of truth; however, there should be some level of consistency across formulations. On the other side of the continuum, there are arguments that formulations should be 'useful' and practically relevant to guide interventions. At this level, formulations should prioritise the client's perspective and then look at theoretical alignment. Butler (1998, p. 21) outlined 'Ten Tests' for a good formulation:

1. Does it make theoretical sense?/Can it be explained by specific psychological theory?
2. Does it fit with the evidence provided by the client? (symptoms, issue, reactions, experiences)
3. Does it account for the four Ps? (predisposing, precipitating, perpetuating, and protective factors)
4. Do others think it is appropriate? (supervisors for trainees, peers, client)
5. Can the formulation be used to make predictions? (about client behaviour, reactions, intervention response)
6. Can the psychologist work out how to test these predictions? (design and implement interventions, anticipate responses, anticipate reactions to events in the client's life)
7. Does the history fit? (regarding clients' 4Ps and other developmental events)
8. Does intervention based on formulation progress as predicted? (see points 5 and 6)
9. Can the formulation be used to identify future risk factors or difficulties the client may experience?
10. Are there other important factors that are unexplained?

Another key test for a formulation is its *usefulness* to the client in terms of how it helps the client understand their issue better or simply. Typically, this provides clients with mastery, a sense that 'I can manage this or deal with it', which improves therapeutic outcomes. Last, it is important that any formulation *does no harm to the client.* Sometimes clients may be in denial or simply not ready to accept their issue, which may prompt a negative emotional reaction. At other times, clients may strongly feel that the psychologist has got the formulation wrong and is trying to shoehorn them into a framework: (a) Formulations should not sound like a judgement, (b) formulations should not be a rewriting of a client's life history based on what the psychologist thinks may be happening, (c) formulations should not be highly rigid with no scope for client involvement, and (d) the psychologist should not reduce the client's autonomy through this process.

A good formulation in applied practice should settle somewhere between a range where we do not claim a perfect, miraculous description of an issue or a 'disaster' where we do not know what is happening with the client. This is an outcome that appreciates context-relevant best practice in applied psychology.

Culturally sensitive formulation

Most formulation has some element of (a) preservation (client quotations or personal language in exact form); (b) deletion, which omits some information which may be repeated; and (c) transformation where some of the information is transformed deictically (i.e., with a referral word (e.g. 'it' or 'that') or may be transformed via paraphrasing or via an empathetic interpretation of client content). When working across cultures, this may often lead to difficulties because of different cultural meanings and/or language barriers. It might be the social and cultural context of a society that might lead to the client's issue (e.g., racism experience causing self-esteem issues).

We draw upon the social inequalities approach to formulation, which goes beyond the individual in emphasising the role of social and cultural contexts in shaping problems. First, structural features of society are acknowledged as playing a role in disempowering some individuals and privileging others. Second, psychology itself is viewed as culturally grounded (predominantly in the West, upper-middle class level) which shapes how we think of what is 'normal', 'healthy' and defines that which is considered as deviant. This is relevant in sport as well, which often has sport-specific micro-cultures. For example, being physical with your teammates is common as a team cohesion exercise in contact sports such as football, American football, rugby, and others; however, it would be seen as deviant in other sports. Sport is also intrinsically multi-cultural, with transfers, player and staff mobility (for example, Coach Zinedine Zidane (French), lead Real Madrid (a Spanish club) to a highly successful three years with a team of players that had a Croatian, German, Portuguese, Brazilian, Spaniards, Colombian, Argentinian, Costa Rican, and a Welshman within its squad). Some key recommendations to underpin your formulation culturally sensitively are as given below.

Cultural hierarchies

If we adopt an interactional view, the self and all the processes related to identity come into being at the interface between the individual and their environment, which includes their culture. We know from research that cultures and cultural hierarchies are different on this planet. It is then only logical to assume that individuals' experience of and relationship with culture will also be different. From birth and after, babies, then children, then adolescents, then young adults, and then older adults all have a complete understanding of their own culture and belief systems. This also extends to cultural hierarchies, which refer to the different values, beliefs, behaviours, norms, and the hierarchical importance that individuals attribute to them. For example, research has shown that there are some levels of similarities in values across cultures, but the importance attributed to a specific value changes (see Schwartz & Bardi, 2001). This has important implications for formulation because if there is a divergence between the cultural hierarchies of the psychologist and client, the sport psychology consultant may miss elements of cultural hierarchies which may be important to clients. For example, Gupta and Divekar (2022) reflected on the similarities and differences in familial support for an athlete with the same characteristics across eastern and western culture. Formulation would need to be cognizant of this, and incorporate this as relevant.

Acknowledge and formulate sources of power

Continuing on from the idea that there are cultural hierarchies, we also start to realise that there are certain elements of culture which have a greater power compared to others. This may be because of dominant discourse, political-economic strength, or even social pressure. For example, there is a relentless pursuit of thinness in certain societies (reflected in media, fashion, and other societal sources) that is identified as a causal factor in a higher prevalence of eating disorders. Some countries have dominant sports like football in the UK, cricket in India, badminton in China, basketball in the US, which may lead to differing levels of funding and support for athletes (i.e., a discrepancy in power structures of governing bodies of sport). For example, a badminton player in the UK will face far more difficulty in securing support services and funding compared to a footballer if all other factors are constant (the football player will also make a lot more money!). Power often manifests itself through the following, which should be considered in formulation:

- **Sanctions:** What is 'appropriate' and what is not. For example, having a non-heterosexual orientation is still considered a divergent position in sport (although it is changing).
- **Norms:** What is the societal script about acceptable patterns of behaviour. For example, verbal abuse is often considered to be 'unsporting' and athletes are told by sponsors not to engage in it since they are role models. This places a censor on expression in a high-stress environment (another example is the racquet smash in tennis).
- **Status and symbols:** What are the symbols of power and what is a 'high status' power holder defined by. These change from culture to culture and from sport to sport. Typically, high-status individuals are key gatekeepers and decision-makers. This could be the manager or coach or sporting director of a team. In sport, especially elite sport, we also have to be cognizant of money and financial security (or lack of it). Sometimes, due to power structures, athletes are travelling to major events on a shoestring budget, with minimal support. On other occasions, and depending on sport, they are flush with cash. It is important to understand if these status/power symbols are important to the client. If they are, they need to be incorporated within formulation and the 4-P's framework within it. For example, I once worked with an 18-year-old footballer who came from an affluent social class. He reported adjustment issues to his new club and a drop in motivation following it. Through formulation, no major social power or status factor came up; however, during a field session when I was in the club, I saw him pull up to the parking lot in a shiny purple Mercedes CLA35 AMG, and overheard comments of 'rich prick' from other players. The individual was completely oblivious to this, and this was duly incorporated within the formulation.

Language, 'normal' and lived experience patterns

This book is written in English. A lot of applied practice is done in English. But, English may be only one language for you as a reader and as a practitioner. It may be the same case for your clients as well. In such cases, pause and check if there are any idioms, words, or even phrases that have gone unnoticed or misunderstood. This is important for certain therapeutic techniques like Socratic questioning, attribution reframing, focusing, two-chair work, empathetic conjecture – all of which use words and linguistics as the core therapeutic intervention. For example, a client may have an anxiety trigger and self-blame thoughts in Spanish or Bulgarian, but when they communicate it to the sport psychology consultant in English, they translate it, and during the translation, the self-blame component disappears.

Another key consideration is: what is considered as 'normal' within the developmental lived experience of the clients. For example, someone who has grown up in the UK will have a 'Tesco meal deal' as a normal part of their lives and lived experience, which will be different from someone who has grown up in Sri Lanka. This automatically means that 'normal' and what is considered as normal is different as lived experience varies. Through the process of formulation, especially as we are trying to get an understanding of the 4Ps and the life history of the client, it is important to consider these lived experience patterns. Typically, the sport psychology consultant is recommended to be cognisant of:

- Gender
- Race
- Religion
- Sexual orientation
- Cultural background (and languages)
- Family orientation (and relational depth within family)
- Cultural power structures
- Early life experience (and barrier experiences or discrimination if any)
- Early sport experience (and norms of sport)

1 **Religion, faith, and spirituality:** There are distinct differences in religion, faith, and spirituality between individuals in a society. This is mirrored in sport environments. It is important to (a) be aware of, (b) understand the influence of, and (c) formulate the interactions of such beliefs with the individual's day-to-day functioning. For example, religious and spiritual beliefs may often clash with the culture of the country where the athlete plays professional sport (e.g., Frank Ribery stepping out of Bayern Munich's beer celebration because of his religious beliefs). At a wider level, religion, faith, and spirituality are an integral part of human culture that helps order the individual's beliefs, values, experience, and behaviours – all the key components we review during an effective formulation.

   a First, remember that some religious/faith/spiritual beliefs are personal and self-defined (i.e., the individual defines their relationship and practices independent of any 'rules' of a community). For others, it is defined by a religious community (i.e., a church, a scripture, mosque, temple, group, etc.). When reflecting and considering this in psychotherapy, it is important to differentiate which level is the individual operating at.
   b Second, it is important to understand where religion/faith/spirituality sits within the wider context. For example, being a practisng Christian in the US will be different from being one in Europe. Similar patterns follow for being practising Islam, Hinduism, Judaism, Buddhism, and other religions across cultural locations.
   c Third, consider how faith-based beliefs and behaviours can be important sources of potential support and obstacles for clients. For example, having the belief that a deity (God) is there to protect you can be incredibly comforting. But within a self-esteem negative spiral, it could also get construed as 'God doesn't care about me, hence everything is going badly'.
   d Finally, how are these themes emerging? These themes often emerge in times of regressive situations, conflictual positions, and transferential feelings (Abernethy & Lancia, 1998). For example, a 26-year-old male swimmer presented with anxiety and negative affect after a major shoulder injury caused him to miss a World Championship event and derail his Olympic qualification chances. He maintained a position that 'It's part of God's plan, there's nothing I can do' which was using an externalised locus of religion and God as a defence mechanism to prevent himself from thinking about uncomfortable emotions and the unresolved conflict within him. This was then triggering unresolved anxiety spirals about his future and the meaning of his life which could not be fully explained by religion alone.

2 **Understand the 'isms':** 'Isms' are the many discriminatory and prejudicial factors that are prevalent in society and have a tangible influence on individuals. These are prevalent in society. However, they may also be manifested via the sport psychology consultant's unconscious perceptions, biases, assumptions, or simply not being aware of something. We have outlined how to reflect with a culture-sensitive perspective in Chapter 5. These isms may

operate on an individual-to-individual level or on a structural level. Some examples of isms are listed below:

a **Racism** (discrimination against people based on their particular racial or ethnic group).
b **Sexism** (discrimination against populations based on one's sex or gender, primarily affecting women and girls).
c **Ableism** (discrimination against populations because of perceived competence, capabilities, or disabilities).
d **Classism/elitism** (discrimination against people of a lower class of socioeconomic status).
e **Xenophobia** (discrimination against people from other countries or culture or anyone deemed to be 'foreign' because of visitor status or immigration).
f **Homophobia** (discrimination against non-heterosexual individuals based on their sexuality).

These 'isms' are often experienced by clients and on some occasions may be a prevalent pattern in their lived experience so far. For example, most female athletes are likely to have experienced sexism in some form in their careers, which in recent times is well documented on social media (Adá Lameiras & Rodríguez-Castro, 2021). From a formulation point of view, it is important to acknowledge these events. However, it is likely that there is little to no control over these structural factors. These isms typically go in the system or external level (see Weerasekara's grid above). *We strongly recommend all trainees to receive multicultural practice and critical inquiry training prior to applied practice.*

Formulation: A concluding note

Formulation is a core skill for any sport psychology practitioner. Like any skill, it is developed through time, practice, and experience. Some people find it easier than others to formulate because of how they naturally engage with information. Others find it difficult to distill the client's experience into a model or framework. Therefore, reflection on the self and how *you* are interacting with the skill of formulation is key. We would also suggest that, as a trainee, you do not place pressure on yourself to be 'perfect' in your formulation process or skill. It is the client's formulation; hence, some degree of mutual collaboration is advised.

Take it step by step. Have fun formulating!

9 Delivering an Intervention

Introduction

'Vamos!'

If you watch tennis, you can probably place the person who said this (Rafa Nadal). Have you ever been tired at the end of a gruelling workout and grunted to yourself, 'Come on! Finish this!'. Maybe you got frustrated with a teammate or a co-worker and had to remind yourself to breathe and remind yourself that everyone makes mistakes. Both these examples represent interventions from a psychological skills perspective. In your work with athletes, you will seek to understand the core tenets of various interventions, understand how to map them, and how to deliver them. These interventions would be the part of the sport psychology consultant's job that allows them to reduce or fix a problem that is occurring in some manner of speaking. So, let us understand what constitutes a psychological intervention in sport, and how to go through developing and delivering one as you build your skills as a trainee.

What is an intervention?

Intervention refers to a combination of strategies designed to produce desirable behavioural, performance, emotional, or cognitive outcomes. Interventions are typically targeted at the individual, group, team, or organisational level. Best practice highlights that intervention development should have a few traceable components that have been developed using theory and can be mapped onto certain expected outcomes. For example, we pick an intervention for a performance routine (individual athlete + behavioural) which is guided by the behavioural regulation theory and is mapped onto the outcome of having a 'reset' before every performance action. The guidance from theory and literature is essential because they help us make sense of complex phenomena by tentatively explaining (a) what is happening (see formulation chapter); (b) why it is happening? (c) what circumstances can we modify it under?

Interventions may be designed by the sport psychology consultant. But usually, sport psychology consultants combine a pre-existing intervention to support a client. Why? Because pre-existing interventions have been validated for their efficacy via research. Therefore, when we pick them, we know it works. A parallel example would be picking up a medication that has been approved by the medical board from a licensed pharmacy instead of cooking up a blend at home. When we are looking at interventions in applied psychology, some key points to consider are listed below:

DOI: 10.4324/9781003367208-11

What is the intervention targeting?

Well-designed and well-informed interventions are focused and have a clear set of targets. Targets may be in the form of a certain outcome we want to change. For example, consider an athlete having precompetitive anxiety. Alternatively, an intervention may be targeted at a group process, such as group cohesion or the social identity of a team. An intervention may also have multiple sub-components. For example, if the goal is overall mental skills and talent development (very common in youth sport work), then sub-focus areas may be something around self-awareness, game skill awareness, emotional regulation, and so on. Use the table below to chart these for every case you have (we will populate one more column of the table in every section).

Target area					
Emotional regulation					

What level is the intervention aimed at?

An intervention has several levels of delivery. Knowing exactly what level an intervention is operating at is crucial because it enables you to work with the stakeholders at that level. This is aligned with the socioecological model of human development (Bronfenbrenner, 1994) and we signpost you to the ecological systems model for athletes and sport (see Purcell et al., 2019, open access). The levels are (a) athlete; (b) microsystem (involving of the parents, coaches, friends, high performance environment of training and any other immediate contact environment); (c) exosystem (the overall elements of an individual sport, such as the culture of sport, power dynamics, which influence the individual); and (d) macrosystem which comprises larger environmental influences such as national sporting body, public, and media influences. Therefore, it is critical to know which level the intervention will operate in because it will directly influence choice of delivery, stakeholders involved, time and expenses, all of which are key to intervention efficacy. Another matter to consider here is the level of control related to intervention. For example, if the target of intervention is 'athlete is having body image issues after social media is trending with a weird, angled wardrobe photograph', then there is an interaction between athlete and macrosystem. Obviously, we cannot change too much at the macrosystem level, but we can work at the athlete level, and work on how the athlete interacts with the macrosystem.

Target area	*Level*				
Emotional regulation Coach-athlete relationship	Athlete Athlete + microsystem				

Who is delivering the intervention?

This might appear to be a redundant question initially. You may wonder, well, of course, it is the sport psychology consultant who is delivering the intervention. But sometimes this may not be the case. At times, the sport psychology consultant is directly delivering an intervention through a 1-on-1 or 1-on-group/team modality. Sometimes, the head sport psychology consultant designs and coordinates an intervention at an entire academy pathway through a team of trainees working under them. On other occasions, the intervention may be co-delivered with some form of involvement from coaching and/or sport science staff. Finally, with the advent of technology, interventions may be psychoeducational, decentralised, and at times even delivered via apps. For example, I (Sahen) once delivered a mindfulness-oriented relaxation intervention using the 'Headspace' app providing the mindfulness script, reminders to client and as a tracking process. It is important to know who is delivering the intervention because it allows you to account for individual variation, delivery styles, different professional philosophies, and other factors.

Target area	*Level*	*Delivery*			
Emotional regulation	Athlete	1-on-1			
Coach-athlete relationship	Athlete + microsystem	1-on-1 with athlete + triangulation with athlete and coach			

What is the research supporting this intervention?

Sport psychology is an endeavour of science. Therefore, we as scientist-practitioners must look at the evidence to underpin and inform our interventions. This typically starts with formulation, where we understand what the issue is. Then we use an existing theory to explain this issue. This linkage to theory also signposts us to how the issue may manifest in terms of its interaction and other elements in the client's life. For example, if the client has an irrational belief that 'I must be perfect all the time', we will probably link it to maladaptive perfectionism theory (Hill et al., 2018), and then link it to cognitive behaviour therapy (CBT) (McCarthy et al., 2023) and rational emotive behaviour therapy (REBT) theory (Turner, 2023).

Target area	*Level*	*Delivery*	*Evidence base*		
Emotional regulation	Athlete	1-on-1	Emotion regulation framework (Uphill et al., 2009)		
Coach-athlete relationship	Athlete + microsystem	1-on-1 with athlete + triangulation with athlete and coach	Coach-athlete relationship 3Cs+1 (Jowett, 2007)		

Is this intervention suited to context?

As much as we would want interventions to be developed and ready for us, sometimes it is not the case. Some sport psychology interventions are tested only in certain sports or in certain populations. For example, ThinkAloud-based interventions have been developed in individual, non-contact, non-reactive sports such as golf, cycling, running (cf. Eccles & Arsal, 2017). While they can be applied in other sports, an 'off-the-shelf' tested evidence base does not yet exist. This is the case with many other interventional modalities. Therefore, it is important to question the context-specificity of any intervention *during the choosing and developing* phase. This is important when considering anti-discriminatory practice and multicultural work as well. For example, most interventions in sport psychology have so far been designed for and/or tested with male, white, Eurocentric, sub-elite sport populations, which represent a context-specific area (Gupta, 2022; Schinke et al., 2009). When working with non-white, non-male (female, non-binary), LGBTQA+ and non-Eurocentric clients, care needs to be taken to reflect on how to transfer an intervention to the specific context at play. Another example would be pausing and reflecting with your client what self-talk to use if they speak various languages.

Target area	*Level*	*Delivery*	*Evidence base*	*Context-specificity*	*Timeline*
Emotional regulation	Athlete	1-on-1	Emotion regulation framework (Uphill et al., 2009)	Female athlete with PCOS	
Coach-athlete relationship	Athlete + microsystem	1-on-1 with athlete + triangulation with athlete and coach	Coach-athlete relationship 3Cs+1 (Jowett, 2007)	Age and stage of coach and athlete (athlete 16 years, coach 45 and used to coaching pros)	

What is the timeline of effect at play here?

Often, we forget about time when we design interventions. Psychological interventions should have sufficient contact time, sufficient time between contact, and a realistic planning around sport/training schedules. For example, what is the expected timeline to deliver the intervention and see changes in the outcome? Measurement tools are helpful when implementing this. See Barker et al. (2013) for single case applied methods for measuring intervention efficacy and Moore (2007) to understand more about evidence-based intervention measurement.

Target area	*Level*	*Delivery*	*Evidence base*	*Context-specificity*	*Timeline*
Emotional regulation	Athlete	1-on-1	Emotion regulation framework (Uphill et al., 2009)	Female athlete with PCOS	8–12 weeks
Coach-athlete relationship	Athlete + microsystem	1-on-1 with athlete + triangulation with athlete and coach	Coach-athlete relationship 3Cs+1 (Jowett, 2007)	Age and stage of coach and athlete (athlete 16 years, coach 45 and used to coaching pros)	3 weeks–3 months

Are we responsible for 'fixing' our clients using interventions?

Working in sport has shown that there is a prevalence of what I call the matrix of 3Fs: 'Find' (find talent of some sort); 'Function' (what are you doing here?); 'Fix' (a problem of some sort). The sport psychology consultant has a minimal role in the 'Find'-ing of talent, but they have a role in talent development (in fact, most jobs are in development performance pathways in sport). We definitely have to answer our 'Function' within the sport environment – why are we important and how do we contribute to athlete development? Often, we are also called upon to 'Fix' problems that may arise. If I had got a pound every time, I heard something like 'Can you sort this player's ...' my entire coffee expenses in a month would be taken care of. This leads us to answer the question, what is the 'function' of interventions, and do we use them to 'fix' our clients?

The function of an intervention can be many things: For example, I conducted a monthly intervention that was centred on the techniques of Psychological Evaluation (PsychEval). PsychEval was conducted with a predominantly mental health focus because COVID was going on. The function of the intervention was to monitor players' mental health and well-being, to triage risk factors and provide additional psychotherapeutic support if needed. The outcome of this intervention was a triage and early detection of insomnia, disordered eating, symptomatic depression and panic attacks within the squad. On many other occasions, the function of the intervention has been solely focused on performance and/or athlete development. So, if we are putting so much effort into developing, designing, and delivering interventions, surely, we intend to fix a problem that our client may face?

This inclination to 'fix' is what Dr Jamie Barker calls 'Luke Skywalker' syndrome (McCarthy & Jones, 2013), which is the representation of a saviour complex – when we attribute a high degree of causality and want to fix, help, or change everyone I come into contact with ('To make a difference!'). This is important since it not only reduces bias within interventions but also protects the sport psychology consultant from overreaching ethical boundaries and burnout.

The role of the sport psychology consultant in an intervention

In the 1960s, during the behaviour therapy movement in psychology, Dr Gordan Paul asked what has since become one of the most widely cited questions on the science of evidence-based interventions: 'what treatment, by whom, is most effective for this individual with that specific problem, under which set of circumstances, and how does it come about?' (Paul, 1969, p. 44). If we were to break this down, it would involve:

- Description of intervention
- Who is delivering the intervention?
- Which intervention is most effective for this individual for the specific problem?
- What are the context-specific set of circumstances?
- How does the intervention affect change?

As we have highlighted above, there are many interventions, each with their pros and cons. The only commonality across the interventions is the role of the sport psychology consultant. For the discussion, we clarify intervention procedures versus intervention processes. Intervention procedures are techniques or methods that the sport psychology practitioner uses to achieve the treatment goals of the client. These goals are not always static, but are always mutually agreed upon. For example, a visualisation script that is being sequentially introduced to develop a mental skill to manage performance planning is an example of intervention procedures.

By contrast, intervention processes are the underlying change mechanisms that lead to the attainment of a desirable treatment goal. One example of this is the client-sport psychology consultant relationship (McCarthy & Moffat, 2024). The intervention process is defined as a set of dynamic, progressive, multilevel changes that occur through the delivery of an intervention that predicts an established sequence towards desirable outcomes. They are *dynamic* because they are often non-linear and may have loops. For example, imagine a six-month intervention to support an athlete's mental health and psychological readiness during the recovery of an anterior cruciate ligament (ACL) surgery. Within this, there would be a clearly established sequence of steps (see Podlog et al., 2014) and times where there can be a minor re-injury or similar setbacks necessitating a change in the sequence and be *progressive* as an intervention. Typically, most intervention processes are also *multilevel* because some targets, processes, and ways of being supersede others. For example, during the ACL rehabilitation, the client has to deal with a major life change, such as a transfer between clubs then that would lead to a multilevel focus because they are related.

The role of the sport psychology consultant in interventions is key because they design and deliver the intervention. To use an analogy, they build the car and, to some extent, drive it. Research has indicated that successful interventions in youth and professional sport include a holistic focus, understanding the person beyond their sport, adaptable co-creation of aims delivered with a clear direction (read more Henriksen et al., 2019). But it is important to note that the sport psychology consultant is a facilitator, not a controller. We are not responsible for fixing the client. Rather, we create conditions which facilitate change.

How do we know if an intervention worked?

'It was perfectly designed and achieved all outcomes' v/s 'it was completely useless and a waste of time'. Most interventions would probably settle somewhere in the middle of this range when we evaluate it, claiming to neither be miracles nor disasters, but appreciating the mechanisms and the outcomes gained. A central part of interventions is the evaluation of interventions. Evaluation refers to the systematic process for determining the factors that led to the outcome of an intervention and a measurement (in some manner) of the chosen outcomes themselves.

This means evaluation has two parts.

- **Part 1:** Evaluating the mechanisms of intervention that worked. For example, if an intervention has self-talk and box breathing to combat performance anxiety. The evaluation can tell us to what degree self-talk and box-breathing worked, which one worked better, and why.
- **Part 2:** Refers to the evaluation of the outcome as well, i.e., the issue/s that the intervention is trying to solve. For example, did the intervention of self-talk and box breathing reduce performance anxiety? Therefore, this is a key part of understanding how to fine-tune interventions and develop them to improve outcomes over months and years.

Life Lived: Evaluating Interventions and Implementing Learnings

I developed my first comprehensive intervention for sport and life skills while working with HIV+ adolescents in India. The intervention had psychoeducational components and an active living element via the sport of middle-long distance running (for intervention, see Sudhesh et al., 2021). The first design of the intervention, which ran for six months, included personality development workshops, psychoeducation on mental health, structured running sessions (with coaches) and leadership development. Evaluation was conducted via questionnaires pre-post and by focus-group discussions to initiate stakeholders' feedback. While the questionnaires showed improvement in the cohort overall, the focus group discussion (FGD) informed us that the intervention was 'too much' for the cohort at times. In version 2 of the intervention, which ran for the next eight months, we reduced leadership development workshops to a minimum and increased unstructured play and running sessions (including a 5-km run to a local mountain). The evaluation post eight months showed a significant improvement via questionnaires and a far more engaged FGD process.

Reflection emphasised the value of doing less. But this was only possible by evaluating the mechanism of intervention in addition to the outcome. In the years since, I have adopted a pragmatic philosophy while doing fieldwork interventions to strike a balance between rigour and what works.

Now that we know the importance of evaluation, how do we do it? Some common methods are outlined below with additional reading resources signposted. It is key to remember that each evaluation metric and process will have its pros and cons. We have signposted you to the best guidance literature currently available for further information.

- **Questionnaires** are self-report measures that involve asking a series of questions regarding a certain phenomenon or variable (e.g., motivation or performance strategies) to measure it. There are several questionnaires that measure these psychological variables in sport. Some examples include TOPS (Test of Performance Strategies), SMS (Sport Motivation Scale), SM-HAT (Sport Mental Health Assessment Test), and others. Read more in the following papers (see Horvath & Röthlin, 2018; Londsale et al., 2006; Vealey et al., 2019)
- **Performance data** refers to any and all data relevant to skill execution and performance in the specific sport. For example, this may include unforced errors in tennis or video analysis in football. Performance data can be both qualitative and quantitative and is typically sourced in collaboration with a performance analyst/coach in a sport setting. This form of data is to test whether a specific psychological intervention is having an improvement on dimensions of performance. For example, I once implemented a CBT-based reattribution training with a tennis player who was struggling with multiple double faults in service. Performance data was used to track his percentage of serves and first serve percentage after double faulting.
- **Interviews** are qualitative means of evaluation that have differing levels of structure. Interviews may be done 1-on-1 with the athlete, or it may be done with many members in an athlete's support network. Interviews are useful to understand details about the lived experience of the intervention and the mechanisms of change within it. Interviews are sometimes combined with similar qualitative methods, such as ethnography (Krane & Baird, 2005) and single case follow-up as well. Some follow-up reading includes Mack et al. (2019), Taylor and Schneider (1992), and O'Halloran et al. (2018).
- **Focus-group discussions** refer to a method of evaluation where a selected group of people discussed a given topic or issue in depth while being facilitated by the sport psychology consultant/external moderator. This provides in-depth information on experiences, beliefs, and attitudes. FGDs are beneficial in team and group settings especially when the intervention is targeting group-level processes such as social identity, group cohesion and other metrics at the psychosocial level. FGDs are the good practice for involving stakeholder participation. Some follow-up reading material includes Millward (2012), Slater and Tiggemann (2010), Palmer et al. (2010), and Hennik (2013).
- **Observation** refers to the system of evaluation that involves using a systematic and structured way to observe an athlete while training and practice. Observations can be participatory/non-participatory and provide rich, in-situ detail about the client's behavioural responses to situations. Observations are typically used as a triangulation measure in evaluation, in addition to one or two other methods. See essential reading: Holder and Winter (2017), Martin et al. (2020).
- **Biofeedback/psychophysiological metrics** include various psychophysiological measures that are commonly used in sport such as heart rate, attentional focus, eye tracking and other measures which are linked to psychological elements. For example, Monasterio et al. (2016) provide evidence on the link between stress reactivity and personality in extreme sport athletes. It is recommended that these be used in addition to other measures and in collaboration with a sport scientist. An example of using this could be to see footballers' effort output and distance covered after making a mistake in open play, which leads to a non-strategic, compensatory behaviour.

These are some methods to use for evaluation data. Remember that it is more important to select a context-appropriate measure rather than trying to evaluate everything. Sometimes, one or two simple evaluation measures keep the process streamlined and provide sufficient data to improve outcomes compared to five different measures, which may only serve to overcomplicate things. The other question to consider is where do we get evaluation data from? This can be done at many levels (see Chapter 8 for socioecological levels). Some sources may be

- Clients (1-on-1 or team)
- Immediate microsystem (coaches, parents, teammates, interaction with sport psychology consultant)
- Clients in different environments of competition and training
- Multidisciplinary team

The primary consideration during evaluation is the (a) proximity of evaluation to intervention; (b) level of involvement in the evaluation; (c) reliability of responses.

Sport psychology consultant factors in successful interventions

In 2020, I was working with a cyclist who had come out of a surgery and suddenly found herself locked in her home during COVID. She was a mix of happiness (she could now recover to make the Olympic trials for 2021) and frustration (she could not recover fast enough due to lack of sport science access). In August 2020, when our work together concluded, she profusely thanked me and I politely but steadfastly did not accept her thanks. I believe sport psychology consultants are mere facilitators to the clients driving their own change. But then she said something which has always stayed with me and I have inscribed it in my diary since, 'Anyone can get on my bike Sahen, but it'll take me to go as quick as I can. Anyone could have done the stuff we did, I've had psychs before, but it took the click between you and me to make it work'.

While this tempts egotistical attribution to success to oneself, I still firmly believe I am not the controller of my client's destiny – they are. But all the research does point to the importance of the sport psychology consultant-client relationship in interventions (Sharp & Hodge, 2011). Therefore, it is a matter to be cognizant of and consider. The sport psychology consultant delivers the intervention and influences its design, delivery, and evaluation. Who we are and how we are does affect the intervention process. See Quartiroli et al. (2019) paper on how self-care is the key to others' care. If you are tired as a sport psychology consultant, you will be worse off on the field. If you are personally invested, you will want to make it work more. Below are some reflections from successful intervention processes and how to be the best and more ethical sport psychology consultant during intervention delivery. These are composites from my reflections and interactions with experienced practitioners:

- **Listen, dive, listen:** In every interaction with reflection and with clients, the listen-dive-listen approach works. The first listen is to do so without active intervention, but rather listening and being as they come. This can be an athlete describing their thoughts, supervisor pointing something out, or your own thoughts after a difficult session. After listening, the 'dive' comprises an entry point where there is a shift from listening to active reflection or questioning. This presents new information, which encourages learning, deeper exploration of the issue, and alternative perspectives. Then I shift back to listening again.
- **Beginnings & relationships:** If we look at the transtheoretical model of behaviour change, eventual change always starts with pre-contemplation and then contemplation. Therefore,

we can summarise that when people think of changing something, they have an internal comparison of where they are at that point v/s where they want to be. They pre-contemplate a change, contemplate on all the actions necessary for that change. Therefore, it is important to focus efforts into initiating a good therapeutic relationship at *beginnings* with client. Remember, you are inviting any prospective client to walk *with you* on a journey of change. This requires active effort, training, and practice. Go seek it!

- **Don't be pigeon-holed:** It is often tempting to neatly categorise athlete clients as being solely involved in sport. However, for every hour an athlete spends in sport, they are probably spending five hours outside sport. It is important to draw on the larger person (holistic practice) and the experiences beyond just the sport. On a personal level, draw upon wider literature in psychology and sport science disciplines to continue your professional development.

Concluding comments

'It's a setback only if I let it set me back' is a great quote which I heard or read somewhere or someone mentioned it to me but do not remember it. This holds true in interventions as well. In applied practice, you will inevitably fail and face roadblocks in intervention delivery. Some of these will be because of your own learning curve. Some of these will have nothing to do with you but because of larger structural and organisational factors. Do not get disheartened. Reflect, seek supervision, have a good peer network, and continue ethically developing and delivering interventions during your trainee years. Much like a complicated Lego set, you will slowly learn about your process and also put the building blocks together in a better way.

Section III

Writing for Assessment and Publication

10 Conducting and Publishing Academic Research

Introduction

Closing the research-practice gap is important to move the profession forward. As someone undergoing training in the profession, your contribution to this can be vital. Trainees can bring new practice-grounded perspectives to research and publication and can use their work in the field with clients to inform their research agenda. Research forms an integral part of all training routes for sport and exercise psychologists and that means an immense body of research is being led by trainees at various stages of their training. We, as a profession, need to push for more of this research to gain publication and reach a wider audience. In a similar way to recognition in the counselling psychology literature (see, for example, Hanley et al., 2012), we have to ask what happens to that vast body of research that is undertaken by trainee sport and exercise psychologists and how can we improve that research – publication link to ensure that findings are making their way to relevant audiences using appropriate dissemination. What we want to ensure is we translate data gathered for research into published material that is available to other researchers, practitioners, coaches, and athletes. If it is not, then how can our research be informing practice and reducing that existing gap?

In Chapter 2, we covered some key issues regarding ethics and confidentiality. In this chapter, we will look specifically at research ethics and the considerations necessary to turn your research into publications before we move on to explore how to write certain types of assessment that could lead to publication.

Research ethics

There is a wealth of information available to you on research ethics. You can source information locally from your own institutional ethics committees, you can use information provided by professional and regulatory bodies, and you can use ethical guidelines from online sources such as the World Health Organisation (WHO) and UK Research and Innovation (UKRI), to name just two. Another excellent source of information and guiding principles is the Economic and Social Research Council (ESRC) Framework for Research Ethics, which outlines six key principles for ethical research (ESRC, 2022):

1 Research should aim to maximise benefit for individuals and society and minimise risk and harm.
2 The rights and dignity of individuals and groups should be respected.
3 Wherever possible, participation should be voluntary and appropriately informed.
4 Research should be conducted with integrity and transparency.

DOI: 10.4324/9781003367208-13

5 Lines of responsibility and accountability should be clearly defined.
6 Independence of research should be maintained and where conflicts of interest cannot be avoided, they should be made explicit.

These sources and frameworks are excellent guidelines for you when you are considering your research and how to undertake it. What can be less clear in the domain of sport and exercise psychology are some of the ethical issues that are specific to the profession and that arise because of working relationships, hierarchies, and consent issues when working with athletes, youth athletes, and clubs/organisations. You can read about these in sources such as West (2020) and Hankes (2012) for a fuller and more in-depth coverage of this area. The following information in this chapter though will help you see the difficulties inherent in the profession regarding ethics and acts as a caution for you to take time to consider the ethical implications and issues of your own work before you start. Once you come to publish, you may have to defend your ethical decision-making, so be confident from the start that you have given this due process and attention. We covered some of the fundamental principles of ethics in Chapter 2. Research ethics involve applying those fundamental principles to your research activities, including all stages of the design, development, implementation, write-up, and outputs. This chapter will focus now on two key ethical considerations in sport and exercise research: (1) consent and confidentiality, and (2) multiple relationships and boundaries.

Consent and confidentiality

The domain of sport and exercise can cover a wide range of populations that you might want to research. These can include youth athletes, elite athletes, and those members of the general population who engage in exercise. This variation in potential populations makes issues of consent more involved than some other areas of research. Counselling and clinical psychology, including others, contain many discussions about consent and make suggestions for improvements or solutions to current limitations, which can be useful to inform our own work in the sport and exercise domain, so read widely to gain the most up-to-date information and perspectives.

It is imperative to inform potential research participants of the benefits and potential risks of any proposed intervention or research project they are considering taking part in. This is clearly outlined by the British Psychological Society (BPS) in their ethical guidelines and should be front and centre of your thought processes in the area. Who needs to be informed of the proposed research and who needs to provide consent can be difficult areas to navigate. If you are recruiting youth athletes for example, you will need parental consent, potential consent from coaches or sporting organisations, and, of course, the assent of the individual youth athletes themselves. The information you provide should be clearly written for the audience you are aiming it at to ensure understanding and informed consent for your research. You may need to consider literacy levels and levels of understanding of any technical terms in your information sheet and sometimes information might need to be conveyed verbally or particular actions demonstrated to express what will be involved. It is also important to consider cultural power dynamics and linguistic familiarity (see Chapter 3).

An issue related to confidentiality and consent is managing multiple relationships and boundaries.

Multiple relationships and boundaries

One aspect of ethics to give particular attention to is the management of multiple relationships and boundaries. As a sport and exercise psychologist or trainee you may work within a club or training centre in a role that requires you to spend a lot of time with clients, not only working with them on a one-to-one basis but perhaps travelling to competitions or being present at practices and sharing travel, accommodation, and meals with those who might at some point be potential participants in your research. In these situations, it can be difficult to separate out your different relationships and to be clear about professional boundaries (see McCarthy & Moffat, 2024). These situations also create positives enabling the building of trust and understanding so are not all bad – but you need to take them into account if you are planning research that might involve these athletes. These potential issues are then compounded with issues of confidentiality. For example, if you are on placement at a particular organisation, it might make sense to carry out research on that sport and to recruit from within that service to ensure your research is aligning with your interests and ultimately being of benefit to the sport. How can you maintain confidentiality, though? This can be problematic in several ways. First, when a coach asks you how a particular player is doing, or whether they are taking part in the research. And second, when it might be difficult to maintain confidentiality in the presentation of your research findings. If an organisation employs you, then your research ethics need to consider how you can maintain confidentiality principles.

Maximising the research publication likelihood

Within most training routes, you will have to undertake research that you then write up as an assessment to meet set assessment criteria, allowing you to progress with your studies and move towards your professional accreditation. On many programmes of study, this research component will require you to write as if for publication. This orientation will help you make a good start on the research-publication path but will not guarantee that your work, even if it gains a high grade within the university course, will then be accepted for publication. As mentioned earlier in this chapter, maximising the amount of high-quality research that gets published is something we want because only then can we help to get our findings out there to the athletes, coaches, and the wider community who can use that information. Publishing your work will also help you at an individual level. You will gain credibility in the field, and it will help to raise your professional profile. Having published your work before your viva voce can often help the viva process too, as a community of your peers has already indicated that the work you conducted holds academic value and benefits the research community. So, there are plenty of reasons for you to want to publish – it can help the wider community, your institution, and your own career. Successfully getting published can be a lengthy and time-consuming process. So where should you start?

The first question to ask is whether your research holds academic value. You might have conducted a brilliant piece of academic work hitting all the assessment criteria, but if it does not add to the existing literature or compare with the existing literature and theory, is not comprehensive, does not provide any solutions or use appropriately designed interventions, then publication might not be possible. Speak with your supervisor and/or colleagues to get a sense of whether they think it is worth your pursuing publication and do not do it alone. Being part of a team whether that is with your supervisor or someone who has contributed to your work is a normal way to proceed and means that you can use the expertise of those who are more used to publishing to help you navigate the murky waters of publication processes. You could also consider starting a writing group to really help protect time for your writing and to get that level of social support in what can feel like a time-consuming and lonely place.

Once you've established that your work is worth pursuing publication for you will need to consider the journal in which you hope to publish. There are many journals relevant to the field of sport and exercise psychology and you should inform your decision-making process by considering which audience you want your findings to reach, what style of journal you favour, and what types of journals in the field publish work similar to that you have conducted. Lists can be useful here, allowing you to compare elements like types of publications accepted; word limits; referencing system used and relative journal impact factors (JIFs). Before we go any further, let us think about JIFs. How much consideration to be given to the impact factor of a particular journal can be difficult to gauge. The JIF is a way of telling how important that journal is in your field and tells you the frequency with which that journal has been cited in a set period. The higher the JIF, the more citations. So, in an ideal world, we all want to gain publications in journals with high impact factors, right? Well, not necessarily. JIF can only be calculated once there is three years' worth of data available, so a new journal will not have a JIF for you to gauge against. That does not mean they are not a useful way for you to disseminate your research. There has also been a great deal of debate in the literature about the usefulness and validity of JIFs to assess quality. Some claim JIFs are a poor predictive tool and are not objective. You can find out more about this debate with a quick google search and consider how important you think JIFs are in any decision-making process you have around which journal to aim your prospective publication towards.

The decisions you make about which journal to aim your publication at may depend on what stage of write-up your research is at. For example, if you are training through a taught doctoral programme, it is likely that your research will have needed to be as a journal article for submission to the course. From this position, you may not have much work to do with your current writing for it to be ready for submission. If, however, you are on an independent training route and have not yet written up your research, then your deliberations will be quite different here. Even those pieces of coursework that are written in the correct format for publication will still require a good deal of work prior to submission because university assessment criteria do not always map exactly onto journal author guidelines and requirements.

Consider who the readers of different publications are and whether that is the correct target audience for your work. Do you want to publish for the academic community, for practitioners and athletes who you hope will implement your intervention or findings, or do you want a mix of practitioners and academics to read the paper? You can use these considerations to help you gather a list of potential journals that you could target. There is also a literature for you to read to help with your decision-making process. For example, Suiter and Sarli (2019) wrote about criteria to consider when selecting a publication journal. Once you've identified possibilities, try to think objectively about them. Again, this will depend on what stage your research work is at. Each journal will have specific author guidelines you will need to adhere to and you should read these carefully, as your submission will need to adhere strictly to these. Failing to do that will mean your manuscript being returned unread. A further consideration is often whether the journal has a publication charge. Many institutions have agreements with publishers, and it is certainly worth speaking with your supervisor to elicit advice on where you could publish without incurring hefty publication fees. Also look to see if there is the option of publishing Open Access in the journals you are considering. This option will mean that your work is free and accessible online, increasing its visibility and the reach of your work. If you still are not entirely sure which journal to aim your work, then compile a clear list showing word counts, referencing systems, table allowances, and other key aspects of each journal's author guidelines. These can often help inform your decision as one journal, for example, may require you to cut too much from your manuscript for you to submit there, or it might not support the type of work that you have undertaken (for example, a process report or case study, or a systematic review). You can also explore if any relevant journals have a call out for papers on a special theme or topic that fits your work. Once you have selected a journal, make sure that you are conforming exactly to all the requirements set out in their guidelines. Also, take time to read similar articles in that journal to give you an idea of the type of work they accept, and the level of detail expected for different sections of the work. If you have written up your research for an assessment at a university as part of your training route, then the bones of your manuscript will already be there. Use any feedback on your work to make changes before submitting to a journal. You will also need to remove any aspects that were required for assessment criteria but do not fit with the journal's requirements.

Life Lived: Open and Honest Conversations

I have worked with trainees in different domains of psychology to turn their academic assessment into published work. This can be a lengthy process and at times has taken almost two years from the first conversation to the appearance of that paper in a published journal. Reflecting on my experience, there is one key tip to share. If you want to turn your assessment piece into a publication, have an honest and open discussion between yourself as a trainee and your supervisor about how the process will work and what each person's roles and responsibilities are. There is a requirement to move from a supervisor-student relationship to a more collegiate one where you are both working on your strengths and moving towards that final goal. In my experience, trainees take with them that perception that they are being assessed, and a fear of admitting when they're stuck into the writing for publication arena and that can be detrimental to progress. Maybe as a trainee you do not want to admit to your supervisor that you are totally stuck and do not know what their comment on your work meant (although I would also suggest that should not be the case), but if you're working together on a publication, you need to make that shift from assessment to collaboration and not be afraid to ask questions. Do not feel that you must take responsibility for every aspect of the publication process. You should lead it as first author, but your supervisor will have years of experience that they can draw on to help you, so do not shy away from asking questions and admitting when you do not know what to do. Not engaging in honest conversation will only result in delays to the process.

Once you have an initial draft of your paper, share it with others for feedback. You want to achieve clarity in your writing, and getting feedback from others is a vital step. You could also consider asking a colleague to summarise the key points from your draft manuscript and use that to check that you are conveying the key message that you have aimed at. Once you have revisited your manuscript and incorporated any feedback, make sure the other authors you have collaborated with are completely happy with the work before you submit. If the journal you are targeting has specific deadlines for submission, then make sure you are prepared well before that deadline. Besides the manuscript, you will need to have included information asked for on ethics, conflicts of interest and also most likely have prepared a cover letter outlining why your research is of value, is suitable for the journal and should be published. Not allowing time for all these aspects will detrimentally affect your chances of successful publication.

Once you have submitted, you can expect to have a reasonably long period to wait while the journal editor processes your submission. Manuscripts usually undergo editorial screening to check that manuscripts meet the criteria for publication, that they are not outside the scope of the journal, that there are not any elements that have not been correctly reported or been detailed enough. If your manuscript passes this editorial review, the editor will then send it out to peer review with at least two reviewers independently reading and reporting on your submission.

These reviewers then report back to the editor, giving their opinion on the readiness and suitability of your work for publication. There are several outcomes here. Often submissions are rejected, and the editor will recommend that you seek publication in a different journal. This is not uncommon, and rejections, although disappointing, are all part of the writing process. You can use any feedback to enhance your work and then look for another avenue for publication. Another possibility is that you will be asked to make either minor or major revisions and they will set a timeline on how long you have to do these revisions. You will receive a list of comments from the reviewers, and your re-submission would have to clearly show how you addressed each of these comments and changed your manuscript. The aim of this process is to produce work that has enhanced clarity and impact and results in higher quality publications. All this takes time, and it isn't unusual for months to have passed between you submitting and your paper finally being accepted.

Summary

In summary, this chapter has tried to convey the importance of publishing and why this could benefit not only to the wider community and domain of sport and exercise psychology, but how it could also benefit you as an individual. If you are considering publishing, expect the process to take a considerable amount of time and speak to your supervisor or peers/colleagues about their own experiences and gather tips and advice from them.

Carefully consider the amount of material that you can include in a single publication. If you are thinking about your entire PhD or major research project for a large research module on a taught university programme, you may have to choose one element to focus on for your publication. Deciding about what is important and which element would be most useful to publish can help you develop a clear line of reasoning around the academic value of your work so will have the wider benefit of helping you gain clarity around that which can be a real asset going into any viva voce.

Do not rush into aiming your work at a particular journal without careful consideration of whether that is the best potential home for your work. Think more broadly than JIFs and also consider the audience you want to reach and the type of impact you want your work to have. Try to write as part of a team and ensure you adhere strictly to any author guidelines and journal requirements. Check your institutional fee waiver agreements and ask for feedback from trusted sources prior to submission. Finally, do not be disheartened by rejection – it is all part of the process of getting published and the feedback gained and other lessons learned through that process can be hugely beneficial to you even if you do not finish with the publication you hoped for.

11 How to Write a Process Report

Introduction

Applying one's theoretical knowledge to one's practice with a client forms a hallmark of a practitioner delivering a competent service. Though a practitioner might relate much theory in a supervision session, its application embraces what supervisors and assessors need to witness, whether being present with the trainee and client, watching a video recording or listening to an audio recording of the trainee and client. Though supervisors and assessors might witness the practice of a trainee, they still do not know what the trainee thought, felt, and reflected upon in their work with the client. In short, they need a method where the supervisee shares theory in practice and reflects critically upon their work.

One method to achieve this aim is using a process report. A process report is a written account to share one's method, techniques, and metacommunication from a therapeutic meeting. The trainee records a segment of a session with a client, transcribes it, and then analyses and discusses the therapeutic process, line by line. The trainee describes and critically reflects upon what they did and why and the effect it traces upon the client, practitioner, and their therapeutic relationship. Process reports help the supervisee reflect on their actions and inactions in a session and how they affect the therapeutic process, which they might not do without this form of inquiry and/or assessment.

In a training programme, a module leader might set a process report with a limit of 3,000 words. The trainee transcribes a ten-minute segment for the assessment. The clue to a process report lies in its name – process or processes – of a session with a client. In this training programme, a trainee following a cognitive-behavioural model of therapy describes the model and the content of the session. For example, the trainee might be in her fourth session with a client who presented with performance anxiety around major competitions. Having completed an intake, assessment, and formulation, the client shares their experiences of the early stages of their intervention. In the opening of your process report, you can describe your therapeutic model and the content of the session before moving onto the processes of your work.

In this chapter, we shall describe the steps of a process report from acquiring informed consent from a client to the practicalities of audio recording, choosing a segment to transcribe, and transcribing. Next, we shall consider the written transcript and note your goals, metacommunication, and dilemmas. Finally, we shall examine and illustrate the headings and content of a process report: introduction, client profile, professional setting, presenting problem, assessment, contract and plan, prelude to session, main body, and summary. The main body comprises the line-by-line analysis and interpretation, linking to a theoretical framework. The main body might explore non-verbal communication, how the client appears to feel, the trainee's thoughts, feelings, dilemmas, reflections, pacing, and evaluation. You can include your supervisor's influence, whether directly related to your work with this client or your overall therapeutic work.

DOI: 10.4324/9781003367208-14

Getting started

A process report focuses on the detail of your work with a client. In short, we are asking ourselves about what is going on in our work with our client moment-to-moment. For example, we might listen to a recording and question: 'What's going on here?', 'Why did I pause there?', 'Did the question I raised have the effect I thought it would?', 'Could I have said what I said, differently?'. The first issue you might notice here is the one-sided portrayal of one's work because it seems it is all about one person, the trainee. A case study, in contrast, captures the details from the other side of the dyad, exploring the details of the client and the collaborative approach with the client. These two halves present a whole picture of the sport psychology practitioner working with a client.

So why do we need to know about what is happening at this minute level from the practitioner's point of view? It is these exact processes, this fine-grained analysis, that show the practitioner, supervisor, and assessor how the practitioner undertakes practice. We, as practitioners, handle our actions during our therapeutic hour for the best therapeutic support for our client and reflecting on our practice remains central to sound ethical and competent practice as a sport psychology practitioner. If we believe in the centrality of the therapeutic relationship and techniques we use, then we ought to examine these parts specifically to improve our practice. If we do not know how we practise, how can we develop? One encouraging element of this process lies in identifying strengths and areas for improvement.

We can divide the procedure of a process report into three stages: audio recording, transcribing, and writing the report. Writing the report consumes most of our time in the procedure.

Audio recording

Without clients to work with, we cannot practise. And if we cannot practise, we have nothing to record. Though these points seem axiomatic, they emphasise how central our clients are to our line of work and our services. With these principles in mind, we remain ethically sensitive to our clients, their needs, and their cooperation.

When we audio and video record sessions, we have an excellent opportunity to learn from our actions. Have you ever wondered about the pitch, pace, and tone of your voice in a session with a client? How do you sound? Do you remember the emphasis a client placed on an issue? Did you miss critical moments? We can track these elements of the therapeutic process over time to see how we are developing our skills. Supervisors use these recordings to open discussions about elements of the supervisee's practice and track changes. For instance, if you were listening to a recording of a cognitive behaviour therapy (CBT) session, which elements of the CBT process might you hear (e.g., mood check, agenda setting, homework). Without these recordings, we can only depend on the selective memories of the supervisee from a session without the richness of the audio or video recording. Being pragmatic, recordings offer detailed dialogues while our memories hunt for sections of a dialogue but usually emerge with content rather than process. In short, without audio or video recordings, the quality of practice and supervision suffers.

Trainees often struggle to get started with their recordings. One prominent reason is the fear of negative evaluation from others (e.g., supervisor). Although feeling concerned about how one sounds and practises might seem overwhelming, the fears fade after a few recordings and with the sensitivity of a skilled supervisor. Rather that viewing recordings as a test, recordings offer you a chance to reflect on your work, select strengths and areas for improvement, notice elements of the theoretical framework you adhere to, and raise your efficacy in relating to your clients. When we record sessions as a usual part of our work, we forget about the recording device and focus on our client rather than ourselves.

Because our recordings depend on the cooperation and consent of our clients, we need to seek their consent sensitively to record a session(s). First, we ought to approach the role of recording as a usual part of the therapy process and highlight the benefits to the client. Second, seeking permission to record ought to be clear and consistent with the benefits to the client rather than a tentative, apprehensive, and self-serving appeal. In our experience, clients wish to help us in our work if they feel it will help them in theirs. Third, we must consider whether our clients' sessions ought to be recorded because of the sensitive nature of their case histories. Finally, although we might record a session, a client keeps the right to withdraw that recording. In all that we do with our clients, their needs are paramount.

Written consent

We need consent to record with our client. The safest process means getting written permission from your client, as you will see in a consent form. A consent form ought to address the purpose of the recording, confidentiality, and how the practitioner might use the information. Once you have gained consent, you can photocopy or scan the consent form, keeping the original stored securely and a copy or scan used for your coursework submission, for example. Remember to redact all elements of the client's details to preserve their anonymity.

Getting started with recording

Over the years, the challenges of recording sessions have reduced dramatically with sophisticated smart phones and dictaphones. Yet, the basics often catch us out. For example, batteries running out during a recording, the recording device set too far away from the speakers, or an incoming call to a mobile device ceasing the recording and so on. It's most like now that trainees store recordings electronically with password-protected access for supervisors and assessors. Trainees store files as MP4 and are easy to access and listen to by the supervisor, assessor, or intended recipient.

After addressing these basics, recording several sessions seems sensible and pragmatic. With several sessions recorded, you can choose which session best represents your work with clients and which segment within this recording that allows you to write about your work. Listen to all your recordings for at least three reasons. First, you become familiar with your work and ways of working which you can take into supervision for a SWOT analysis (i.e., strengths, weaknesses, opportunities, threats). Second, you might use your recordings for a self-assessment of your skills in practice choosing areas to improve. Finally, listening to your work offers a chance to notice the feelings and physical responses emerging with particular segments. You might notice feeling 'tense', 'excited', 'embarrassed', or 'chuffed', and this last reason often finds its way into a process report to understand the 'why' of doing what you do. Because this is a process report, you will write about the process rather than the content. It is easy to be drawn into content issues and away from the process. If, for example, you were completing a process report following a CBT modality, the assessment criteria would normally address

1 Professional and ethical demands
2 A critical and conceptual basis of CBT
3 Your goals – what you are trying to achieve in your work with your client
4 Link your practice with theory and research

5 Your effectiveness as a practitioner
6 How you cope with unexpected challenges

With these assessment criteria in mind, you might choose a segment in which you encountered an unexpected dilemma or a challenge you and other practitioners face in practice, or a specific issue with interrelated issues. In this way, you will have much to analyse, evaluate, and synthesise in your report. A client might relate issues of a relationship breakdown with a coach or a transition from one team to another. Though these issues seem quotidian, your challenges within the session are what the assessor pursues. The challenges you face might relate to culture, race, ethnicity, status, gender, and so forth. Keep in mind the distinction between content and process because you can easily slip into a theoretical debate about ethnicity and forget to engage with how this issue affected the course of your work with the client.

Transcribing

You need a transcription for a process report because you illustrate to an assessor a verbatim transcribed dialogue in which you critique your work in a session with a client. The verbatim dialogue represents the authentic depiction of your work. Transcribing a session takes time and can often feel uncomfortable listening to your voice and interactions; however, there is much to be gained from the transcription process. A 50-minute session might take four hours to transcribe depending on your typing speed following a line-by-line format, so you might wish to transcribe in one-hour segments or shorter. Each line contains statements from the client or from the practitioner, which is why we separate them onto different lines to specify the speaker. We recommend double-line spacing so you can run through your transcription and identify the elements of your session (i.e., your purpose and goals for the sessions). A 50-minute session might have up to 30 pages of double-line spaced text, so you might need to choose six pages for your process report segment.

Reading your transcript

Once you have your transcript, you can review the dialogue between you and your client. Some trainees, especially at the beginning of their training, feel uncomfortable with the balance of dialogue because they notice how much they spoke or how little they spoke in the session or the differences in dialogue between the opening and closing sections of the session which were not their intentions or goals for the session. Perhaps following a CBT format, you set the agenda for the session with the client but forgot to review the homework from the intervening week. Listening to our sessions and reading transcripts allows us to make sense of our practice.

To read a transcript, like reading a book or journal article, we need to know which questions we are trying to answer to gain from the text. The questions you ask are about: What is my goal here? Or what am I trying to achieve? And what is the effect? Or how does the client respond? This process rolls from you to the client and back again because what you say, for instance, influences how the client responds and perhaps how you respond in return. It is these exchanges we analyse and evaluate. A transcript often misses intonation and feeling. Reading a transcript, we are not sure about the feelings conveyed. A client might express 'I don't know how I feel about the move to a new club to London' with frustration, sadness, or doubt and we could not tell from the dialogue. We can note the feeling as we experienced it or perhaps recalled it from the recording in the transcribed text. Verbatim text transcripts also do not contain the metacommunication in your work with your client. Metacommunication comprises all the non-verbal communication (e.g., eye contact or lack of it; fidgeting or stillness) that influences our professional judgement and decision-making in the session. Sometimes there will be pauses, silences, or perhaps interruptions that influence us and the client. Perhaps you intended to raise something in the silence and the client broke the silence so you let your thought or feeling go or perhaps you made a note of it in your session notes.

Process reports explore the practitioner's thoughts, feelings, goals, responses, and so forth. Few practitioners are clear on these all the time; rather, it is most likely we have points of uncertainty, a change of pace, a change of direction, mixed feelings, and reflections upon these. These dilemmas form engaging and provoking segments for a process report. As an assessor or supervisor, we wish to understand the trainee's moment-to-moment reflection on their thoughts, feelings, and actions. A trainee might reflect up his choice of response to a client and perhaps how he feels differently now about his choice. The trainee reflects on his own experiencing and suspected experiencing of the client. Choosing one segment from the whole transcription usually means locating material that seems challenging, engaging, and insightful.

Life Lived

When I (Paul), began my training in person-centred therapy, one of our early assignments was to write a process report. I had some ideas of what they entailed; however, I had no experience of conducting them. Thankfully, a recently published book by Andersen (2000) helped me understand how experienced practitioners practised and offered an illustration of how to do sport psychology. The commentary and interpretations helped me to hear how sport psychology in practice sounds. I had also just begun my doctorate, conducting qualitative interviews and focus groups, so I carried my Dictaphone everywhere. It took me six recorded and transcribed sessions to feel comfortable with an excerpt for my process report. I was trying to 'get it right', rather than understand what the process report meant at that stage of my training. The process report should show my method, technique, and metacommunication illustrating my ability to put theory into practice and critically reflect on my work as a sport psychology consultant.

Writing the process report

All good written process reports follow with a beginning, middle, and ending. In the beginning, you introduce your aims: What am I trying to achieve in my process report? The middle, or main body, achieves your goals, and the ending summarises your process report. We need to remind ourselves that the process report reflects the practitioner's method, techniques, and metacommunication in the therapeutic work with a client. Trainees put theory into practice and critically reflect on their work as a practitioner, especially on how their actions influence the therapeutic process. Knowing that you, as a practitioner, influence the therapeutic process means you play an active role and a reflective role. We can easily slip into content-related issues rather than process information, so we need to remind ourselves to 'stick to the process'. With the process in mind, you can question yourself: How am I seeing things? Why am I seeing things this way? Are there other ways to see this part? What is influencing my view here? The scientist-practitioner moves from hypothesis to hypothesis, tests each one sequentially, seeks alternatives, notices the possibility of several processes unfolding contemporarily.

One key challenge to remember is the length of the process report. If the assessor sets it at 3,000 words, then we need to use our word count wisely. We cannot delve into every issue, so we can choose a few issues and perhaps one central dialogue.

The beginning

In the introduction, we need to tell the reader about our theoretical approach and aims of the process report. We also need to orient the reader to our client about the usual elements, such as the working organisation, referral, client profile, assessment, presenting problem, contract, and formulation, before leading into the current session.

Setting the scene for the reader means introducing the reader to your work setting (e.g., private practice, national governing body, professional sports club) so the reader recognises your position within the organisation and the limits in your work practice, approach, and outcomes. Your setting also helps to understand the referral process (self-referred or other), the understanding and expectations from the person (e.g., coach, parent, general practitioner) referring the client to you. The support offered as a practitioner to a client in an Olympic sport (e.g., swimming) might differ from what is possible, practical, and affordable for a client whom you see in private practice. We ensure anonymity for the client by using a pseudonym, and we also used pseudonyms for people and organisations involved. We can disguise specifics for the client (e.g., age, location) to reduce the chances of the client being identified. Maybe your client plays as second row forward in rugby and you change this detail to the back row. We try to conceal the identity of the client. We introduce the reader typical specifics such as age, gender, ethnicity, appearance, and perhaps your general feelings on meeting the client. The client will share the presenting issue; however, a referral letter might also hold specifics. The client's view of the presenting issue might differ significantly from the notes in the referral letter. What matters here is that you describe the problem as presented and how the problem affects the client. Next, we can move to the initial assessment and formulation to orient the reader to the main body. The assessment and formulation ought to be comprehensive because you describe your understanding of the problem while hinting at what might arise in the main body of the process report. Sound scholarly work joins practice (i.e., assessment and formulation) with theory and research, so these citations inform the reader of your leading edge understanding and synthesis of scholarly publications.

Depending on your workplace setting, it's likely that you will have agreed a contract for your work with your client. Sometimes these are formal, sometimes informal. For instance, you may have agreed to six sessions with a client that fits with your organisation's stipulations. The contract will contain the time (e.g., Monday 4 pm) and number (e.g., 6) of sessions, and goals and focus of the therapeutic support. The main body of your report might be session four of six, which allows the reader to understand what has happened to this point, with details of the previous session and relevant information (e.g., homework) for the upcoming session. Also, explain where the upcoming segment fits within the overall session (e.g., beginning, middle, or end) and what preceded it in the session. Also, you can note any specific progress or lack of it for the reader in the presenting problem.

The middle

Different assessors request different formats to present the main body. Some assessors will require the dialogue to be attached as an appendix, while others request the dialogue to fit within the text. When we attach the dialogue as an appendix, we need to cross reference with the appendix (e.g., In line 22, I ask whether …). When we present the dialogue in the main body, we can critique following each segment presented. The main body houses your goals (i.e., what I am trying to achieve) and its effects (i.e., what effect it had on the client). Sometimes the effect matches the goal, sometimes it does not. The key process remains to identify what has happened and alter accordingly. It is this rolling process of goals and effects which we critique in the process report. Trainees often feel they need to 'get it all right'; however, the goal is to reflect critically on our work, not try to be 'perfect' and say all the 'right things in the right way'. What a process report allows us to do is to improve our techniques of working with clients so the assessor will wish to see our ability to critique dispassionately. We need to explore the dialogue with an openness to learn that harbours strengths and areas for improvement. You might ask yourself questions like 'How was my response received?', 'Did my intention work out as I planned?', and 'How did the client's response influence me?' To answer these questions means joining practice with theory and research. For example, how did your chosen theory match with your decision to respond here? Did you use your theoretical framework to make sense of the response that followed from the client? Taking your client's response, how does it fit with your guiding theory?

You might slide away from your guiding theoretical frameworks for several reasons. The key here is to recognise and reflect upon this departure. Maybe the clients' response confused you or perhaps their frustration put pressure on you to offer advice. What matters here is your ability to recognise what you did and make sense of it. After all, you are asking yourself why something happened, not trying to get everything right.

The difficulties or dilemmas we face draw upon how we decide. What did you decide to do? How did you decide? Which factors influenced the decision-making process? Sometimes we align with our theoretical framework, sometimes we deviate from it. What readers and assessors seek in a process report is how you explore your choices, reflect upon them, and consider alternatives.

The process report offers us an opportunity to reflect within a theoretical framework. It offers us an opportunity to present alternative responses. Perhaps our goal achieved its intended outcome; however, we can consider alternatives. If you are following a cognitive-behavioural approach in your work, you might have a client who feels concerned about challenging her coach so you explore the thoughts behind those feelings. Some alternatives might be an imagination exercise, role play, or recall instances where the client challenged other authority figures.

While process reports might seem to only deal with the words in the transcription, they capture so much more about the client and practitioner. A few examples would be the pacing of the session, non-verbal communication and feelings of the client and you, the practitioner, and perhaps the influence of your supervisor and supervision on your work. With pacing, the client and practitioner try to move together through a session. Often, however, the client might wish to speed or slow, which is at odds with the practitioner's judgement. The stage of one's development as a practitioner often influences pacing because at the early stages of one's career, a practitioner might feel results are paramount and ought to be immediate or perhaps a new client feels frustrated with the pace of a session because he is not getting to the intervention phase fast enough and has concerns about an upcoming performance. These processes ought to be discussed and how they might present themselves and influence the therapeutic process. Noticing the pace of a session gives us a sense of how a client might present themselves (e.g., animated, fidgeting, minimal eye contact). A client presenting with performance anxiety fidgets when you mention the national championships or a client experiencing a performance slump sits defeated in her chair with her gaze to the floor when she tries to recall her strengths. This non-verbal sharing of one's feelings alongside silences, paralanguage (e.g., pitch, tone, pace of speaking), and facial expressions ought to be shared in the main body. You will notice changes or lack of changes in your client's mood across the session from your interventions with them. Of course, practitioners' feelings also rise, fall, and change, perhaps exploring a challenging topic or how the practitioner receives the client in session. In our goals and outcomes working with a client, we gain greater sensitivity to our thoughts and feelings which are in the room alongside those of our client.

The ending

The summary of your report allows you to summarise what you covered and offer an assessment of your work and an overall evaluation of your session. You can also provide a statement about the outcome of your service delivery with your client. When we acknowledge our strengths and areas for improvement, we keep a sense of efficacy about our work and a desire to keep improving. Finally, we adhere to the references, any appendices noted in the report, and proof-reading your document. Though these tasks may seem tiresome, these finishing touches reflect the discipline, diligence, and can care you offer for your work. Whatever work we offer in writing, we ought to reference theory, research, and practice from the literature. If we stated in our introduction that we work within a CBT framework, then our written work should follow suit.

Summary

Process reports, like all new skills learned on a doctoral programme, for example, are daunting initially. With practice, however, they become easier to conduct from beginning to end, especially writing that shares the overlap of you as a person and a professional. We recommend practising recording, listening, and transcribing sessions as part of your ongoing supervision. We recommend reading Moffat and McCarthy (2023) for examples of the details of the stages of a process report and key tasks. Also, you will find questions to guide you through a process report, along with an applied example of mapping core themes on to a transcript and an extract from a process report.

12 How to Write a Client Case Study

Introduction

A client case study, like a process report, captures how a sport psychology practitioner blends psychological theory, research, and practice experience with clinical skills when working collaboratively with a client. Because the practitioner writes the case study, the slant within the case reflects the practitioner's interpretation of the events of their interactions over several sessions. And the case study also mirrors the practitioner's ability to write sensitively, clearly, and coherently for students, trainees, and professional colleagues. In short, writing and publishing a case study discloses much of what the practitioner wishes to reveal and perhaps keeps hidden. After all, a case study declares to its readers one's professional competence and clinical skills in professional practice and one's ability to write.

Client case studies offer a chance for professional growth. For trainees, they will need to write several case studies to satisfy accrediting organisations such as the Health and Care Professions Council (HCPC) and the British Psychological Society (BPS). This opportunity to write to persuade assessors about your practice competencies ought to be seen as an engaging challenge rather than a foreboding threat because you can express openly and honestly how you practise. To achieve this stage of writing about how and why you do what you do means investing in developing your theoretical and research knowledge and clinical skills while you practise. The consequences of writing a poor case study pose a threat to trainees, so they often feel overwrought in their drafts writing about what happened; however, there are no perfect case studies. Rather, there are opportunities to write and learn about your personal and professional development as a trainee practitioner psychologist.

In this chapter, we shall address five key aspects to assemble a client case study. First, we lay out what you need to write about within a case study. Next, we consider how to choose a suitable case to present for assessment. Then, we explore the contents of the case. After these steps, we write the first draft before revising it. Finally, we submit for assessment or review (if we are seeking publication) and respond to the feedback. Before we address these elements, we shall open with a justification for case studies in applied sport psychology.

Why do we need case studies?

Applied sport psychology encompasses a broad church of practitioners with diverse approaches to practise with athletes, coaches, and teams. Yet, our knowledge and understanding of their methods and the evidence base supporting their approaches remain insufficient (Cotterill, Weston, & Breslin, 2017). In short, without case studies, for instance, we do not know how or why sport psychology practitioners do what they do. This gap in our knowledge base means trainees and qualified practitioners cannot read and learn from the experiences of others working

DOI: 10.4324/9781003367208-15

with a varied client base in diverse settings, which lessens their armoury working in an assorted and eclectic field. Though most students are general psychologists first (undergraduate studies), and sport psychology consultants second (postgraduate studies and training), experiences from the territory (i.e., working in the field) capture the imagination and steadfastness more that the details on the map (i.e., learning through postgraduate degrees and training programmes). Case studies assemble such experiences about practising in the field, learning through experience and the role of supervision. Published case studies make us vulnerable because we open ourselves to criticism about our work, yet our authenticity grows through such experiences. We are not flawless and invulnerable – we are flawed, and vulnerable as well as wonderful. And, like our clients, we need to tell our stories as psychologists and as storytellers (Andersen & Speed, 2011).

Case studies allow us to develop theory and practice, yet equally, we seek a rigorous and unbiased method to observe, analyse, and write case studies. In the sport and exercise psychology literature, we have behavioural case studies ('N = 1' or single-case designs) reflecting the scientist-practitioner model tracking change over time in one or a few variables. Sometimes case studies help develop theory or narrative case studies, which encourage the client or practitioner to tell their story of therapy. The challenge, however, lies within the credibility and usefulness of the work undertaken.

Case studies sit alongside other research methods, such as interviews, surveys, autoethnography, and autobiography.

What you need to write about within a case study

A case study offers you several opportunities to display to your supervisor and assessors that you are a safe, independent, and professional practitioner in your field. Supervisors and assessors do not see you working in the field, rather, they see a portrayal of your work in writing. This portrayal does not mean we write dishonestly and smooth our story to fit the assessment criteria; instead, we write honestly and persuasively to exemplify how we work to the best of our ability for the benefit of our client and those we serve in service delivery.

Most assessors set assessment criteria with which to judge the competency of your work as a trainee practitioner. You might discuss these assessment criteria with a course tutor or a supervisor to prepare your case study. Case studies are flourishing within academic journals so you can read how others practise in sport and exercise psychology. The assessment criteria with your course of study might relate to a specific therapeutic modality, such as cognitive behaviour therapy or person-centred therapy, and your case study ought to reflect this modality.

We write case studies with our focus on the assessment guidelines and criteria. A case study written by a trainee offers the assessor a chance to assess the trainee's work. The trainee, therefore, occupies a central platform alongside the client and presenting issue(s) within the case study. The assessor needs to see psychological theory, research, and practice woven through clinical skills and professional reflexivity. Although some description sets the scene for the assessor, at this level of scholarship, the assessor needs to see evidence of how you integrate theory with your clinical practice; the assessor needs to see evidence of analysis, synthesis, and evaluation. You can demonstrate these competencies by explaining and justifying why you did what you did in your work with your client regarding theory, research, and practice. This interconnectedness of a theoretical orientation (e.g., CBT) and practice ought to be clear in your work and within the case study you write for assessment. Remember the following:

a Be clear and consistent on the therapeutic model you are using.
b Bring the assessor along logically through your case study by explaining and justifying how and why you did what you did.

c Remember your assessor needs to know you are a safe, independent, and professional practitioner who learns from theory, research, professional practice, personal experience, and supervision.

Whether you are registered on a taught doctorate, professional doctorate, or independent training route, all require case studies. All the work trainees undertake with clients form independent case studies within their practicum placement. A practicum placement ought to be suitable for case work. Several case studies are available within the sport and exercise psychology literature to guide your writing and presentation with Case Studies in Sport and Exercise Psychology as one example of a dedicated journal to case studies from the Association for Applied Sport Psychology.

Choosing a suitable case to present for assessment

Undertaking therapeutic work with several clients on practicum placements means you can choose which case best represents you as a safe, independent, and professional practitioner who learns from theory, research, professional practice, personal experience, and supervision. Let the assessment criteria guide your choice here. What remains critical with all your work with clients is how you keep client notes, reflections, and supervisory meetings.

Cotterill, Schinke, and Thelwell (2017) outlined three objectives for submitting case studies within the journal, Case Studies in Sport and Exercise Psychology: (1) Sharing in a community of practice. (2) Situated approaches. (3) Situating the self. These three objectives allow practitioners to share their experiences (i.e., successes and challenges) working in the field. And though underpinned by theoretical rigour and criticality, stay open to creativity and innovation while situating oneself personally and professionally within a context. The person (e.g., age, gender, culture) and the professional (e.g., education, training, professional orientation) knit their way into, and through, the case study especially in their thorough and critical reflections (Knowles & Gilbourne, 2010). It is this metacognition (i.e., thinking about our thinking) which allows trainees to think critically and exhaustively as a practitioner and applied researcher in the field. In keeping with good case studies, the authors present the context, case, and reflections which illustrate how and why they work as they do, leaning on philosophy of practice, assessment, formulation, intervention, evaluation, and communication. Through all these experiences, the thread of reflection helps them to learn from their experiences, understand what they could change, and how they will become better practitioners.

In summary, the case you choose to present shows your ability to know, comprehend, analyse, synthesise, and evaluate theory and research and apply clinical skills in practice. Writing clearly, coherently, and persuasively is the medium through which assessors and reviewers appreciate your proficiency and competency as a practitioner in sport and exercise contexts.

The contents of the case study

Because a case study illustrates the cycle of professional practice, it reflects ethical values (e.g., respect, competence, responsibility and integrity) and five core skills: assessment, formulation, intervention or implementation, evaluation, and communication. To explain, we assess and establish agreements to work with a client. Next, we formulate with the client their needs and problems before intervening or implementing solutions. Then we evaluate the outcome of our work before communicating and reflecting on the outcomes. The web of how sport psychology consultants work (e.g., reflective practice), where they work (e.g., remotely), and with whom they work (e.g., multiple clients) draws several strands of standards, processes, and issues such as legislation, safeguarding, contracting, referrals, informed consent, managing data and confidentiality, and responding when things go wrong (e.g., managing conflict and complaints) (BPS Practice Guidelines 2017). Not all of this information fits explicitly into a case study; however, implicitly, it lies within your practice and the assessor is keen to know that you know these foundations even if it is one sentence to explain how you secure consent or establish a contract with a client.

The central features of a case study outlined by Cotterill et al. (2017) reflect sharing in a community of practice, situated approaches, and situating the self. These parts stitch the core skills of assessment, formulation, intervention or implementation, evaluation, and communication to show how theory, research, practice experience, and reflection sit alongside clinical skills when working with a client. Not only do you, the practitioner, outline and detail the course of service delivery using theory and research to justify your choices and actions, and reflective practice to make sense of what unfolded, but also your deep and considered personal and professional development in the field.

One question students and trainees ask is how sophisticated should the case study be for assessment. There are at least two answers to this question. First, it depends on your stage of study. For example, an introductory case study at Master's degree level will differ from a doctoral degree level case study on aspects of knowledge, comprehension, analysis, synthesis, and evaluation of theory and research and application of clinical skills in practice. Second, sound basics, when applied correctly, demonstrate sophistication because your chosen therapeutic modality, its facets, and drawbacks are presented with clarity. You are not mixing approaches and concepts unless you are presenting an integrated model of practice, for example. The assessor will wish to know how you are learning, developing, and reflecting on your strengths and areas for improvement.

Presenting a theoretical position

One's philosophy of practice is ever unfolding; however, it is a typical requirement in assessments on the path to professional status to share it in writing. Because of this requirement, trainees need to have a coherent philosophy which they can describe to others. One's philosophy of practice will include theory and philosophy of therapy, theory related to their working context (e.g., sport and exercise), research, and clinical practice. Stitching these together presents several challenges because of the tug-o-war between head and heart. To explain, any training programme undertaken to achieve professional status as a sport psychology consultant emphasises aspects of the head such as assessment, evaluation, evidence, and critical thinking perhaps above aspects of the heart such as open-heartedness, warmth, love, simplicity, untutored innocence, and defencelessness (Feltham & Dryden, 2006). Any case study presented for assessment, despite the work undertaken with clients in the therapy room, needs to show orientation and detail of one's stance (i.e., philosophical, theoretical).

University training programmes, for instance, spend many lecture hours, seminars, and skills classes introducing students to the theory of their chosen approach (e.g., person-centred therapy). Trainees undertake their own reading, peer-led discussions, and essays to make sense of the presented approach. Their skills classes allow them to practise safely with fellow trainees before completing a fitness to practise assessment and taking their tentative steps into the real world of applied sport psychology. One's theoretical foundation, therefore, though elaborate, needs to fit into one section of your case study and core theoretical principles guide practice from beginning to end. Writing and rewriting this section helps you to familiarise yourself with the core principles of your work but also embeds the directions you need to work well with clients. Rewriting the core principles of your work usually means refining and polishing your stance, and it opens up an opportunity to share your summary with peers, a supervisor, or a tutor. Occasionally, trainees learn about their therapeutic approach best by contrasting it with other approaches, highlighting a higher-order cognitive skill.

A theoretical summary does not need to be exhaustive, rather, it exemplifies your core theoretical position, perhaps with an overview, basic assumptions, and origins and maintenance of problems, and the process of change (Tudor, 2017). The following is an example of a theoretical summary for a person-centred approach.

A person-centred approach

- **Overview:** Emerging from the work of Rogers, person-centred therapy focuses on the whole person and being of the client and rests on the view that therapy is the relationship between the therapist or sport psychology consultant and the client. It influenced, and was influenced by, the humanistic psychology becoming the most influential of the humanistic approaches to therapy. *Basic assumptions:* First, the human organism actualises. Second, a non-directive approach and attitude from the therapist support growth and change. Finally, the client and therapist create the conditions for growth, challenge, and change.
- **Origins and maintenance of problems:** Incongruence exists when a person's tendency to actualise diverges from one's self-actualisation. From full congruence at the beginning of life, experience enters awareness without distortion or denial. When faced with the possibility of threat, disruption, disapproval, or rejection, a person may feel anxious because of the need for positive regard from important people in their life. The person's perception of themselves (i.e., self-concept) is shaped by these adverse experiences, so they internalise conditions of worth and try to guard themselves from similar events. The self-concept that is formed through conditioning can be so strong that a person may lose all sense of their true self and the goals they had set for themselves. A state of disharmony has been created, causing psychological distress.
- **Process of change:** To promote therapeutic change, particular conditions that are not just necessary, but are also sufficient enough to permit the client's self-actualisation to be more powerful than other drives, like defensive forces of their self-concept. Rogers identified unconditional positive regard, empathy, and genuineness as being the core qualities of a therapist.

Choosing a suitable case

With several cases to choose from practicum placement, which case best suits the needs of your assessment? The answer is twofold. First, the case that allows you to persuade the assessor that you are as a safe, ethical, and professional practitioner who uses a core therapeutic model (e.g., CBT) alongside theory and research related to the context of sport and exercise to undertake service delivery with a client. Second, does the chosen case allow you to meet the specific assessment criteria (e.g., working with child and adolescent athletes using a CBT orientation). A suitable case from your caseload allows you to show the doctoral criteria, for example, in your assessment. These criteria typically require a theoretical model, core theoretical principles of your approach, details of an evidence-based approach, sufficient sessions with the client, a challenging rather than simple case study, use of supervision, and reflection.

Writing the first draft

A case study ought to follow general headings that steer you and the assessor through your case study. These headings guide you through the major elements and ensure you do not miss significant features of your assessment. We offer six specific headings, and a suggested word count in brackets: introduction (500), therapeutic beginning (600), therapeutic middle (900), therapeutic ending (400), and conclusion (600) followed by references and appendices. These headings and suggested word counts can be adjusted to your chosen therapeutic modality, which might emphasise specific elements (e.g., assessment) over others (e.g., relational dynamics).

Suggested headings and contents for your case study:

1 Introduction

    a Introduction to case
    b Summary of chosen theoretical orientation
    c Setting – context for the work

2 Therapeutic beginning

    a Referral (if it applies) and communicating with other professionals
    b Assessment session
    c Presenting problem and initial formulation
    d Contracting and aims of therapy

3 Therapeutic middle

    a Co-created formulation
    b Therapeutic intervention plan and techniques
    c Content and progress of the case
    d Process of the case between client and practitioner
    e Challenges of the case (e.g., reformulation)
    f Use of supervision

4 Therapeutic ending

    a Therapeutic ending
    b Evaluation of process success and outcome success
    c Communicating outcomes with other professionals where necessary
    d Plans for follow-up

5 Conclusion

    a Reflection on professional learning about sport psychology service delivery
    b Reflection on personal learning as a sport psychology consultant

6 References and appendices

    a References
    b Tables, graphs, and diagrams relevant to the case study
    c Formulation diagram for the case study

To get started on a first draft, we need to familiarise ourselves with all the material related to the case, such as referral letters, correspondence to and from other health professionals and third parties, number of sessions attended and missed, case progress notes, and contract(s) with the client. Most intake assessment sheets gather biographical data from the client ranging from age, sex, sexual orientation, ethnicity, occupation or programme of study, physical health, medications, and previous contacts with psychological services. Most clients who seek the services of a sport psychology consultant have personal relationships (e.g., family) and multiple professional relationships (coaches, teammates, support staff, agent) that require (e.g., parents, manager) correspondence across the helping process.

Because you have completed the work with the client, you will be familiar with the content and process of the case; however, writing about the experiential process means fitting your information (i.e., evidence) into the right places and making sense of the whole. The suggested headings and contents for your case study turn an unwieldy challenge into manageable parts and offer small wins as you complete each (Weick, 1984).

Another challenge trainees face when writing case studies is what to include and what to exclude. A simple rule is to categorise your paragraphs and sentences as essential, desirable, inessential. If the sentence(s) is essential, then it is addressing the assessment criteria directly and the progress of your case study. If the sentence(s) is desirable, it is addressing a minor point relating to the assessment criteria and can be included if space permits. If the sentence(s) is inessential, it does not add relevant information to meet the assessment criteria of the case study. We recommend writing your first draft and then revising using this system of inclusion and exclusion.

In summary, a case study represents the story of a client's work with you. The client holds a primary role in the story arc. You, as a practitioner, do too. Also, most trainees focus on the content of the case study (i.e., what the client brings) and forget or lose sight of the process (i.e., what unfolds between the client and the practitioner) through the helping journey. Although a process report is an analysis of a therapeutic encounter where practitioners question their intentions, actions, and effect, the intentions, actions (or inactions), and effect of one's practice are also considered in the case study though to a lesser extent.

Revising your draft(s)

You will see several examples of case studies written for publication. These case studies typically emphasise a theme or issue particular to the sport and exercise context (e.g., working with child athletes) focusing on a specific problem (e.g., unhelpful attributions) or intervention (e.g., attribution retraining) that has, hitherto, not been addressed in the literature. Though much of your caseload might include familiar presenting problems, familiar theories, and therapeutic approaches in familiar settings, each case will be unique in its own way.

We typically represent the structure of knowledge in one of four ways: factual, conceptual, procedural, and metacognitive. In a case study, we might present factual knowledge (e.g., basic element within the discipline), conceptual knowledge (e.g., the interrelationships among basic elements in a larger structure and how they work together), procedural knowledge (e.g., how to do something or use skills), and metacognitive knowledge (e.g., awareness and knowledge of one's own knowledge) (Krathwohl, 2002) at different junctures.

But what is most important is that your scholarly writing emphasises the complexity and specificity of your learning at your level of study (e.g., master's or doctorate) by including theory and research and applying clinical skills in practice. In our case study, different sections require different cognitive skills such as to remember (i.e., present basic concepts), understand (i.e., explain concepts), apply (i.e., use information in new situations), analyse (i.e., draw connections among ideas), evaluate (i.e., justify decisions), and create (i.e., produce original work) (Krathwohl, 2002). Though most trainees remember (e.g., recall), understand (e.g., explain), and apply (e.g., implement a procedure) in their case studies, they do not analyse (e.g., differentiate), evaluate (e.g., critique), and create (e.g., generate) as much as assessors would expect. As a useful guide, you might use the checklist of these six cognitive processes to read and revise your case study. Each sentence is usually playing one of these six roles, so while we need to remember, understand, and apply, we need to ensure we move up the hierarchy to analyse, evaluate, and create. In the next section, we shall outline how you can craft persuasive arguments using a five-step formula that blends the structure of knowledge and cognitive skills.

Fitting the pieces together

This five-step formula helps you to remember that we usually explain to the assessor what we did and how, where, when, and why we did it. In our argument, we make a claim, support it with reasons, and back it up with evidence, acknowledge, and respond to other views and explain our principles of reasoning (Booth et al., 2016).

- Step 1: We make a *claim* (what do you want me to believe?).
- Step 2: We provide a *reason* or *reasons* (why should I agree?) for our claim.
- Step 3: We offer *evidence* (how can you back it up?) to support our claim and reason(s).
- Step 4: After presenting our evidence, we *acknowledge* and *respond* (but what about ...?) to alternative explanations or counter arguments.
- Step 5: We explain our *principles* or *warrant* (how does it all add up?) of our reasoning where necessary before moving to the next paragraph.

Academic writing represents one of several critical skills developed while studying at university. Academic writing in a case study persuades the reader of the reliability and validity of your arguments, as well as representing yourself as a safe, ethical, and professional practitioner.

A helpful first session with a client ought to begin with a comprehensive assessment (claim) because an assessment allows the practitioner to establish the boundaries of a presenting issue (reason 1 support claim one/claim 2). When an assessment stretches to the boundaries of interview, observation, and psychometric data, it increases the chances of correctly identifying the presenting issue(s) alongside predisposing, precipitating, perpetuating factors, and protective factors (reason 2 supporting claim 1 and claim 2). Together, these factors establish a formulation or working hypothesis of the client needs and problems to create an intervention or implementation of solutions. When assessments are insensitive and overly demanding, however, some clients cannot form a dependable therapeutic bond with the practitioner.

Submitting for assessment or publication

Good writing within a case study persuades the assessor or journal reviewer that you are a skilled and capable trainee who practises safely, ethically, and professionally. Assessors and journal reviewers only have the words on the pages to know how and why you combine a therapeutic modality, psychological theory, research, and practice experience with clinical skills when working with a client. Pay close attention to the submission requirements so that your communication reflects your professional standards. Whether as an assessment for a university training programme or a manuscript submitted to a peer-reviewed journal, attend to all details (e.g., word limit, headings, referencing style). If you are submitting an assessment requiring the presentation and style set in the *APA Publication Manual 7th edition*, then checking for clarity and precision is work that you ought to do rather than have an assessor or journal reviewer do for you. Assembling a reference list is an example. The references in the text must correspond to the references in the reference list.

One caveat, however, relates to time. Writing a client case study might be one of several commitments on your course and you may well have other personal commitments outside your course (e.g., work, family, sport). Putting a time limit on your submission will help you hand your work in on time and leave sufficient time for other obligations. For those wishing to pursue publication, a time limit also helps because several trainees with excellent case studies fear the rejection that is a normal part of the publication process. With this fear of failure looming, the case study never gets submitted (so could never be published) and so the trainee misses out on the feedback from the publication process. Feedback, however, is our friend when we accept it with the intention in which it is (usually) given.

Responding to feedback

Feedback for an assessment or manuscript means different things. For a training programme, passing or failing has repercussions for your training pathway, while pursuing publication has fewer consequences. The emotional fallout means you might be pleased and relieved or disappointed and befuddled. If it is the latter, taking some time before reading through the comments will allow you to hold a measured response to the outcome of the assessment or publication and the comments. We encourage trainees to welcome feedback as an opportunity to learn. Remember, the assessor can only award marks or credit for what is written in the client case study and their interpretation of those words. Often, learning to express ourselves clearly in writing is time well spent. Reading comments gives you a chance to categorise the feedback as minor or major. For example, minor comments might relate to clarity or expression in a sentence, or incorrect referencing style, whereas major comments might relate to core elements of the therapeutic modality you misunderstood. We call these major comments because they usually require reading, understanding, and perhaps discussing with your tutor or supervisor. Often, students understand, for example, the principles of a therapeutic modality, though they do not express it clearly in writing, which leads us back to how critical written expression is to our professional communication. Our guidance for students focuses on learning to write for academic purposes, and there are multiple resources available to help you on your way.

Summary

Writing and submitting a client case study for an assessment or publication is a beneficial and necessary challenge for trainees.

13 Presenting at a Conference

Introduction

Whether you are undertaking a postgraduate research degree, engaging with a taught programme at a university, or progressing through an independent route to qualifying as a sport psychology practitioner, presenting at a conference is a key milestone in your professional development.

Why should you present your research?

Before covering the 'how to' aspects of this chapter, we underline why presenting at a conference is so significant. Have you taken time to reflect on why attending a conference and presenting at it could help you? There are many ways in which engaging with conferences will benefit you during and after your training. As part of your professional development/training, no matter what route you are taking, you will engage in research in your chosen field. If you do not present your research findings to an appropriate audience, then you are not disseminating it effectively and will not benefit others by imparting your findings. Presenting at a conference provides you with the perfect medium for communicating your research to a wide audience of experts in your field. Not only that, but attending a conference can be really inspiring and always offer insights, new ideas, and reminds you why you were enthusiastic enough about the field to embark on your training. Attending a conference helps you to keep up-to-date with the developments in the area and to see who is involved in the type of work in which you are interested. Conferences are inspirational, and they can revive you.. You will find your motivation rises and it can also help to generate ideas for how your current research could be developed, implemented, or used by practitioners and researchers. Presenting your findings will raise your visibility and can help you network with future colleagues, potential employers, and also potential research collaborators. People who hear your work or see your conference poster might then want to read your future publications, so this is an excellent way to get that recognition from others in your field at an early stage. Presenting can help to get your name known in relevant academic circles, increasing your chances of gaining future employment positions, developing collaborations, and getting your foot in the door. Do not underestimate the power of networking. Presenting will help you refine your research ideas and develop your future research agenda. Feedback on your presentation or questions asked at the conference can give you vital feedback on your research that you simply would not gain from any other medium. This feedback can be hugely beneficial not only to your training but also to your viva voce and your future employment prospects. Conferences also offer perfect learning opportunities to see how others present their findings and to give your ideas for how you can develop your own ability to present and to pitch ideas – something that will always be useful to you as a sport psychology consultant.

DOI: 10.4324/9781003367208-16

Finding the right conference

Before you even think about how to present, you need to take time to make sure you are choosing the right conference for you. This choice can depend on several factors and you will need to weigh them up before you decide. You want to choose a conference that presents you with opportunities to network and that will also offer you the opportunity to raise the profile of your research and the visibility of what you do. It might seem like a good idea to attend a large conference to maximise your chances of meeting many people. Networking is key at conferences, and they offer you the opportunity to meet new people and widen your network. Give the size of the conference some consideration. Might your work fit better at a smaller, more focused conference? Might people at a smaller conference share your interests and be more willing to conduct research with you in the future?

Another consideration is: who is presenting at the conference? If there is a well-known name in the field who you want to meet, then attending the conference and presenting at it could be a good decision; however, conferences that attract well-known researchers and practitioners are often expensive to attend, so you will need to find a balance there. It is also worth examining whether the conference organisers offer discounts to trainees or whether there are any bursaries or scholarships available to help you, either those provided by the conference organisers or by your own academic institution or professional body. Speak to your supervisor too. They will often be able to advise you on the best conference to aim your work at.

Consider the networking opportunities offered by the conference and make sure that it offers you what you want and need at the current stage of your professional training. Look at the timing of the conference before you decide. Often you have to submit your abstract several months before the conference, so you need to be confident that you can write an abstract that will translate into a polished presentation in the time between your submission and the conference. The abstract submission guidelines will be available to you, so go through them carefully to make sure you can meet the standards required for the peer review process.

What type of presentation should you give?

At this stage, you should also consider the type of conference presentation that you want to give. Different conferences will have different options available, including symposia where several individuals present on a particular topic or theme; workshops or roundtables where people share professional practice aspects; traditional presentations where a single individual speaker presents their research or applied topic; panels where experts present information; and posters. If you are not an experienced presenter, then consider a poster presentation. The conference organisers often display these for a good period of time, and if you are nervous about presenting in front of an audience, these allow for a much more relaxed and one-to-one interaction with those who come to read your poster. Alternatively, you can think about a presentation where you will be given a set amount of time to showcase your work to an audience and then answer questions that arise from that.

Life Lived: Reflection on a Conference Presentation Format

I recently presented at an international teaching conference where I was reporting on the results of a project to enhance a postgraduate programme through the creation of an initiative to foster experiential skills practice. The project had been completed, and the team had data from both the postgraduate students who had used their coaching skills and the undergraduate students who had been the recipients of that coaching. The results were hugely positive, and we were keen to expand the programme and to share our findings showing how increasing that theory-practice link for postgraduate students could add to their experience and how it could also be beneficial for others. There were many conferences we could have presented these findings at, including practice focused conferences, psychology domain-specific conferences, and broader teaching and education conferences. Reflecting on the project, its findings and the implications of that meant that an international education conference was chosen. We not only wanted to share our findings, but to make sure that others in higher education were receiving our clear message that the student experience could be enhanced through this type of initiative. We wanted to share the practical aspects of that project, the training we offered the MSc students, the supervision we provided and how we assessed the outcomes. That meant that instead of a traditional presentation format we led a roundtable, a 90-minute session where we could share information on the project, share some of the training materials we had developed, and open up the floor to discussion of how this could be adapted to different university programmes. Thinking about what message you want to convey and who you want to convey that message to is a vital first step in choosing the conference you want to submit your work to.

Making the most out of your conference attendance

Once you have identified the relevant conference and successfully had your abstract accepted, you can then prepare. Prepare well before attending the conference. Do not wait until you are there to plan, but read the conference programme well ahead of attending and give thought to what sessions you want to attend. You cannot plan out every hour of being there, but you can make sure you are aware of what really interests you. You can also think ahead about particular individuals you want to meet and whether you know anyone who could offer an introduction. If not, then think about how you could introduce yourself – perhaps commenting on how you are using their research or on how vital their work has been to informing the direction of your own research or practice. If you do not want to approach someone you do not know, then think about other ways to network. For example, if you have identified researchers whose presentations you want to attend, then think about a relevant question to ask at that session. Asking such a question at the presentation will show that you are knowledgeable and interested in the presenters' work and it can also facilitate opportunities to start conversations later on. This is also true for paying attention to who else asks questions. You can use their question to start a conversation at a social event later in the day if you remember who they are and what they asked. Conferences offer amazing opportunities for meeting like-minded people, but preparing in advance can make it all seem much easier. In the run up to the conference, prepare a short 'elevator pitch' that encompasses the key aspects of your own training so far, your current research and plans. You will not have time to give a full rundown of everything you have done and preparing ahead can help to make sure you do not miss out on key information when you are meeting new people. It can be difficult to start conversations when you feel you don't know anyone – but remember, others will be in a similar situation, so you are not alone. The temptation to stick with people you know can be strong, but try to use the opportunities afforded to you by the conference and push yourself to meet researchers who you would not otherwise have access to.

Creating your presentation

What you want to do is effectively get across the main findings of your research – the 'so what?' message from your work. You want those attending your presentation to be focused on your research and your findings, not on your presentation skills. To do so, you need to understand where your research sits within the wider context (i.e., what it contributes to the large existing body of research). You also need to know what your take away message is, what you want to get across. You cannot possibly cover everything in the allocated time, so make sure you have selected the most important elements of your work and highlighted those.

Preparing for a poster presentation at a conference

Presenting a poster can be quite daunting, but effective preparation helps. Posters are unique in giving an opportunity for one to one or small group discussion and require their own form of presentation. Make sure that you understand everything you have put on your poster. You should have a good understanding of all the diagrams, figures, and text included and be able to expand on any aspects that are included. When you are designing your poster, be aware of how it will look from a distance. You want people to read it from around a 1.5-m distance (and to see the subject from even further away) so choose a suitable font size. Make sure keywords and the title are visible from a distance and that the title engages people's interest and makes them want to approach and uncover more. Avoid revealing the findings in your title. You want people to be interested in discovering more. Keep the design simple and do not have clashing colours or changes in font size and style. Ensure your poster has a good flow to it. For example, presenting it in columns often makes it easier for people to digest the information quickly. Avoid being over wordy in your poster, often presenting key ideas in diagrams can be more easily digestible quickly and can avoid your poster being overcrowded. Seek feedback from multiple people before you complete it. You want honest feedback that you can incorporate into your poster design to maximise your chances of pulling people in to talk to you at the conference. Poster sessions at conferences are approximately 90 minutes and you need to be prepared to stand alongside your poster for the entire time. Make sure your name and email address are clearly presented on your poster just in case you need to be away from it for a few minutes, as that then allows anyone interested to contact you. Try to remember that it is exciting to share your research with other people and to be enthusiastic about discussing your work. The poster acts as a conversation starter, with people moving closer to have a quick scan and speak to you. They might not want to read the whole thing, so it's important that you have your 'elevator pitch' at the ready should they require a quick synopsis of what is contained in it. Try to be welcoming, smile, and say hello to people as they pass. Do not be afraid to engage with people, but also be prepared to give people space to just read your poster if they want to. It is often a good idea to ask people if they would like you to talk them through your poster or if they have questions. If they want you to talk them through your poster, then you can give them your prepared 'elevator pitch'. This should be short, just a few minutes maximum, and should convey your topic, your findings, and the implications. You are not trying to tell the reader everything about your work, you are trying to draw them in, elicit their intrigue, and leave them wanting to discover more. What you say about your poster and your research is equally important as the content of your poster, so knowing what you're going to say ahead of time is key to a successful poster presentation. Once they have that interest, they can ask you questions and you can expand on your narrative and give them more detail. You need to be sure about what you are saying, though, and again, practice and preparation are key elements here. In the run up to the conference, practise discussing your research, make sure you can expand on all the details included in the poster and that you can talk confidently and succinctly about your research and your findings situating them in the existing field. You can also ask if you have explained yourself well or if the audience would like any more information or detail on any aspects of your work.

Sometimes people have copies of their poster as a handout to give to people. These are not strictly necessary but if you would like to have a handout, then make sure it's readable if it's simply a smaller version of your poster, or perhaps consider just having the abstract and your name and contact details on a handout instead of a full replication of your poster. Handouts are not required but can be a good way to pass on your contact details to others in your field. You can use it as a business card and a reminder to anyone after the conference of you and your work.

Preparing for a single-speaker presentation at a conference

Those giving a presentation as a single speaker are usually referred to as speakers, with the term presenter being used for those providing input to other types of sessions, such as roundtables or workshops. The following considerations really help:

1 The first thing to consider and to be clear about before you even start thinking about the content of your talk is the time you have to present. Often, conference presentations are brief, approximately 20 minutes, including time for questions. There is no leeway for going over time at conferences. You will be stopped because they have to run on time. Not only will it look unprofessional, if you cannot stick to time, you will also lose the opportunity for questions and this is a key opportunity for you to get feedback on your research and to gain insight you might not otherwise have. Thinking back on the other reasons to present outlined at the start of this chapter not sticking to time will also detrimentally affect those. You want to create a good impression on those in the field that you might want to work with in future and if you cannot stick to the guidelines, then that will not happen. Once you've established the time that you have for your presentation, then the next step is to consider what to present.

2 In a 15-minute time slot, you will not present an entire PhD or even the entire component of a 60-credit research module, so you need to be selective here. You will need to choose one element or aspect of your work and then consider how to present a clear narrative around that. You should also take time to think about who is your audience. These are people who have a lot of experience in the field, so what do they know already? People will attend various presentations during the conference, so you want to make sure yours is clear, concise, and memorable, offering a clear take home or "so what" message that the audience can remember. Do not start with basic information that those working in the field will already be familiar with. Be mindful of the knowledge already in the room and pitch your presentation appropriately. It can help to break down your thinking into easy steps first considering what issue or aim are you wanting to convey; what approach did you take to addressing that, what are your key findings and finally what conclusions or implications did you draw from that?

3 You want to have that clear thread of a narrative running through your presentation that makes it easy to follow. There should be a clear beginning, middle and end, and the structure of your presentation needs to be clear to the audience. Do not be tempted to include too much information as this will not engage the audience or give clarity to your presentation. Instead, have a clear focus. Present your aim so that it conveys the importance of your work and then provide the context for that through using the existing literature/theory.

4 Present your findings clearly and use slides to add to your narrative, not replicate what you are saying.
5 Finally, have a clear 'so what' or take-home message showing why your work is a significant contribution to the field. Consider leaving that take-home message up as your final slide while inviting questions from the audience. It is tempting to move onto a slide that invites questions but instead verbally inviting questions while still displaying your key point can help people internalise your findings and ask relevant questions that will help you move forward with your research.
6 Avoid the temptation to have too many slides containing too much information because you want people to find the content of the slides easy to digest, so rather than having a lot of dense text consider how that information could be conveyed in a more visually engaging manner. You do not want to be reading off slides or repeating what is written on them, instead you want a visually pleasing, easy-to-understand slide you can add to with your narrative. You will only need one slide for every two or three minutes of your talk. Having too many slides will be off-putting to the audience and they will lose interest.

Key to a successful presentation is confidence and practice. Assume that people are interested in your work (they would not be there otherwise) and build on that interest by demonstrating knowledge and enthusiasm for your work. Although it's tempting to avoid rehearsing your presentation in front of a live audience, the importance of doing that should not be underestimated. Ask peers, friends, supervisors, staff at your institution, or anyone you can find to come to a practice run through and treat it as though it were the conference. Presenting in front of a live audience differs from running through your presentation alone, and this will give you a taste of what it will be like. It will also give you the opportunity for feedback from people who are knowledgeable, and you can use that to tweak your presentation ahead of the actual conference. You will also gain an idea of the questions that might be asked and that will let you prepare potential responses again, helping you appear knowledgeable and articulate on the day.

Think about your presentation skills and the content of your talk. Do not underestimate the way key presentation skills contribute to the overall effect of your offering. A speaker who makes eye contact with different people in the audience, who stands confidently and avoids using notes or looking at the screen, will make a much better impression on the audience and will be perceived as being more competent than someone who appears nervous. It is not just what you say that is important, but how you say it can be equally important. By practising your presentation multiple times, recording yourself and listening back, requesting feedback and advice from others, you can improve the quality of your presentation before the conference. This type of practice helps you to present more confidently, to reduce the amount of filler words you use and to be comfortable with a pause or with varying the pace of your speech all of which will make you and your message much easier for an audience to take in.

Nerves can often be an issue when you are presenting, but practice will help with this and there are other practical ways to reduce your nerves, too. One key method is to scope out the room you are presenting in ahead of time. Ideally, go along ahead of your programmed session time and have a good look around the room so that you have a certain familiarity with it. If you can then listen to other people present in the room ahead of your own session, that will give you an idea of how the room works, where the audience sits and what things to incorporate or avoid in your own presentation. A final tip is to arrive early to the room. This serves a dual purpose of letting you become used to your surroundings and enabling you to chat with people as they come in to get an idea of the interests and expectations of your audience.

Summary

Presenting your work at a conference has many potential benefits and can be a vital part of your professional development during your training. Conference presentations offer a real networking opportunity and one where you can convey the importance of your own research to those in the field. Preparation is key to effective conference presentations and choosing the conference, the type of presentation, acquiring feedback before attending and taking the time to make the most of your attendance will generate a valuable experience and one that will boost your motivation and reinvigorate your research giving you a multitude of ideas for future work and collaborations.

Section IV

The Supervisory Process

14 Seeking Supervision and Flourishing through It

Introduction

Supervision in applied sport psychology erects a stable substructure of good practice for those training and practising in an applied setting using two podia: first, care for the athlete-client, which lies at the heart of this supervisory process, and second, the sport psychology practitioner growing into a competent, knowledgeable, and ethical practitioner (Van Raalte & Andersen, 2000). One assumption we claim to here is that supervision meets some minimum standards set by a regulatory body (e.g., Health and Care Professions Council in the UK) so that trainees gather awareness, knowledge and understanding of themselves, and their work with client-athletes. This 'archaeological dig' with a supervisor throughout one's training helps the trainee to understand their needs, how they meet their needs in functional or dysfunctional ways, and their current knitting of theory and clinical skills in their practice with clients. Together, these intertwining elements of personal and professional development run throughout one's supervision. Supervision encompasses care for the client-athlete and care for the trainee. We cannot truly have one need met (e.g., caring for the client) without the other (e.g., caring for oneself as a trainee). For this reason, we need supervision to work for us. In this chapter, we outline how to seek supervision that works by establishing a contract, working to your goals and tasks, reviewing progress, addressing difficulties, and harnessing the power of good supervision.

Seeking supervision – What is it? And what do I need?

Inskipp and Proctor (2001, p. 1) presented supervision as: A working alliance between the supervisor and counsellor in which the counsellor can offer an account or recording of her work; reflect on it; receive feedback and, where appropriate, guidance. The object of this alliance is to enable the counsellor to gain in ethical competence, confidence, compassion, and creativity in order to give her best possible service to the client. This definition guides and helps us to understand the detail of supervision, but we need not leap too far to know that we, as human beings, need to feel cared for and safe in supervision. When we rush off to seek a supervisor, we fall into unfamiliar territory and our anxiety grows. Simple criteria might guide us: availability and affordability or perhaps accessibility and experience. But do we consider how we will feel cared for and safe? If we are fortunate enough to find a supervisor holding those elegant Rogerian qualities of unconditional positive regard, warmth, kindness, and genuineness, we feel safe again, and critically, we grow. Because many training programmes stipulate the nature and frequency of supervision, we know we shall spend much time in supervision with our supervisor. Not only are you learning as a supervisee but also the supervisor is learning as a supervisor through one or a combination of four learning modes: reflection, conceptualisation (thinking), planning, and concrete experience (feeling and doing) (Milne, 2009).

DOI: 10.4324/9781003367208-18

But what does it mean to supervise or to be supervised? Supervision means different things depending on the context (e.g., in training, post accreditation, or registration). In sport and exercise psychology, supervision forms an integral part of the training process, usually supported by teaching and, for some, personal therapy. For the supervisee, supervision is typically evaluative: monitoring the development of competencies and submitting work (e.g., logbooks, case studies) for assessment. Post-accreditation or registration, some practitioners continue with supervision; however, others do not. At this stage of professional development, supervision is consultative rather than evaluative as practitioners move through their professional career.

For the supervisor, thinking, feeling, and behaving like a supervisor often means translating your background knowledge, skills, and experience into your supervisory role. Through different phases of education and training, in one's master's and independent training, or doctoral programme, a supervisor supervises trainees leaning on substantial training and experience. In sport and exercise psychology, this training and experience includes various elements of professional practice: therapeutic modalities, assessment approaches, helping skills, change interventions, ethical and legal guidelines, and social and cultural competence. Typical taught elements include theory and research on developmental and social processes, individual differences, cognitive processes, psychological skills and strategies, participation and well-being, and research methods. The supervisor will usually have much experience working in sport and exercise settings with various clients, bringing their training and practice together to supervise a trainee. Some supervisors also have teaching and research experience to add to this collection of roles, skills, and knowledge (Borders & Brown, 2022).

Different supervision forms

Several forms of supervision are available to trainees, though most are familiar with one-to-one supervision, which often occurs for supervision of research projects at the undergraduate level. These forms of supervision range from self-supervision, one-to-one, group, dual, live and remote or electronic (McCann, 2017). One might conceive of self-supervision as a process unfolding throughout a training programme where the trainee sets out their training within a host organisation on a day-to-day basis with one-to-one or group supervision from a supervisor operating quarterly. Self-supervision might emerge and develop through self-reflexive practice in which the trainee is in a developmental trajectory, for example, moving from the content presented by clients to the processes within therapeutic encounters. One-to-one supervision is a popular and sought-after form of supervision, especially for trainees in the early developmental phase of their training because it offers trainees much needed confidence and guidance regarding each element of their client work. Clear roles and responsibilities mean the supervisory support and input meet the needs of each party. This form of supervisory support, however, is time consuming and some supervisors opt for group supervision involving several trainees and one or more qualified supervisors. Group supervision holds advantages and disadvantages. For instance, one advantage is that the group members offer social and professional support to each other by presenting and discussing cases and dilemmas. Peer feedback increases reflexivity about one's personal and professional development. One potential disadvantage of a group supervisory approach is addressing and meeting individual needs if there is no one-to-one support, besides group supervision. The developmental needs of each trainee might go unaddressed, leading to frustration and worries about one's competence and confidence in working with clients.

Occasionally, some trainees seek supervision from two sources or avail of the supervision available in a practicum placement and at university. Dual supervision works well with clear roles and responsibilities, though it can also present conflict through different methods of supervision and ways of working therapeutically with clients. Some trainees seek supervision from a supervisor with specific experience working and supervising other trainees (e.g., in an Olympic or Paralympic sport) with different theoretical orientations. It seems prudent to set and agree boundaries between the supervisors and meet periodically over the supervision period.

Most training programmes require live supervision (i.e., a supervisor observing a trainee working with a client) as part of supervision or as an assessment and evaluation. These live supervision sessions ought to unfold with a clear aim and purpose because they will involve clients willing to take part in the live supervision. The aim and purpose of live supervision ought to present the trainee with a chance to learn and reflect upon their experience. Many trainees seek opportunities to observe their supervisor, perhaps in an intake assessment or a treatment session. We can undertake these sessions with a client or in role play within a classroom setting.

Remote or online supervision is following the trend of the digital era in online therapy comprising text, e-mail, messaging, and video calling. Through the benefits of greater flexibility and availability of supervisors and the autonomy to choose a supervisor geographically less accessible (i.e., living in another part of the country), we balanced against the drawbacks of an unreliable link or issues of confidentiality.

A model of supervision

The good supervisor also has a model (or models) as a framework to organise knowledge and skills for conducting supervision. Models capture the 'what', 'how', and 'why' of supervision for the supervisor and supervisee because without such coordinates, supervision drifts and seems unlikely to meet the needs of the supervisee. For the practice of supervision, van Ooijen (2013) divided models into four major categories: reflection, developmental, psychotherapeutic approach, and supervision-specific. Exploring all these models is beyond the goals of this chapter, however, each category holds benefit. For example, trainees might find it helpful to begin reflection using Driscoll's reflective cycle (Driscoll, 2007). This is a three-step method for reflection or problem solving comprising:

- **What?** The trainee selects an event from placement. From this event, they select some elements for further reflection, e.g., What purpose do I hold for reflection on this situation? What have I and/or others observed or accomplished?
- **So what?** The supervisee analyses the event and focuses on any learning from it, e.g., How did I feel then? How do I feel now? What went well? What was difficult?
- **Now what?** What have I learned? What might I do differently next time? If I need to act now, what can I do?

As we explained in Chapter 4, reflection forms a key component of professional development which allows the supervisee to learn from practice and for the supervisor to explore and note the supervisee's development as a sport psychology practitioner. This point leads us to developmental models, which focus on the development (or educative function) of supervision. These models draw on cognitive learning theory and psychosocial development theory. This approach makes intuitive sense as supervisees gain experience, moving from one developmental milestone to the next. One example is Stoltenberg and McNeill's (2010) Integrative Developmental Model (IDM). It comprises four stages or levels with guidance for supervisors about how to work with supervisees within these stages. For this chapter, we focus on one model by van Ooijen (2013).

A three-step approach – What, how, and what now

Though there are several models with which one might work as a supervisor and supervisee, aiming for parsimony sounds sensible and intuitive at this stage of your training cycle. Simple in its presentation, the three-step approach by van Ooijen (2013) joins theory with practice, consolidates previous learning, frames new learning, and works as a reflective tool to enquire about one's own practice. At its heart lies a cooperative relationship. The 'what' in the three-step approach focuses on what the supervisee wishes to explore and what happened in the client session. The 'how' relates to how the client session developed. For example, how each person thought, felt, and the dynamics between them. The 'what now' relates to how can future sessions with clients be different through reflective learning from the supervision session. The three-step method means there is flexibility in whichever theoretical framework one prefers and the methods and tools one wishes to use within the supervision session. Also, the basic boundaries of time, place, regularity, privacy, among others, fit within it. The structure affords order, and the order affords safety.

Supervision comprises at least three functions: support, monitor, and develop/educate (van Ooijen, 2013). These parts work in lockstep to create a safe, ethical, and professional supervisory relationship where trainees meet their supervisory needs. This last part means the supervisor needs to know what the supervisee needs from a session, otherwise, time might pass without development.

What (focus on facts)?

This first step focuses on the number of clients that a supervisee wishes to speak about, how much time each requires, what the supervisee wishes to achieve, and how the supervisee wishes to feel after discussing these cases; however, the strings holding these parts together are the working alliance. The working alliance, therefore, comes before discussing tasks, qualities, and skills. Placing the focus on the person, how they feel, how they feel their work is going, develops a sense of trust and respect between supervisee and supervisor. As the sessions unfold each week, this emphasis on the working alliance means each person gets a sense of the other, especially the compassion and empathy of each person's role and the wider scheme of their working world. The emotional labour attached to practising and supervising in the healthcare and performance professions can easily swell to unmanageable proportions, leading to high turnover and burnout.

The qualities of openness, respectful curiosity, and relationship building offer the supervisee a chance to be open, honest, and trusting in the relationship. From here, the supervisee can emphasise the tasks by selecting the topic, their needs, wants, and hopes to get started on the work. The task for the supervisee is to describe their presenting case(s) and remain open to questions. For the supervisor, helping the supervisee to describe, summarise, and focus through active listening brings a clarity and focus to questions or other tools, methods, and techniques such as role play, use of props, drawing, or writing. Because the client is selecting topics, identifying needs, wants, hopes, and fears, they ought to come to the session prepared. This preparation might include reflection on specific aspects of their reflective log or case notes.

How (focus on feelings)?

The decisions and content of Step 1 drive the intention and process of Step 2. Once the supervisee and supervisor settle on the outcomes of the session, the tasks, qualities, and skills follow. For example, the supervisor can create a reflective space that encompasses thinking, feeling, physical sensations, intuition, and the rational and irrational. Within this space, they can integrate theory and practice with a feeling of safety and working together. Through this process, the supervisee develops their internal supervisor, self-awareness, and works together with the supervisor towards best practice. For the supervisee to develop self-awareness, openness, honesty, and learn how to tolerate and accept not knowing with these same qualities within the supervisor. The supervisor judges when to challenge supportively, when to reflect on challenging material, when to use creative methods alongside models, theories, and practice.

Reflecting on one's experience means an openness to learn new knowledge and discover different ways of seeing one's experiences. Within this process lies an openness to let go of some things and pick up new things. For instance, the motivation theory we learn about in class manifests itself in practice through the story told by a client-athlete. This story blends with our experience of their story in the session, and we relate it back to theory, putting theory into our experience and our experience in theory (van Ooijen, 2013).

Getting into the details of you and your work means balancing content (i.e., what the client brings) with process (i.e., the relationship between you and your client). Exploring the content of a case also means exploring the relationship between the supervisee and the client. In sharing content and process, there is also a process between the supervisee and the supervisor. The supervisee might share an experience that troubled them and left them with a dilemma; however, in sharing the experience, the supervisee might experience the supervisor as pleased, unconcerned, or perhaps not relating the empathy the supervisee expected. Setting some time aside to reflect on 'process' between you and your supervisor seems sensible, but how do we have time for everything? It seems practical to make sense of all these moving parts in supervision with a guiding model. One possibility is the seven-eyed model presented by Hawkins and McMahon (2020), which offers seven eyes or lenses to look at what the supervisee brings to supervision. The seven-eyed model comprises two matrices (i.e., circles), one for therapy and one for supervision, each with three eyes or modes (i.e., smaller circles) in each matrix. Each of the eyes (i.e., smaller circles) link with the next. The first mode focuses on the clients, what they bring, and how they present. In the second mode, the focus is on the strategies and interventions used by the supervisee. Next, we have the relationship between the client and supervisee in the third mode. In mode four, the focus is on the supervisee and the supervisory relationship is the mode five. Mode six is the supervisor focusing on their own experience and mode seven focuses on the wider context within which the work happens (cultural, organisational, political).

This seven-eyed model captures the 'out there' (i.e., what happens in therapy) in the therapy matrix and the 'in here' (i.e., what happens in supervision) in the supervision matrix. Depending on the developmental level of the supervisee, it seems utilitarian to move at the pace and level of the supervisee. For instance, the client's story (mode one) and the supervisee's interventions (mode two) might be the focus of supervisees beginning their journey of service delivery in sport and exercise psychology. Many of these trainees feel compelled to 'fix' or 'do' something that makes the client's life better, or perhaps so that others will see how competent they are as practitioners. A more experienced trainee of the developmental trajectory might focus on their relationship with their client.

What now (focus on action)?

It can feel like a supervision session ends when we complete the 'what' and 'how' sections. Together, without monitoring one's time, the 'what' and the 'how' might consume the entire supervision session, perhaps because of interest in what the supervisee brings; however, the last part 'what now' ties the first two parts and helps us evaluate, monitor, set goals, gather evidence, and continue learning (van Ooijen, 2013). Without these elements, it is difficult to understand what we have achieved in Step 2 and how we can move to action based on what we learned.

Similar to Steps 1 and 2, Step 3 involves the active participation of supervisee and supervisor. Some supervisors, without realising, might spend the last section of the supervision session telling the supervisee what to do with a particular client based on their experience because time is running out and they feel better having established a plan of action for the supervisee. With a little more preparation, we can set aside time for Step 3. Step 3 includes learning, evaluation, monitoring, action, and evidence. Each of these components does not take a lot of time yet add significantly to the supervisory session.

The first task of Stage 3 is to for the supervisor and especially the supervisee to be clear on their thoughts, feelings, and views and consolidate the reflection from Step 2. Both supervisee and supervisor evaluate the effectiveness of the session. For supervisees, most, if not all, practice logbooks for assessment require a reflection on supervision and supervision sessions. Supervision sessions need to meet the needs, wants, and hopes of the supervisee and for supervision to work for the supervisee. The notes and reflections in the logbook are evidence of what happened in supervision. In practical terms, the supervisor and supervisee can judge whether their work together met the goals for the session and acknowledge the central themes and outcomes. Each can give and receive feedback on the process and monitor ethical practice. This monitoring allows good therapeutic practice to shine and limit unhelpful therapeutic practice. After learning, evaluating, and monitoring, the supervisor and supervisee move to action. They use what they reflected upon in the session to drive ideas for action and undertake that action. Finally, they compile evidence, which entails keeping notes of the session. In summary, of the five tasks in Step 3, learning, evaluating, monitoring, action, and evidence, each has their own place and requirements of the supervisee and supervisor.

Life Lived

A trainee sport psychology consultant, upon following a thread of persuasive arguments from contributors on a social media platform, sought supervision from a practitioner who 'has been there' rather than one with wide-ranging supervision experience, models of supervision to choose from, and those polished Rogerian qualities of unconditional positive regard, warmth, kindness, and genuineness. From the outside looking in, it seemed the chosen supervisor had the requisite experience in the field working in professional sport for several years. This guiding principle of supervision from one who 'has been there', however, though sensible in part, meant superseding several key criteria relating to therapeutic approaches, evidence-based practice, approaches to learning, roles and responsibilities, boundaries, and workable, regular meetings. The supervisee, wishing to ask questions, debate, and explore topics bumped up against a supervisor who felt the supervisee ought to listen and not question their methods. This power struggle meant the supervisee had to forego opportunities to learn, develop, and progress as a trainee because the supervisor's authoritarian and didactic style kept the trainee in a repetitive pattern of raising cases followed by a sermonette about the supervisor's experiences in the field. After 18 months of frustration, the supervisee sought another supervisor. This time, however, based on the difficulties of the past 18 months, the supervisee knew what she sought and what she knew she sought to avoid.

Preventing difficulties before they arise

Setting out on one's supervision journey means laying out one's knowledge and understanding of various facets of competence as a practitioner, such as therapeutic modalities, assessment approaches, helping skills, change interventions, ethical and legal guidelines, social and cultural competence, and so forth. Without knowing where you are now, it is difficult to plan a sensible and manageable journey for the months and years ahead. Each stage of the supervisory process will require a requisite number of hours to complete within the practicum placement(s) settings. Placement might begin with observational work before moving to work directly with clients and specific client groups. It is a joint responsibility of the supervisee and the supervisor to review progress on the goals and tasks set out at the outset of your supervisory journey. Many of the difficulties arising in supervisory relationships find their genesis in flimsy boundaries, undefined roles, and blurred responsibilities at the outset of the supervision process and few periodic check-ins thereafter. Good supervision means putting the supervisory relationship at the heart of the work between the supervisor and supervisee to ensure an understanding, empathic, and mutually beneficial connection emerges. Though one might assume a hierarchy in the supervisory relationship, it benefits both parties to witness and honour a collaborative alliance that benefits each person. Getting off to a good start in your search for a supervisor to fit your needs means seeking answers to questions that will influence the quality of your supervisory experience throughout your training. Each trainee will have different needs they wish to meet; however, setting out a list of those questions seems wise. You might wish to know: Is the supervisor experienced as a supervisor? Does the supervisor practise in the field currently? Is there a fit between the supervisor and the trainee's approach? Is there evidence-based practice within the supervisory process? Does the supervisor know how I learn best? Are my goals for supervision clear? Are we compatible? How shall we evaluate the outcomes of our work together? Regardless of the form of supervision, you will need to establish a contract for your supervision. You will see an example contract in McCarthy and Moffat (2024) outlining key considerations for your work with your supervisor. You can build in the goals and tasks of supervision following Carroll's (1996) guidance, including:

1 creating a learning relationship,
2 teaching,
3 counselling,
4 evaluation,
5 consulting,
6 monitoring administrative aspects, and
7 monitoring professional and ethical issues.

Summary

The metaphor of a journey captures so many life experiences and perhaps life itself. Supervision represents a journey for the supervisor and supervisee and perhaps for the supervisor, one of many journeys each year with several supervisees. It can be tempting as a supervisor to keep supervision simple. What I mean here is that we can use our experience as practitioners to guide supervision; however, supervision is a unique journey and a unique journey for each supervisee demanding requisite knowledge, skills, and practice. In short, supervision benefits from a guiding model of supervision, feedback from supervisees, from reflection and action to make supervision better for each supervisee and so on in the supervision journey.

15 A Supervisors' View of Training and Supervision

Introduction

In the previous chapter, you learned how to seek supervision, establish a contract, and work with the person you chose or secured to supervise you as you train. What this chapter covers is the perspective of the supervisor. We shall consider the reasons supervision works or does not work, what can help the supervisory process and the challenges that are frequently encountered during supervision. We hope that sharing these experiences will help you prepare for and make the most out of your own supervision.

Supervision is a vital element of effective practice. If you want to practise safely and effectively, then supervision must form part of your working life. Supervision is not a legal requirement once you are qualified and you should not see it as something that you have to do, but should be something you see as valuable and integral to your own self-awareness, reflective practice, and professional development. There is a myriad of benefits to be gained from supervision and your engagement with supervision should be a lifelong engagement, not just something that you do because your training course mandates it. As a supervisor, you cannot work effectively with a practitioner who does not see or understand the value of supervision. Your training programme will mandate supervision but do not see it as a chore or something that has to be endured, instead embrace supervision and make it work for you.

As a supervisor, it is extremely challenging and frustrating when a supervisee attends a supervision session and claims to have nothing to talk about, or does not fully engage in productive discussions during supervision. Something that is important from a supervisor's point of view is that supervisees realise that the breadth of supervision is vast. You can bring anything you want to supervision: issues with your research project aligned to your training; issues with how to carry out a particular session with a client or to improve your intake sessions; issues with your own practice development or CPD; concerns you have about upcoming sessions; reflections of sessions you have already had; work with a specific individual, issues with working as part of a team; a systematic review you read that sparked thoughts; questions about different formulation techniques, models, or approaches. The list goes on. So, what concerns a supervisor is when a trainee claims they have nothing they need to explore, which often relates to concerns that trainees might have about supervision, which results in a reluctance to share and embed themselves and the challenges they face within that supervisory relationship.

Start as you mean to go on: Make it work for you

As a supervisor, you are there to work with the supervisee, whether that is in a group setting during training or in a one-to-one setting. Effective supervision depends on there being a solid foundational relationship between the supervisor and the supervisee. The most effective

DOI: 10.4324/9781003367208-19

supervision occurs when the supervisor-trainee relationship mirrors that of the trainee-client relationship with that mirroring allowing the focus to be on whatever area the trainee feels is necessary or important, and the supervisor working with them to foster competence, confidence, and ethical practice. There is a literature that you can access on effective supervision in sport psychology training, and within this you can read about different models of supervision and how these apply to the sporting domain (see, for example, Foltz et al., 2015). Take time at the start of your supervisory relationship to talk through theoretical orientation, models of supervision, and how you want supervision to work for you. From experience, supervision works best when the trainee comes to supervision prepared and open to discussion. As a trainee, be sure to get the most you can out of supervision – make it work for you. We recommend thinking about what you need supervision to do for you before you attend and to spend time with your supervisor contracting and ensuring that you have set up a clear but flexible model of supervision that will be adaptable to your needs (see Chapter 14). Sometimes this can be difficult within the confines of your training route, but try to ensure your supervisor works in the mode you are working in or at the very least be open to discussion with your supervisor about theoretical orientation and how you intend to work together. Clearly contracting at the start of your supervisory relationship will help sessions to run more smoothly, manage expectations, and set the tone for a challenging but ultimately useful and developmental supervisory relationship. Without this discussion and contracting, you both might find the supervision lacking focus and direction and, in that case, it cannot possibly fulfil its aim to help you practise safely, develop self-awareness, and develop the competencies needed as an effective practitioner.

Challenges and benefits of group supervision

As a trainee, we hope you experience individual and group supervision and the authors of this text all have experience of delivering both types of supervision. Individual and group supervision cater to different needs and it is worth considering what is unique to each and what you should think about before engaging with both types of supervision. Before we move on to explore some challenges commonly encountered during individual supervision, it is worth considering supervision as a group activity and reflecting on our experiences of issues that arise here. By group supervision, we mean small groups of between four and six trainees who meet regularly (this could be weekly or monthly depending on the training route you are on) with a supervisor and discuss case presentations and client issues. Here, supervisors have dual roles as practitioners and academics who deliver content on the programme. This dual role can be challenging as a supervisor, and the time constraints can be a source of frustration from both supervisor and trainee perspectives. We usually divide these group supervision sessions into small chunks of time to allow multiple trainees to contribute. One example is a structure for one trainee to present a case or issue and others then discussing the presentation that is brought.

As mentioned above, for individual one-to-one supervision, you want to discuss your contract with your supervision and talk though the modality (e.g., cognitive behaviour therapy (CBT)) you will work in and the expectations and roles and responsibilities of each person in that relationship. Group supervision is the same and trainees should collectively consider the ground rules of group supervision and consider how best to make this work for them.

As a supervisor, group supervision differs from individual supervision in several ways. For example, think about your own experiences of group work to date. Have you used group work for personal or professional development before? Have you worked effectively in a group setting before and, if so, what made this effective? You will find similar elements are important in group supervision as in other group-based learning activities, but group supervision can be a place to not only reflect on your own practice but also to learn from the reflections of others. You can engage in discussion around theoretical or conceptual issues, and you can also reflect on any skills-based elements encountered during your studies. Challenges from a supervisory standpoint of group supervision can be trainees seeing these as the opportunity for personal therapy or seeing them as placement meetings and wanting to discuss issues that a placement coordinator or someone with responsibility for placement-related issues should address.

Another challenge of group supervision that we have encountered during our experiences is trainees who come along to group sessions unprepared. If trainees do not bring issues to supervision; if they do not read around the subject area; and if they are not up to date with the current state of the literature and theory, then discussions will not be rich and will not benefit the wider group. These group supervision sessions can provide a wealth of information, but only if everyone is clear about the purpose of the groups and comes prepared. There are many benefits to group supervision and again you can access the relevant literature on group supervision to help your preparation and engagement with these groups. For example, Valentino et al. (2016) discussed the benefits that group supervision can bring that you cannot get from individual one-to-one supervision (peer feedback skills; interpersonal skills; ethical recognition) and these chime with the authors of this text in terms of suggestions of ways for you to prepare well and engage well in group supervision opportunities. Reflect on your peer feedback skills and how others might perceive you when you enter discussions. Is there a chance they will perceive you as being confrontational if you are congruent with your communication? Alternatively, if you feel uncomfortable contributing to a group, could they perceive you as being disengaged and bored? Besides these perceptual challenges, group supervision can fail to produce effective developmental results when group members are not clear about the process of the supervision and what their aims are for supervision.

Life Lived: The Importance of Ground Rules

Reflecting on my experience of supervising groups, a key factor in their success is setting clear ground rules as a group at the outset. In my (Lindsey's) experience, this is crucial and without that buy in from all group members, the group processes will not work well. It is normal to assume that we all know how to behave in a group setting, but group supervision is a unique context and from my experience I would actively encourage you to include a discussion of group processes in your contracting or ground rule setting for your supervision groups. Groups are difficult to be a part of at times and when professional practice is being discussed group supervision can invoke feelings of self-consciousness, lack of confidence, and anxiety. As a supervisor, I have witnessed defensive behaviours resulting from group supervision and recommend that you spend time before group supervision thinking about your own defence mechanisms and how you might recognise these at play during group supervision. Examples I have encountered include trainees turning up late for group supervision; trainees becoming quite competitive during group supervision; individuals withdrawing from the group; individuals becoming overbearing and increased rates of self-disclosure. Take some time now to think through the implications of all these types of behaviours on the group supervision process. If you were a member of a group where one of these things happened, how would it make you feel and what do you think the potential consequences for the group would be?

We would urge you to consider these types of possibilities before attending a group supervision session and to be aware of your comfort zone and how you might act or change your behaviour if you feel you're being pushed or feel slightly out of your comfort zone during group supervision. Reflecting on how we have seen trainees develop it is almost inevitable that you will feel a certain level of discomfort during group supervision and this challenge can touch positively on your professional development as you are called on to articulate difficult experiences during practice or to consider other points of view carefully.

For a supervisor, it can be challenging managing a dual role of academic and supervisor, and this is true for group and individual supervision in some institutions. Expect your supervisors to have a coherent conversation with you about the expectations and roles of each party and to be open with you about any routes for complaints. If a supervisory relationship is not working, it can be difficult for the supervisor and the trainee to raise this because of concerns with the knock-on effect on other aspects of the training. Do not use that discomfort or concern as an excuse not to confront any instances where supervision is not working, though. Being able to engage in tough conversations again adds to your professional repertoire and will hopefully result in improvements being made to your supervisory experience. A final challenge to note relating to group supervision can be that trainees might not feel as though they want to share something in a group setting and will try to 'keep' something for individual supervision rather than presenting it during the group session. This often happens if the trainee considers the issue to be serious or thinks they have not handled a situation or presentation in the most effective way. In our experience, we would recommend sharing these types of scenarios in group supervision because learning from your peers and developing skills in engaging in tough conversations can be crucial to your development as practitioners. As mentioned above, we cannot gain these opportunities for professional development through one-to-one supervision alone, so our advice is to get the most you can out of these group supervision opportunities.

Reflecting on challenges encountered during individual supervision

Besides what might be weekly group supervision, most training programmes expect you to engage with individual one-to-one supervision during your training. This supervision might be provided through the organisation you are training with (and therefore might also include dual role challenges as mentioned above in the section on group supervision) or might be something you need to source yourself. There are unique challenges to individual supervision that we have encountered as supervisors during our careers to date. Before we outline some of those, it is worth highlighting the benefits of these supervision sessions though and why we would encourage you to not be afraid to share things with your supervisor but to be open and honest in your presentations and reflections to ensure supervision works for you. Supervision is a place where you can discuss in depth anything from your training that you want to explore. As a supervisor, it is a privilege to see trainees develop their practice and their critical reflection during supervision and to grow as professionals. Different supervisors will approach supervision differently, but being able to provide a sound scaffolding for trainees individually is a tremendous benefit of one-to-one supervision. Besides carefully considering how to work with each other and roles and expectations as suggested above, there are other aspects of one-to-one supervision that are important to highlight. The British Psychological Society (BPS) defines supervision as being 'personal interaction between the trainee sport and exercise psychologist and their supervisor for addressing the trainee's needs and performance in relation to the requirement of the accredited programme' (BPS, 2019). This is a huge scope and can cover a whole multitude of areas, as we have already established. It can be difficult to know what to bring to supervision as a novice supervisee and often trainees need a more structured approach to their supervision when they are just starting out. From our experience, this structured approach can help trainees to gain confidence in process and themselves. One-to-one supervision allows for that growth and lets supervisors provide an approach that begins with a logical structure and enhanced support for those trainees who are new to supervision. Each individual supervisor will approach supervision differently and there are many tools or methods such as case studies, journal articles, and role plays that are used by supervisors, and your supervisor will probably prefer the sort of methods that work for them or have worked for them in the past. Reflecting on our own experiences we would describe ourselves as employing an enabling model of supervision finding that works effectively. If one takes a directive approach, it can remove a sense of agency from trainees and create dependency. We find that discussing potential solutions allows for the development of critical analysis skills and provides the opportunity to work longer term with a trainee assisting their development, fostering independent thinking, and allow them to develop a sense of confidence in their own decision-making and a sense of trust in their developing competence. Without that, it is difficult for trainees to use supervision effectively and to meet the overarching aims of supervision. With this in mind, we caution you against expecting that your supervisor will take the lead or will provide solutions to issues you encounter. To help challenge you and to push you to develop your skills we find a less directive more enabling model works best, so do not mistake that approach for a lack of interest or understanding by your supervisor – they may just be ensuring that you develop during supervision and are challenged appropriately to think through different solutions to issues to develop your competencies.

You should discuss the nature and frequency of supervision with your supervisor and these might differ depending on your stage of training and your identification of specific learning needs. Challenges can arise when you do not consider these aspects. Do not expect that your supervisor will lead the supervision session. You need to direct these sessions and make them work for you and your training needs that you have identified. Be clear with your supervisor how you want to record the content of supervision (i.e., will you take notes and write these up after each session and send them on to your supervisor?). You also need to schedule sessions far enough in advance that you can find times to suit both parties involved. This can be difficult with conflicting schedules. Do not be tempted to move or cancel supervision if you can help it. Short-term gains in getting assignments completed, for example, will not help your overall performance in the long run. Related to this example is our observation of trainees not wanting to share experiences that might not reflect well on them. For example, if they believe they did not provide the best support for a client, feel overwhelmed by the emotional peaks and troughs displayed by the client or feel a sense of imposter syndrome, trainees may be reluctant to express this during supervision. Sometimes, this can be linked to a power imbalance where the trainee is concerned that this will reflect poorly on the impression the supervisor has of them as a trainee practitioner. Or it can be related to an incorrect perception that the supervisor will judge them. This can be the case when the supervisory relationship is embedded in a university training programme. If your supervisor is also a lecturer on your programme, you may become concerned that if you report challenges during supervision that this knowledge will be transferred to the supervisors' other interactions with you. These potential power differentials can negatively affect the supervisory experience and reinforce the need for discussions about how supervision will work before engaging in that. If you are concerned about presenting something during supervision, look to the literature for examples of how qualified practitioners use supervision and this should comfort you and give you confidence that presenting challenges does not always lead to a negative impression of your ability by your supervisor. For example, Sharp et al. (2021) outlined various challenges that sport psychology consultants reported, including boundaries, multiple relationships, confidentiality, and religious or spiritual issues. They also highlight the necessity of supervision for qualified practitioners and report it to be an essential element of applied practice that enables boundaries to be monitored, provides support and promotes self-care and awareness. So do not be afraid to share arduous experiences during supervision – without doing so, you will not experience the full benefits that supervision can offer.

Summary

In this chapter, we aimed to outline the importance of supervision from the perspective of the authors and their own experiences of supervising trainee practitioners. We outlined the need for supervision, the reasons trainees may find it difficult to engage with supervision, and some challenges that we encountered during our own provision of supervision in group and one-to-one supervisory settings. These have included reluctance to share, defence mechanisms triggered by group work, misunderstandings of the role of supervision, and the issues inherent with potential power differentials when supervision is provided through a university and the resulting dual roles; however, if used correctly, supervision is an excellent and unique way to improve your competencies, to learn from yourself and others, and to become a practitioner who sees supervision as being an ethical imperative and something integral to their professional identity and ability.

16 A Trainee's View of Training and Supervision

Introduction

So far in this book, we have covered all the key skills, competencies, processes, and plans a trainee needs to undertake for their development. The journey to become a sport psychology practitioner, is one of learning (from research, books, and reflective experiences), developing and refining our skills, and developing as a person and professional. There are many textbooks that tell us how to study sport psychology (e.g., Andersen, 2005; Gardner & Moore, 2004; Moran, 2013 and Moran & Toner, 2017). There are books which inform us about the therapeutic skills of CBT (McCarthy et al., 2023), REBT (Turner et al., 2023), acceptance commitment therapy (ACT) (Hayes et al., 2006), and volumes on reflection and reflective practice (e.g., Bolton, 2018; Cropley et al., 2023). There are a few autobiographical reflections and accounts, but the field needs more. As argued by McCarthy and Jones (2013), reflections and autobiographical stories may seem like 'unadulterated self-indulgence… but is necessary… we are on balance responsible for our profession' (p. 3). Sport psychology thankfully is no longer a dark science or mystic arts. But the journey and experience of becoming a trainee sometimes feels like it is. So, this chapter will present to you the unadulterated experiences of being a trainee (from recently finished trainee Sahen Gupta's perspective and his interactions with others between 2019 and 2023). I write this chapter in equal parts with honesty and authenticity. There will be vulnerabilities, frustrations, and successes. I hope you the reader find it instrumental as I reflected on these (and not be too harsh a critic on my trainee journey, nor on yours).

About this trainee

I am from India. I was born in Kolkata, and raised in a nuclear family, with close ties and quality time spent with both sets of grandparents and extended family. I was at the same school for the entirety of my early and middle education. I was actively involved in sport growing up with formal training-competition in cricket, and tennis. I moved 1,800 km to Bangalore, India, for my Undergraduate Education engaging in a Bachelor of Arts (Triple Major) in Psychology, Sociology, and English. During university days, I lived in a hostel with four roommates and learned how to live independently (like most people do). I also held various leadership positions at the department and then the university level through the course of university. By the end of my three years of undergraduate studies, I had built a bank of applied psychology experience, leadership skills, and research skills (including two publications). In 2019, I decided to pursue sport psychology, but there were no institutions to pursue sport psychology in India. Despite financial constraints, I applied to the UK for MSc programmes (since applications

DOI: 10.4324/9781003367208-20

were free!). I found the doctorate course at Glasgow Caledonian University but did not initially apply since no one I knew 'skipped' an MSc or had an integrated course. Eventually, after someone pointed out I had nothing to lose, I applied. After two rounds of interviews, I was accepted and in 2019, moved to Glasgow to pursue my doctorate in psychology (DPsych Sport and Exercise Psychology) with a British Psychological Society (BPS) and Health and Care Professions Council (HCPC) qualification. I am a male, from a Black, Asian, and Minority Ethnic (BAME) background, from a different cultural and linguistic background. My trainee journey has a pre-COVID, during COVID, and post-COVID element. I have held and currently hold an academic position and applied psychology position. My research and practice have been in diverse cultural contexts of multiple countries (India, Sri Lanka, UAE, South Africa, England, Scotland, and Spain). I can practise in three different languages and have worked with clients across the spectrum of race, religion, gender, and socio-economic status. My professional philosophy (at present) is integrative, founded on humanistic philosophy, cognitive-behavioural approaches, and emotion-focused techniques. I identify myself as a cisgender male and my pronouns are he/his/him.

Key skills from a trainee's view

Trainees are taught several skills and competencies across the years of applied psychology training. In the beginning, most of these skills look vague and are not clear to the trainee. Sometimes, trainees struggle with what these skills and competencies might look like in practice. How do we distil this knowledge into simple, clear processes?

The technique I used was rooted in the HCPC competency criteria that all training adheres to in the UK. Depending on your training programme, these may be broken down into 15–20 criteria that you may have to clear sequentially (i.e., year on year) or at the end with a final assessment. In the table below, I have used the 10 HCPC criteria that are adapted for sport and exercise psychology within my taught doctorate and simplified them with a case example of how it looked like in lived experience. *Keep in mind that these are examples to showcase, not pathways to follow.*

HCPC criteria		*What does it mean?*	*Example*
1	Demonstrate a clear and critical understanding of their professional identity as a practitioner psychologist	I can answer the question who I am as a practising psychologist across cases and situations	In an intake session, I can clearly outline my training, style, and philosophy to a client
2	Demonstrate a deep, reflective awareness of how their personal experiencing relates to their professional stance as a practitioner psychologist	I know my strengths, weaknesses, and biases	I know I am a supremely competitive person and sometimes need to be aware of this tendency to compete when working in the field
3	Demonstrate critical, detailed, and potentially leading knowledge within an applied psychology domain	I can critically engage with knowledge and interact with it to be an applied practitioner	I can differentiate between models and theoretical orientations based on the context at hand
4	Critically reflect on the complex relationship between the personal and professional spheres within their specific domain of practice and the tensions this presents as a practitioner psychologist	I can tell when my life experience and professional training intersects during my work	I can speak Hindi or Bengali to a client, but I have to mentally translate my training in English to this context

5 Critically reflect on personal functioning in professional practice (e.g., autonomy and accountability, fitness to practice, development needs, resilience) and to engage positively with feedback from fellow students, supervisors, and tutors	I can understand my developmental journey and all the things that played a key role within it	I hold myself to high standards, try to meet them, and am hard on myself when I fall short of them
6 Critically analyse and integrate research, theory, and practice to address complex professional dilemmas and generate innovative solutions to these drawing on a creative and original personal stance		
7 Reflect on and critically evaluate professional practice in relation to ethical and anti-discriminatory values and principles		
8 Critically appraise the factors impacting upon employability as a practitioner psychologist and the development of an innovative, personal strategy regarding career planning		
9 Demonstrate a high degree of autonomy and initiative		
10 Demonstrate the capacity to communicate at the standard of published academic and/or professional work (including appropriate referencing)		

What does the trainee see practice to be?

Throughout the course of training, your supervisors will nudge you to define what is applied practice for you. This opens up a variety of questions. 'Why sport psychology?' 'What does the sport psychology consultant do?' 'How do I want to help athletes?' 'Which domain or sport do I seek expertise in?'

Typically, sport psychology consultants are individuals who have a strong passion for sport and/or were involved with sport themselves (some are ex-athletes). They then get educated in psychology via undergraduate and postgraduate degrees, before transitioning into specific training. Each individual will have a different idea of what practice is, how to help athletes achieve their goals, which athletes to work with. Start reflecting and visualising on (a) your idea of effective practice; (b) reflect on your practice during your trainee years and learn from it. Often, this process is tricky. Based on my experience interacting with trainees, these are some perspectives on how sport psychology consultants practise

1 **Traditional psychological skills enhancement:** Psychological skills training (PST) is one of the most widely researched and used elements of sport psychology. These encompass interventions on mental skills such a visualisation, self-talk, anxiety-arousal management, performance routines, and others. Trainees often rely on rigid PST delivery structures as a 'manual' for practice. This serves two functions (neither wrong): (a) it acts as a contained plan that would be effective as long as it was followed; (b) it allows trainees to have structure

which helps avoid self-doubt. While psychological skills are needed, and often need to be delivered with this structure, it may not be relevant in complex cases where psychological skills alone may not address the issue.

2 **Sympathetic friend and motivator:** Within this conceptualisation of practice, the trainee identifies issues and provides emotional support. They often provide broad outlines and processes of interventions based on reading and experience with superficial awareness of power dynamics, role of relationships, and the self-in-practice. In sport, this often leads to overcommitment to the role and blurred boundaries where the sport psychology consultant is doing many things that may or may not be linked to their job role. The trainee at this stage may also find it difficult to challenge clients, often relying on positive reinforcement from clients. Because there is so much focus on being the sympathetic friend and motivator, the sport psychology consultant has limited understanding or acknowledgement of the context of work, and the larger dynamics at play.
3 **Considering individuals and uniqueness:** The sport psychology consultant considers practice as beyond the PST approach and the motivator who identifies problems and begins to consider individuals as the individual. This typically acts as the catalyst for the skills of formulation, assessment, and critical reflection to begin within the sport psychology consultant. The practitioner slowly goes beyond what the client reports and starts formulating (see Chapter 8) the problems and the larger maintenance factors of the problem. For example, a cricketer presents with the common problem of 'not scoring enough runs', but the actual issue at play was a cycle of self-doubt which prevented risk-taking because of a fear of failure. This was revealed by formulation and allows the sport psychology consultant to go deeper rather than simply look at implementing a PST intervention.
4 **No man person is an island:** John Donne's quote, while adapted here, is an important consideration for practice. Practice often involves working with many people ranging from coaches to parents. In recent times, it also involves wider community in terms of social media. The practitioner begins to appreciate this at the level of the client (their family, coaches, sport environment, and others). But it also allows the practitioner to understand their own reflective learning and working process. For example, I actively work with coaches to identify issues at the team level, and work to secure buy-in from the entire support staff for team level interventions. In this context, practice may consider factors beyond the individual themselves. This is particularly relevant when working with equality, diversity, and inclusion factors (see Chapter 5).
5 **Fixer or skilled helper?:** The fixer in practice is what I call the 'Avengers' syndrome. I had it myself too. The idea that I, as the psychologist, am there to help fix problems that arise. However, with training, this idea of practice has shifted. The Avengers syndrome happens to us all. It may arise due to our need for control and reinforcement for our competence. Or it may be because 'I am relevant in this scenario'. Whatever it may be, if it resonates with you, do reflect on it. The other end of the spectrum is conceptualising practice as being a 'Skilled Helper'. In this stage, the sport psychology consultant recognises that they are limited in what they can do and stay focused on being a helper to the clients in their journey to achieve their goals. The practitioner recognises that people present with similar patterns, but acknowledges and respects the uniqueness of individual stories, which includes how they may have tried to solve the issue themselves. Typically, this leads to the sport psychology consultant being slower to offer solutions, but rather formulate issues *together* with the client and *explore solutions together*. Being a skilled helper allows the sport psychology consultant to understand what the client needs. This may be a structured PST intervention. For example, an Olympic sailor I worked with found a structured goal-setting intervention massively helpful

Table 16.1 Hart and Nance (2003) framework of supervision styles

	High support	*Low support*
High direction	Supportive teacher	Directive, expert teacher
Low direction	Counsellor (interpersonal support)	Consultant

to navigate endurance races. But the same individual during post-season just wanted to have an emotional sounding board and support system, not solutions. Creating that safe space was the intervention itself within my role as a skilled helper.

Supervision: From the trainee's perspective

Before we go any further, remember that not all supervisors are similar. Bernard (1997) outlined three clear roles that the supervisor may adopt; (1) task-oriented teacher; (2) consultant; (3) interpersonally sensitive counsellor. This was developed further by Hart and Nance (2003) who distilled this into a framework of supervisory styles that could be understood in a 2 × 2 matrix of high-low direction and high-low support. This framework (see Table 16.1) is a helpful way of understanding supervisory styles. You can use this to reflect which style you would prefer or if you have a supervisor, what style do they adopt? This provides a language to both the trainee and the supervisor to deliberate on an effective process of supervision that aids the trainee's development.

In the teacher role, the supervisor differs based on how much support they provide while they are both high in direction. On the other hand, the other styles are characterised by low direction (i.e., flexible, but one has high support and the other has low support).

Matters arising in supervision

The supervisor-trainee relationship is an important pillar that supports the development of the psychologist. It is fundamental; however, we often need to look at how to manage the relationship, since it is a two-person system. Supervision assumes that trainees can develop therapeutic skills, can practise them under supervision with ethical frameworks, and are motivated to learn. Supervision assumes that supervisors have the relevant skills to aid this development process. This has an essential working alliance to facilitate learning and development. From my reflection and discussions with trainees, these are some points to consider during supervision:

1 **Resistance:** Refers to non-engagement with plans, tasks or processes, typically because of some perception of threat. This may come as resistance to the process of supervision itself, resistance to openness, resistance to conflict resolution, or other interpersonal dynamics. For example, the trainee may feel that their supervisor is too directive and has a problem-solving orientation while they have a need for more emotional support for their practice anxiety. This may cause a misalignment, which may trigger resistance.
2 **Trust:** A good supervisory relationship must be anchored in trust. Trust is *mutual* and bidirectional. This trust means that both parties find each other to be dependable and linked to a positive developmental experience. The greater the degree of trust, the more engaged the trainee is likely to be. Trust is a process, it is not an automatic, all-or-nothing phenomenon. It is earned through several interactions and has some degree of a shared interpersonal risk.

Communicate these elements to your supervisor and slowly communicate factors that affect trust with your supervisor.

3 **Countertransference/transference:** Refers to the projection of the supervisors' feelings into the trainee or vice versa. This may arise from similarities in gender, life experience, and training patterns. They may also be due to 'seeing oneself in the other'. While the supervisor-trainee experience inherently has an emotional orientation, there also needs to be a boundary between supervisory processes not becoming therapeutic ones. For example, your supervisor will probably discuss your anxiety with a client, or a personal trigger during client work, but will not be your therapist to help you manage that anxiety.

4 **Dual-roles:** Within training pathways, it is common to see overlapping dual-roles that the supervisor may have in wider training and education. Your supervisor may be your professor in a teaching/marking capacity, your co-author on a research project, or a stakeholder in a working group or project. It is important to reflect and communicate what the rules of engagement are in such scenarios. For example, my supervisor graded my work, and we communicated on how to set 15-minutes of a session to discuss the feedback and loop it into my developmental progression.

5 **Agreement of tasks-goals:** There should be typically a strong agreement between the short-term, medium-term, and long-term tasks and goals between the supervisor and trainee. This is key since it links to the trainee's developmental level and allows them to progress accordingly. At times, the task-goals are strictly linked to the client case being discussed, where interventions or formulations are discussed. But there should also be a clear focus on wider professional development in terms of therapeutic modality, professional practice philosophy, style, ethics, and wider development goals. It is helpful to set timelines for these (for example, I set six months to develop skills to be comfortable with deep emotional processing with clients), so that they are trackable and allows troubleshooting.

6 **Attachment style:** Supervisor-trainee relationship is an adult-adult relationship. But because of the difference in knowledge (i.e., the trainee learning from the supervisor), the trainee might have an anxious-attachment style and be reliant on the supervisor for constant support and want to be the supervisor's favourite. In another way, a trainee who has a history of compulsive caregiving may have a tendency of 'rescue' or 'fixing' clients may also look for approval from the supervisor. In another example, the trainee who is highly self-reliant may refuse or resist help or guidance from the supervisor. It is important to (a) reflect on your natural attachment style; (b) reflect on how and why resistance/conflicts in your dyad has played out.

7 **Guilt, shame, and pride:** Guilt, shame, and pride are self-conscious emotions that every individual experiences. Shame is focused on the evaluation of self that triggers a desire to hide or protect the self ('I am not good enough'). Guilt is act of thought or feeling of an action that motivates a desire to repair ('I have messed up' or 'I have done something wrong'). Pride is focused on feelings of accomplishment from action ('I am happy and satisfied with how I acted'). As psychologists we work with individuals and our emotionally deep work may often lead to these emotions. Supervision then asks us to expose and reveal them to prove them. These emotions are not a bad thing, they arrive because we are invested in our client work. Typically, with these emotions the trainee responds with submissively by taking an extended accountability or aggressively by being overtly defensive. These may lead to withdrawal, avoidance, attack, or shift of blame or attack on self via excessive self-criticism.

8 **Performance and developmental anxiety:** Part and parcel of being a trainee is being opening yourself up to new experience. Some of these will be challenging, some of them will be anxiety provoking, and some of them will involve making mistakes. It is normal to

feel anxious and threatening with failure. It is important to have a good balance between feeling challenged in our capacity's vs perceiving a threat of failure within the therapeutic relationship.

9 **Shadow motives:** Refer to the self's blindspots or insecurities projected to a situation or others. Trainee psychologists have many shadow motives. Some common ones include need to be competent, need for success, need for status, need to be valued, need for validation, or need to have their own emotional needs met.

Conflict and conflict resolution

Within the trainee-supervisor relationship, we consider it is, in fact, a relationship. There are fluctuations that occur over time, and those that lead to conflict. We can also view conflict as a breakdown or rupture in the collaborative working alliance. In supervision, this may also be in the form of impasses (i.e., stalemates, where trainee and supervisor may be stuck on an issue or a process of work). Interestingly, Nigam et al. (1997) examined supervisory impasses and found they last around 3–4 weeks which 40% of trainees having experienced it at least once. These may be because of philosophical disagreements, personality factors, or other reasons. So, what do these conflicts look like?

- **Conflicts from miscommunication or misalignment:** This may lead to disagreements or a lack of communication around evaluative feedback. The supervisor evaluates the trainee's ethical and competent practice and provides feedback conducive to their development. There may also be a misalignment between the supervisory style/role and the expectation of the trainee. For example, the trainee may expect greater support, but this is in contrast to the supervisory style.
- **Normative developmental conflicts:** Some conflicts within this relationship are normative and expected with changes to the supervisee's developmental level. For example, conflicts are typically low when the trainee is in their early days, but increase as trainee's become advanced with an oscillation between confidence and insecurity in their identity development. The supervisor should typically expect this and plan for it.
- **Participants' interpersonal dynamics:** The participant in this case refers to both the supervisor and trainee. This may include other life concerns, personal concerns, or even a major disparity between standards of conduct or professional expectations. This may happen during a particularly stressful period in either parties lives, or a consistent cycle of poor communication.

Resolving conflicts in supervision

There will be inevitable conflicts or friction points in a supervisory relationship. This is part of the process. It is, in fact, a helpful part if there are certain pre-emptive steps taken to address conflict in the supervision process.

1 **Supervision contract:** A supervisor typically provides a contract outlining the purpose, objectives, styles, evaluation, and feedback process of supervision. This is very similar to a confidentiality and mode of practice document that psychologists use with clients. Having this document before supervision allows a clear understanding of (a) how supervision will help develop clinical competencies; (b) how feedback will be provided; (c) the general style and pattern of supervision; (d) clarity on the supervision process itself. This document also provides

an outline of the duties of both parties. For example, if the supervisor provides written feedback, then it is agreed in this document. Or if the trainee is supposed to be audio recordings of the sessions, how will they be used for learning within ethical boundaries is highlighted here.

2 **Method of evaluation:** Supervision is an evaluative experience because the supervisor is responsible for the ethical practice and development of the trainee. Key considerations that *must* be brought up for discussion are: (a) what types of formative and summative evaluation methods are in place; (b) is there a process of marking and grading involved for clinical degrees; (c) what psychotherapeutic style and professional philosophy is used to undertake feedback (for example, a trainee may be a person-centred practitioner, but the supervisor may be integrative-eclectic with person-centred as one domain). An agreement and discussion are repeatedly evaluated to evolve as the trainee progresses over the months to better align to what the trainee needs for their professional development. For example, I needed support in the design of the intervention linked to formulation in my first three months as a trainee. After that, the next seven months of supervision were focused on developing my comfort, skills, and facilitative ability to engage non-directively with clients to process deep emotion and not problem-solve. A minor conflict came up midway through those seven months as my supervisor indicated that my client presentation was ill-suited to such work, and I disagreed. Here, we returned to our contract to troubleshoot and pave the way forward.

3 **Acknowledge the conflict:** If we, as trainees and supervisors, do not acknowledge that there is a conflict, then we are likely to do little to resolve it. Conflicts that arise from emotional countertransference are the most common area when defensiveness, guardedness, guilt, shame, and other inhibitory emotions arise. This leads to emotional and procedural needs of the trainee being unmet, causing frustrations or social comparisons. Remember that **supervision is for you**. Therefore, you need to be accountable to communicate what you need out of it, what is working for you, and what is aligned with your identity as a psychologist.

4 **Specialist supervision and learning curve:** Sometimes trainees want to learn a very specific therapeutic style or want to learn from a specific school of intervention. Typically, this means that they have to follow, learn, and develop the skills mandated by it. For example, a colleague of mine doing a counselling psychology doctorate went through EMDR (Eye Movement Desensitisation and Reprocessing) therapy training which required him to adhere to a very specific training process and supervision process to be an accredited practitioner in EMDR. He discussed how EMDR supervision (specialist) was very focused on EMDR skills and client analysis in EMDR therapy, whereas his larger therapeutic training was focused on other things. Conflicts arise when there is no clarity around what specialist supervision will comprise or expecting specialist supervision when it falls outside of the supervisor's skill competence. Similarly, there is a conflict (usually out of self-esteem or imposter syndrome) when the trainee is attempting a specialist training course. Reflection and the supervision contract are essential in these elements.

5 **Process orientation vs developmental identity orientation:** Some conflicts will establish themselves within the process of therapy and supervision. Trainee defensiveness is natural, since they are putting their work under a scanner. Trainees differ in their coping styles. Some deal with defensiveness by 'doing more', others try to change their opinions to match their supervisor (people pleasing) while others try to assert their own opinions forcefully. This is okay! Reflect on this, and try to engage in the following development process-oriented steps: (a) clarify the source of the problem – 'is it my issue with how I am receiving feedback?'/ 'can my supervisor provide better feedback to me?'; (b) go beyond the immediate conflict and identify other barriers (am I stressed, is my supervisor stressed, is this client triggering me, etc.); and (c) establish a common goal and take mutual agreements to reach there.

Other conflicts may be developmental-identity oriented. This is about what kind of psychologist you, as a trainee, eventually want to be. Sometimes you might want to be exactly like your supervisor (because it is easy to mimic than negotiate your own identity). Sometimes you might want to be nothing like your supervisor. Most times, trainees arrive at a point where they understand their authentic elements of self and also adopt some elements from their teachers, supervisors, and other role models as they finish clinical training (this changes as they professionally develop). Larger conflicts of developmental-identity may be because of professional practice modality. For example, I knew a trainee who struggled to adapt to cognitive-behaviour therapy and its structures because they held the belief that it was detrimental to individual differences. However, CBT was a key part of their training programme and evaluated via the licensing board making her forced to engage with it, and an ensuing conflict followed. On a personal level, I still consider most psychological evidence to have a western Eurocentric bias, and the origin of research proves my point. This led to an internal identity conflict that I had to engage with in supervision around cultural competence and practice with different languages (for context: my supervisor only speaks English, I practice in three languages – each with their unique frames of reference).

Feedback and self-assessment

Feedback and self-assessment are key parts of training and supervision. This allows us to track what we are doing well and areas we need to improve. Here are four key elements of effective feedback and self-assessment. We encourage you to discuss and outline these with your supervisor so that you can get the most out of supervision.

- **Learning competencies:** Feedback and feedback goals should be based on competencies and skills that the trainee needs to develop. These should be agreed upon early in supervision and be periodically reviewed (typically every 6 months or 50 hours of 1-on-1 client work, whichever is earlier). Trainees should try linking all feedback to their learning competencies (Mind Maps are helpful!)
- **Delivery of feedback:** Feedback should be a balance between support-reinforcement and critique-challenge. Any extreme feedback is typically poorly received and ignored (this goes for self-assessment and reflective feedback that trainees provide themselves as well!). Corrective feedback is also a key part of supervision, usually provided on skills and should be delivered on behaviours, case analysis, sample of work submitted in a timely and non-judgemental manner.
- **Feedback and self-assessment is not a test:** Unlike submissions where there are pass/fail criteria, feedback and self-assessment to development as a psychologist is rarely that way. The only pass-fail criteria in applied psychology training related to ethical principles in practice, everything else, is a process of development with little inclination to be 'perfect'. Feedback and self-assessment should be like taking steps towards a destination, not a dichotomous right-or-wrong. Reflective self-assessment and brainstorming with the supervisor should be to identify further areas of development or even areas they feel uncomfortable in so that they can be the focus of supervision.

'I' as 'I' and 'I' as 'Psych': The interactions of person and professional

It is quite tempting to create an artificial boundary within our professional and personal self. While a boundary is necessary, it is important to recognise that the process of training to be a psychologist will impact you and change bits and pieces of who you are, how you view the world, and how you respond to things. Similarly, who you are (your values, thoughts, beliefs, ways of emotional coping, etc.) will impact your professional development and identity as a psychologist. Too much crossover is not helpful. Too little may reduce authenticity. So where do these interactions find a healthy balance?

Typically, training courses last for 3–7 years (part-time route of study extends the time and allows more work and life experience in the middle). There will be a combination of traditional education (seminars, workshops, lectures, assessments), skill-based training (1-on-1 psychotherapy training), supervision, and reflective work. I did mine over three years. I had seven other people with me. I ended up graduating with one other person as people moulded their own timescales: this is an important reflection; you can do it on your own timescale of development!

I met my supervisors biweekly for supervision, and we had a peer led professional development group every Friday for 90 minutes where we combined literature with case presentations. I had numerous assessments. Most of them were applied and required some casework and client presentations to be analysed, reflected upon, and synthesised so that effective practice was visible (e.g., process reports, client studies, intervention plans, etc.). My supervisor and I had a process of self-assessment which we returned to every six months. Finally, we had a professional practice logbook that had client records of every hour of practice and supervision (approximately 700 hours of 1-on-1 work), and a yearly reflective professional development essay. Throughout this course of training, it is an *undisputable fact* that I (and every trainee I knew) changed. I have listed some reflective prompters for you to explore how 'I' as 'I' and 'I' as 'Psych' are interacting for you. Then, there is a 'Life Lived' box to share my experience.

- How are my values showing up in my day-to-day applied work?
- What are moments of friction and discomfort that I am having with myself?
- Are there specific people, things, clients, organisations, scenarios where I feel at extremes of comfort? (Super comfortable to uncomfortable), why is that?
- When did my job as a psych 'leak' over into my personal life?
- I want to reflect on when a particular event in my psych life triggered me due to something that happened or was happening in my personal life.
- In terms of how I view the world, and what actions I am most comfortable in, do I always have that in my profession? (when I don't, how do I respond?)

Life Lived

I like structure, but I am also completely fine without it. I am particularly irked when there are structures and rules that are inefficient and those that make little sense. Most of my psychotherapy training had structured exercises as starting points for experiential learning (linked to client work). Before starting, I had planned my doctorate out – to the month! It was going splendidly till February 2020. In this period, I was also unaware that I was satisfying my shadow need for high control. Then, in March 2020, COVID lockdowns happened, and everything went for a toss. For 15 days, there was nothing. I went back to working on my research, which was the only thing I could control (logical right? I thought so too). I felt completely divorced from the world, in my little bubble, doing research and crunching numbers. I helped a clinical crunch some basic numbers and stats too (my friend was a medical assistant there). Over the next six months, I (a) moved back to India;

(b) started remote education and online practice; (c) had to adapt and change 50% of my programme of research; and (d) deal with being unemployed and having little money. All my best laid plans went out of the window, no more satiating of my need for control. I have since reflected and reflected a lot. I have realised and slowly let go of my clutched grip on absolute control. I still need some sense of control (my research on resilience does also point to mastery being an adaptive factor). But I work with an active Socratic dialogue and situational control, rather than absolute control. That's the change in 'I' as 'I'. How did it affect the psych? Well, it changed my perception of how to work with clients who present with fragile processes and those who present with anxiety due to low control in their lives. I no longer feel the urge within me to promote control all the time – rather I recognise that sometimes, there is no absolute control in the short term, life is going to take you for a rollercoaster ride.

Some Other Reflections of the Trainee Journey on 'I'

- I realised I truly do not seek approval from others.
- I am fundamentally comfortable with conflict, but rarely initiate it.
- I am always curious and ask questions (even when people might not be ready to answer them).
- I can compartmentalise areas of my life efficiently.
- I sometimes struggle to work with people who 'settle' and do not want to improve things.

I have a high compulsion to be accountable and responsible (as my supervisor pointed out, 'you are accountable to your client, not responsible for them').

Section V

Endings and Beginnings

17 Referring a Client

Introduction

Referring a client to another service provider might seem like a simple operation. You, the trainee, recognise that the presenting issue (e.g., eating disorder) lies outside your competency, so you decide to refer to a physician or clinical psychologist, for instance. When we consider the processes in client referral, however, a knot of complexities arises for the client, the practitioner, and the organisation for whom the practitioner works. We shall unravel this knot within this chapter.

One of the first queries a trainee raises in training is about their competencies: what lies within my competency and what lies outside my competency. This apparent sharp divide between what lies within and what lies outside masks the intricacy of what lies in between. If sport psychology practitioners work within performance enhancement and well-being, what exactly do those terms include? And, if presenting issues (e.g., eating disorders) lie outside my competency, how do I decide what makes up an eating disorder? Within one's training, it is probable that you will receive referrals, accept referrals, reject referrals, and make referrals through the boundaries of competence. In this chapter, we shall explore receiving, accepting, rejecting, and making referrals. We shall begin by exploring boundaries of competence for an applied psychology practitioner.

What is a referral?

In sport and exercise psychology practice, a referral means when a sport psychology practitioner directs a client, or potential client, to another professional for services (e.g., psychological; medical; nutritional) (Van Raalte, 2010). But why do we refer? We refer to another professional for services to meet the ethical responsibilities we hold as practitioners to treat clients. Our training and competence erect boundaries to keep the client (or potential client) and us, the practitioners, safe. Knowing that we ought to refer does not mean that we make referrals when we should make them; however, if we build some cases, we can see how referral is an ethical, professional, and sound choice for the welfare of the client.

For instance, issues of competence, experience, time, availability, travel, interest, and others mean that a referral is necessary. At a more detailed level, a practitioner might lack the skills and experience to work with a client of a particular age, culture, disability, ethnicity, gender, sexual orientation, or socio-economic status (American Psychological Association, 2002). As an illustration, a sport psychology practitioner might not be available to meet a client's needs to meet for a face-to-face meeting on a Monday morning because the client flies to her next professional tournament on Monday evenings and the practitioner fulfils a contract at a professional rugby club on Mondays. On other occasions, a behavioural or psychological (e.g., generalised anxiety disorder) concern might lie outside the practitioner's knowledge and experience.

DOI: 10.4324/9781003367208-22

Occasionally, we will feel unsure about the exact conditions to refer. If we consider the referral process as a series of decisions, we first need to decide whether we need to refer a client whenever it might arise in service delivery. As a decision-making process, we might explore our training and professional competencies and take our case to our supervisor. But if these cases arise only occasionally, we might not be ethically sensitive, reasoned, or motivated to refer. In a survey of 18 sport psychology consultants in Canada, Gayman and Crossman (2006) reported that, on average, respondents were not dealing with athletes with clinical issues. A related finding was that other professionals rarely referred clients to them. Without adequate training, clinical skills, and supervision, it is likely that a practitioner would not recognise signs (e.g., objective things we can see like a plaster over a cut) and symptoms (e.g., subjective experiences a person describes like feeling pain) of anxiety or depression, for instance. Referral works when we recognise clients need support (e.g., we recognise the risk factors) from another professional to address their needs. Beyond issues of training, clinical skills, and supervision, another reason a practitioner might not refer a client is because they are unaware and unsure of how to conduct a referral and having developed a working relationship, for example, wish to continue for pure (e.g., to help) and shadow (e.g., a drive for power) motives. Many practitioners might not be aware of their motives for acting as they do and this limited self-awareness ought to be addressed in one or a combination of personal therapy, peer group supervision, personal supervision, or through self-reflective practices. We might hold shadow motives like a drive for power, a need to be liked, a wish to heal, a need for reflected glory, and a need to maintain one's income. These less than ethical reasons remind us of our impairments as practitioners and the need for safeguards in our practice to safeguard others (Andersen & Brewer, 2000). In the next section, we explore a core personal and professional issue of boundaries, which arise in training and supervision and have a profound influence on the quality of personal and professional relationships in sport, exercise, and performance psychology.

Boundaries

Boundaries define those things for which we are responsible. We can consider boundaries as those dividing lines between us and others – what is me (my responsibilities, my body, my feelings, my property) and what is not me. In relating with others, boundaries communicate how we wish to be treated and what we believe is okay or not okay (Martin, 2021). Being a healthcare professional, however, you might consider others' needs ahead of your own and this concern for others might mean you lose sight of your needs because you focus so intensely on what others want or need. One outcome might be that you feel exhausted, frustrated, and unappreciated.

Though we might recognise physical (e.g., body, property) and sexual (e.g., right to consent) boundaries, we might not recognise (or see) emotional or time boundaries so readily. Our emotional boundaries protect us from emotional harm (e.g., invalidating one's feelings). Time boundaries help us manage our time and workload so we commit to what is manageable and achievable for us rather than saying yes to everything because we do not wish to offend others. In psychotherapeutic work, we differentiate the client from the practitioner. We recognise the client and practitioner are unique, autonomous individuals with their own identity and responsibilities. There is a healthy separation between the client and practitioner that allows each individual to be themselves and choose what is right for each person.

Though we each have our thoughts, feelings, values, beliefs, goals, and interests, a lack of boundaries might mean we feel unsure of what we need, what matters to us, or what we believe in. Gaining a sense of our identity and boundaries means we do not get swallowed up by others' feelings, needs, and wants. It can be tempting to rescue others in our helper role as sport psychology practitioners by taking responsibility for a client's problems and trying to solve them. Though we can provide support and guidance for some problems, the client ultimately holds control of their problems and they are the client's responsibility. How others think, feel, and act is their responsibility, not ours. Yet, in helping relationships, we need to consider our emotional safety because a client or third party might blame, shame, or criticise us unfairly. They might yell, belittle, or bully us. Our boundaries protect us from these threats and set limits on what we accept from others and how we wish them to treat us.

In sport settings, personnel (e.g., coaches, athletes) normalise working, giving, and volunteering beyond what seems reasonable. Sport, like other settings, has people over-working, over-committing, and being taken advantage of because of the perceived prizes at the end of all of one's efforts. But our resources (e.g., time, energy) are finite and so we need to decide how to allocate our resources. Saying yes to projects at work that lie beyond our current capacity often leaves us feeling weary but also angry at ourselves for allowing the situation to escalate.

Life Lived

Tom checked his weekly schedule and realised how busy the week could get. He seemed to have so many back-to-back client sessions across the week, staff workshops, parent workshops, team meetings, administrative duties, and his own young family at home. Tom's workload increased year on year as the only sport psychology practitioner at the football club. Some budget cuts meant the Board of Directors shelved plans for another sport psychology practitioner to help with the academy squad. Tom felt emotionally shattered by the weight of struggles players and staff shared with him. To cope with his workload, Tom started going to work earlier and leaving later. Though he used to swim each morning before work, he felt he had to leave it go because he did not have the time or energy for it. His relationships at home suffered because he saw his wife and kids less and less owing to his workload increase. All his time and energy went into an unmanageable workload.

In Tom's case, he set no boundaries at work. Tom and his family felt the consequences because his work exhausted him, leaving him little time or energy for his family, and he felt aggrieved that an organisation would act so irresponsibly towards him. Tom lacked boundaries with time, energy, and emotions, leaving him vulnerable to absorb their feelings (e.g., sadness, anger) and issues.

Boundaries of competence

From the moment a trainee enters a training programme, we, as supervisors and instructors, introduce them to ethics, boundaries, and competencies. Using various methods of assessment and supervision, we monitor and evaluate competencies, boundaries, and ethical practice. In the locker rooms, training sites, and competition arenas, we and our clients challenge these interrelated concepts each day we deliver services to clients. Through feedback, reflective practice, personal, peer and group supervision, we gather a sense of clear professional development with client welfare sitting at the centre of our concerns.

This structure of assessment, supervision, and reflective practice brings us, as trainees and practitioners, closer to understanding what lies within and outside our competency. Inherent within these processes, however, lies a sense of unease about our responsibilities to our clients. But this sense of unease authenticates one's competencies and leads the practitioner to address gaps in skills or knowledge at that stage of training as part of one's professional development.

Training programmes in sport and exercise psychology allow trainees to integrate the skills necessary to perform one's role as a sport psychology practitioner. These training programmes build on undergraduate and postgraduate studies to apply this knowledge to professional practice settings where trainees make informed judgements on complex issues in specialist fields. Trainees also undertake pure or applied research while developing professional skills and responsibilities in varied contexts.

Sport psychology practitioners follow an ethical, empirical, and theoretical orientation often conceived within a scientist-practitioner perspective. Ethical, empirical, and theoretical developments continue throughout one's career, so practitioners must continue to develop professionally like other psychologists. Although sport psychology practitioners have services to offer, these services must meet the needs of service users (e.g., athletes, coaches, teams, officials, parents, of athletes) from different populations, diverse settings, and be responsive to their presenting problems.

In simple terms, practitioners work to understand, explain, predict, and improve the performance of participants (e.g., athletes, coaches, officials) in individual and teams sports. But this work cannot happen without applying psychological theory to maintain and improve physical health and psychological well-being, whether in a sport setting or as part of an active lifestyle. Therefore, performance and well-being form central pillars of the work of a sport psychology practitioner. What lies within these pillars?

Receiving and conducting referrals

Referrals are a critical process in service delivery because the sport psychology practitioner will not always fit the needs of all clients and all their presenting issues. Instead, the most appropriate professional ought to be the one working with the client because several issues arise before and during service delivery that dictate a referral. These reasons might be legal, ethical, medical, psychiatric, psychological, social, and so on, which emerge at different stages of the helping process and are not a reflection of the incompetence of the sport psychology practitioner; rather, it is the best professional for the presenting issue. On other occasions, the sport psychology practitioner will receive referrals from other professionals (e.g., coach, physician) and will need a process or protocol to manage the referral process.

Some sport psychology practitioners feel that all presenting issues ought to be within their professional competence; however, this demand upon oneself is extreme and unfair. In these situations, feelings of shame and embarrassment mean some practitioners do not refer the client when they ought to, and for others, they feel so diffident; they refer too quickly or feel unable to accept a referral from another professional. The possibility of referral in service delivery ought to be raised at the outset of the helping process so clients know they might need to be referred to another professional. It might come as a shock to some clients in a session to learn that they are negotiating a referral with their practitioner and feel overcome with feelings of rejection or abandonment. There are several reasons a practitioner might not raise the possibility of referral. For example, they might believe a referral is a relatively rare practice in service delivery or being part of a multidisciplinary team with other practitioners (e.g., physician, clinical psychologist) would mean that the referral is a smooth process among members of the same multidisciplinary team. A third reason is that a client might present with problems in performance and later reveal other issues (e.g., eating disorder, martial breakdown) that require a referral. In the next section, we shall explore when a professional or third party refers a client to you and then when you refer a client to a professional.

Receiving a referral

The sporting milieu teems with well-meaning administrators, coaches, backroom staff, parents, and friends, all wishing the best for their athletes. On the one hand, their suggestions to seek help (e.g., I think you should see a sport psychology consultant) show how much a person (e.g., coach) wishes another (e.g., athlete) to succeed but there is often a need to control another or deal with one's own anxiety. To illustrate, as we explained about boundaries, their purpose is so that you can take care of yourself, not control others. Though we might seek control as coaches because sport is meaningful and treasured, yet unpredictable, we might encourage, demand, or threaten an athlete to seek help against their wishes. Someone might shame an athlete to control them by saying, 'The problem with you is that you're too selfish; you're only thinking about yourself and not the team'. These moralistic judgements highlight how another person is bad (or hopeless or lazy) because they do not act in harmony with another's values. In sport, as in life, blame, insults, criticism, and prejudicial comparisons alienate one from another because the rightness or wrongness of things leaves people in a world of judgements (Rosenberg, 2015). Or someone might feel anxious about an athlete's performances or the likelihood that the next performance might not go well and feeling anxious about this circumstance persuades or cajoles the athlete to seek help.

Regardless of the prevailing circumstances, a coach or physiotherapist might telephone or email requesting you see a client-athlete. The process might unsettle the athlete because they might feel that if a member of the staff is suggesting a referral, there must be something wrong and if one does not attend an arranged appointment with a sport psychology practitioner, which sanctions might unfold? As with Leah, we could address the misunderstandings and inaccuracies of her coach.

Life Lived

A well-meaning coach contacted me on the telephone to arrange an appointment for Leah, one of his professional track athletes. The central message was that the athlete 'needed to relax' and the athlete was 'keen to attend'. Part of the ongoing contractual arrangement with the national squad was that a member of the coaching and backroom staff could arrange a referral (typically an initial meeting) on behalf of their athletes, and the athlete would assume responsibility from that point tracked by follow-up contact with the coach or backroom staff, thereafter. During the initial meeting, it emerged that the client had listened to her coach and his advice seemed sensible, but more critically, he reassured her that this was the only way to go to address her recent poor performances. Being compliant and not wishing to displease her coach, she attended. As the initial meeting unfolded, it emerged that she had an ongoing dispute with a coercive and controlling landlord. She did not wish to tell her coach about her 'personal problems' because ultimately it was just one troublesome person making her life difficult and she could deal with him. What she did not recognise was the effect of this ongoing dispute. For instance, she struggled to relax in the evening and sleep at night. She did not like staying at her flat and did not feel safe. Although it began as a practical problem, it became an emotional problem that affected her everyday life and her performances as a professional athlete. She had ended her contract with her landlord the previous week and had secured another place to rent. Leah explained to her coach what had happened. She learned that troublesome people, like her landlord, want to be in control. He often argued with her and created conflicts to avoid undertaking his duties as a landlord. He seemed to enjoy the conflict, and he drew Leah into a power struggle.

A referral begins a process rather than a discrete event between two (or more) professionals. When a sport psychology professional receives a referral, it sets off a decision-making procedure to consider the source of the referral, time, fees, and suitability of service delivery with the referred client. To explain, the sport psychology practitioner needs to consider their trust in the professional referring the client, whether the practitioner has time to support the client, the fees the client has to pay, and if service delivery is possible and suitable. On a broader note, the referral process means considering boundaries, confidentiality, ethics, countertransference, and professional networks (Shapiro & Ginzberg, 2003). One example of countertransference occurs when a practitioner receives a referral from a perceived higher status practitioner or professional. To impress this professional, a practitioner might take on the client even with a gruelling caseload or see the client at an unsuitable time.

Making a referral

A key component of a referral process is having a professional network to whom one might refer a client. In sport, a sport psychology practitioner might refer a client to a physician, psychiatrist, or clinical psychologist, for instance, and so it is time well spent locating, meeting, and established working relationships with these professionals. It is also likely that with a good working relationship, they will refer clients to you.

Most professionals conduct referrals using a written format and because a written format is a static form of communication, professionals need to be precise and comprehensive in the information they share. Hartveit et al. (2013) suggested recommended content of referral letters from general practitioners to specialised mental healthcare professionals using a qualitative multi-perspective study. Seven headings covered the major themes arising from the study: (1) Personal information and contact information. (2) Important introductory information (check-off points). (3) Case history and social situation. (4) Present state and results. (5) Past and ongoing treatment efforts, involved professional network. (6) The patient's assessment. (7) Reason for referral. This structure for content helps the professional to whom you are referring your client to understand what the client is presenting, what we expect of the professional, and what might help the client address their presenting problem(s).

1 **Personal information and contact information:** This section requires correctly determining who the person is, their contact information, emergency contact numbers, and where they live. This section also provides details about the psychologist, including their phone number, email address, and workplace.
2 **Important introductory information:** In this section, the practitioner addresses the check-off points (i.e., yes, or no) of the risk of the client specific to mental health. For instance, is there an immediate need for compulsory care? Is the client suicidal? Is the client a threat to others? Is the client responsible for the care of children? Does the client have a drug problem or addiction? These questions determine the client's current needs.
3 **Case history and social situation:** The case history highlights alterations such as deterioration of a condition over time and the extent of the condition. Any episodes of violence, former suicidal risk, guide the reader and the broader context of the client's psychosocial circumstances, such as economics, employment, residence, social network, and activities.
4 **Present state and results:** Here we hold four categories of information: (1) function, symptoms, and limitations, (2) somatic health, (3) test results, and (4) medications. With function, symptoms, and limitations, we present the problem and the present mental status of the client. Where a loss of function reveals itself, we present the level and duration of the loss. The

present state of symptoms and their duration ought to be outlined as well. One's somatic health includes any diseases or comorbidities. Some organisations ask clients to complete specific questionnaires relating to anxiety and depression. For example, we could include test scores from these questionnaires and any notice of medications.

5. **Past and ongoing treatment efforts and the wider professional network:** Here, the referring sport psychology consultant presents what they have tried so far and any current interventions alongside other supportive services that the client uses.
6. **The client's assessment:** Here we include the client's experience of the situation, desire, and motives for treatment, and attitude towards treatment.
7. **Reason for referral:** The sport psychology consultant outlines a goal for treatment along with the reasons for referral.

Summary

Referrals, like so many other elements of applied sport psychology, are a process, not an event. Referrals often mean an end to one working relationship and beginning to another working relationship. These endings and beginnings are part of personal and professional life circumstances; however, we all respond uniquely to such experiences. Referrals are also multifaceted and this complexity of communication and proceedings among professionals and clients means unsettling feelings emerge in the procedure, which means all parties hold responsibility for their role and sharing how they are feeling and growing through the experience. Attending to the details of referral, communicating openly and sensitively means all parties can contribute to successful outcomes. On a broader note, referrals in sport and exercise psychology have received little empirical exploration, yet they are a critical part of successful sport psychology service delivery. Perhaps referrals might spark your interest as a topic of research during your training.

18 Preparing for and Sitting Your Viva Voce

Introduction

So, the day has finally come; you have set a date for your viva voce. This is what you have been working towards since you applied to your training route. The end is finally in sight, the culmination of so many months of hard work and dedication – so it should please you, should it not?

What we usually find, though, is that the overwhelming response to being close to a viva voce is fear or anxiety. Regardless of whether you are preparing for a viva on a taught route or one on a research only route, it is normal to feel anxious about your viva. One positive aspect to reassure you right away, though, is that you are in the right domain of psychology to think positively about this upcoming experience. Where better to learn about the importance of mental preparation and confidence under pressure than the academic world of sport and exercise psychology? The literature is abundantly clear on the importance of preparation for performance, so learn from this, extrapolate what you can, and take comfort from knowing that your profession has demonstrated that being mentally prepared and rehearsing aspects of performance result in enhanced outcomes. The literature tells us that self-confidence is key to performance success. Motivation as a driving force for successful activity and self-efficacy have both been shown to be instrumental to outcomes in sporting contexts. In fact, self-efficacy, emotional intelligence, achievement motivation, personality, and time perspective are all elements associated with performance and with differences between elite and non-elite athletes (Mitić et al., 2021). Keep this information in mind during your preparations and use the evidence base from your profession to help you prepare successfully for your own upcoming performance while remaining calm.

Preparation is key – it will enhance your confidence and increase your ability to cope. Preparation is also individualistic. What works for one athlete when preparing for competition is not what works for everyone and we can say the same for your viva preparation. You need to find what works for you. We have suggested some key areas in the writing that follows, but remember you should engage with the activities or preparations that are a fit for you. Just because someone you know did a certain activity to prepare for their viva does not mean that will work for you, so take time to think through your preparation strategy and allow time during the run up to the viva to prepare thoroughly so that you are going into the viva feeling confident.

How to prepare – Some suggestions

There are many ways to prepare for your viva and we will cover some in more detail than others. Consider our suggestions and mull over which of them you deem relevant for your own preparation. As a general rule of thumb, there will be a few months between you submitting your completed thesis and your viva if you are undertaking a research PhD. This time frame might be

DOI: 10.4324/9781003367208-23

much shorter for those of you who are on a taught or professional doctorate route or the independent route. Map out the time that you have and consider what you can do most productively during that time. The academic literature is something that you are familiar with and we would direct you to that literature here to build your confidence. There are many published articles about viva voces: how to prepare, the utility of mock vivas, their benefits or challenges, and recently a useful literature on experiences of online vivas. For example, the article by Wisker et al. (2022) on examiner and candidate experiences of online doctoral vivas.

Life Lived: Reflecting on Viva Preparation Sessions

As a programme director, I led sessions on viva preparation with trainees and gathered feedback on which aspects of those sessions were most helpful. Reflecting on that, the most useful input for trainees is usually the opportunity to speak with someone in their field who has been through the viva process recently. I find that this can dispel concerns and give a real sense of focus and purpose in a much quicker and more convincing way than reading material on viva preparation or discussing potential questions with peers or supervisors. Having a chance to ask questions of someone who has recently been through a viva and hearing that person offer hints, tips, and reflect on their own experience are invaluable. Often trainees approaching viva are apprehensive about what the experience will involve. Gaining that first-hand knowledge of the process and having positive aspects of the experience highlighted can be a real short-cut to becoming prepared because it provides information, allays fears, and provides a real insight into the potential for a viva to be enjoyable. Demystifying the viva is probably the best way to help trainees prepare. If you don't know anyone who has recently been through a viva, then speak to staff at your institution or to your supervisor and see if they could arrange a brief session with someone who has that experience. Reflecting on my efforts to help trainees prepare for viva nothing I can share with trainees will have the same impact as someone sharing their recent lived experience.

Staying calm

A crucial part of your preparation to reinforce is to stay calm. No one knows your work as well as you do, and while questions during a viva can seem challenging, no examiner goes into the viva to trip you up or catch you out. You have spent a considerable amount of time on this training route and developed your competence as a practitioner psychologist over a considerable time period. The viva can be seen as your opportunity to discuss your body of work with people who are interested in it, have read it in its entirety, and who have knowledge of the domain. So, practice staying calm (e.g., breathing techniques) and remind yourself that you know your work and that your work is of a sufficient standard to pass at viva otherwise your supervisor would not have put you forward. That you have made it to viva should be reassuring in itself.

If you become anxious during your viva, then it is okay to be open about that. Your examiners will understand that this is an arduous process and will not mind repeating a question or rephrasing something if you are not quite understanding what is being asked. You can also pause and ask for a minute to think about your response to a question or to have a drink of water and give yourself the moment you need to take a deep breath and get your nerves under control.

Read your work over

It is daunting to re-read your work ahead of viva and sometimes students become so worried that they will spot mistakes they shy away from reading it. Do not let those worries put you off. You need to be familiar with your work and if you notice any errors, then note them so that you are prepared if one of your examiners has also spotted them. Do not underestimate the amount of preparation required by examiners and the degree to which they will have read your work and considered it. Reading your work through can ensure you are also familiar with it all, even the aspects of it you may have written quite some time ago. It will help remind you of the big picture and help you think about where you would like to go next with your work. Another thing it can help you with is to see any gaps between what you have written and any new publications that have come out since you submitted. Being acquainted with that new literature is important at viva and will mean that you sound knowledgeable about your area and interested in the field. You do not want the examiners to see you as not being engaged with the recent updates in the area. A last thing that reading the work over can help you prepare for is that opening question that will surely be asked. Examiners will start off with an ice breaker type question, probably asking you to summarise your work or to highlight your main findings. This opening question is usually something that examiners think will be easy for you to answer and will help you settle into the viva itself. Unfortunately, because it is often an open question, it can make candidates nervous, as they feel maybe the examiners are looking for something specific. So, do not be put off by this type of question, but prepare for it and try to give a detailed answer that shows your contribution to the field. During your preparations, make sure you are reading through an identical copy to the one that your examiners will have. Having the same page numbers could be vital so that you can track questions and refer to your document, confident knowing that what you have on paper in front of you is identical to that the examiners are referring to.

One last thing to highlight and for you to remember at the start of your viva is that, if possible, try to enjoy it. That might sound unlikely given your nerves and the importance of the viva but you do not get many opportunities in your career to discuss in depth a piece of work that you have carried out with experts in the field who have read your work and have aligned research interests. So, make the most of that opportunity to share your contribution, experiences, and hopes for the future with people who really understand the context within which you are working. Speak to other people who have recently been through their viva – many of them will tell you they enjoyed the opportunity to discuss their work and reflect on all they had achieved.

Check your institutional or training programme policies

It is always helpful to read through the policy documents around viva for your institution or training programme. Be clear about the outcomes from your viva, the role of the internal and external examiner, and the likely duration and time frames involved. Some institutions will be happy for examiners to tell you at the start that having read your work, they feel confident of a positive outcome, but other institutions' policies will prohibit this declaration. It is good to know this possibility because you should remember that just because the examiners do not give you any sign at the start, it does not mean there will not be a positive outcome, it might just be a policy recommendation from your institution or one from their own institution that they are used to working with.

It is also beneficial to be familiar with these policies because they will give you a clear idea of how the viva will progress, who usually leads it, whether there will be a sport psychology consultant as chair or convenor for proceedings besides your internal and external examiner, and useful information for preparation such as if your supervisor may attend. If your supervisor may attend the viva consider if you want that. Some students find it reassuring that their supervisor is present, whereas others find it just introduces another layer of worry or anxiety and would prefer their supervisor not be present. Knowing the institutional policy will help you identify areas you need to think about and plan and any conversations you need to have with your supervisor ahead of the viva.

Research your examiners

One thing that is important to consider is who your examiners are (lightly stalk their work and their professional background). As someone reading your thesis or the assessment you have prepared for viva the perspective of the examiner will determine their questions. With that in mind, find out about your examiners and what their areas of expertise or interest are because those will probably be the ones that they will want to ask questions about. For an external examiner especially knowing their area of expertise and having knowledge of their published work can be key to expecting questions and to helping you to prepare. Understanding their point of view or the lens through which they are reading your work will help you make sense of the questions they ask and to provide an informed response to those questions.

Prepare questions and practise, practise, practise

We have already mentioned the initial ice breaker question and the need to prepare for it. We suggest preparing a coherent list of questions besides the ice breaker question and outline answers to them ahead of your viva. There are many books and websites dedicated to viva preparation and you can make up a list of questions from those and from asking people who have recently been through a viva themselves for the questions asked of them. Write a list of questions from these generic ones provided online and think about how these could be tailored to your own work that you submitted. Make them specific to your own topic and submitted work and then plan answers to these questions. Do not stick to the straightforward questions either, include those that you are hoping they will not ask you, and the ones you are dreading. Avoiding these questions will not help you in the long run, but doing whatever preparation you can will help. To help you keep on top of the potential questions, we recommend organising them into different areas, for example, general questions that an examiner might ask at the start of the viva: how the field has developed since you started your work; your method; your analysis; questions on your main findings, etc. You can then think through short concise answers and more detailed in-depth responses to each. When thinking about your answers to these questions, try to keep your focus on your contribution to the field. What you really want to convey during your viva is what you have contributed that makes your work 'doctoral'. We don't have time here for an in-depth exploration of the concept of 'doctorateness' (see Poole, 2015 if you are interested in the progress to date and arguments around the concept) but try to think about your contribution and how you have added to the field, the unique contribution that your work alone has made, and how you can best convey that during the viva. So not only do you need to report what you have contributed to knowledge, but also how that fits with the existing state of knowledge and how it differs from what was already known.

Another thing to note is that often, when we are preparing for these types of events, we write potential answers. While that might fit well with your usual working style and be a good way of keeping information together in one place, the viva is an oral examination so you need to verbalise your responses and for them not to sound rehearsed or stilted. Practise responding out loud to questions because giving verbal responses differs from providing a pre-rehearsed written response. If you have only ever written responses to practice questions, then you might struggle during the viva when you're feeling under pressure to remember those and to reimagine them into verbal responses. Practising the oral delivery ahead of time will be invaluable. We also suggest avoiding writing an answer to questions as though it's the only way to answer them. If you write out a response, learn it verbatim and aim to regurgitate that in the viva then you are setting yourself up for difficulties. Recall can be negatively affected when we are under pressure and trying to remember what you want to say is much more taxing than having the relevant knowledge in your head and verbalising it coherently that fits the question. We suggest you prepare but that you avoid over-preparing, which can be detrimental. That type of over-preparation can also result in your providing an answer to a question that you thought you were going to be asked rather than an answer to a question that they asked you.

Whether to have a mock viva

There are different recommendations around the use of a mock to prepare for your viva. Some people believe a mock is essential to the preparation process, others feel it can provide an unrealistic sense of preparedness and reduce the level of spontaneity shown in the viva itself. Some also think it can increase anxiety levels if it does not go as planned or if feedback from it is not wholly positive. Our advice would be to consider whether a mock will help your individual preparation. To return to the point we made in the introduction to this chapter, a viva is a unique experience and each person's preparation will also be unique. You are the person best placed to decide on the value to you of a mock viva. Do not avoid it just because it seems like it will be a scary experience, instead try to think objectively about the usefulness of a mock viva for you. If you decide on a mock (and some institutions might mandate that for you), then to maximise the benefit to yourself and your preparation make it as realistic as possible. If you have a mock exam where the questions are all straightforward and easy to answer and the people who are your 'examiners' are not experts or do not have the experience of being examiners, then this is unlikely to help prepare you for the actual event. Using a setup that mirrors that of the viva in terms of processes and location can help reduce any nerves you have about the process and unfamiliarity of the viva itself. That can be hugely beneficial to some people. For others, the benefit comes from verbally responding to questions and trying to articulate their findings or experiences. Think about the overall aim of a mock viva for you and what that should entail for it to be an effective means of preparation Similarly, if you decide to go ahead with a mock, then speak with your mock examiners to make sure that they understand what you are hoping to gain from the experience.

As mentioned above, try to make the mock as realistic as possible. If you're concerned about the actual process, then make sure you are replicating the scenario as it will happen. If your viva is going to be face to face, then make sure your mock viva is too, but if it is going to be online, then make sure your mock is online and that you're using whatever platform you will use in the real thing to help you troubleshoot any technological issues and to make sure you are familiar with the platform being used and the process involved.

If you decide that what you actually need to help you prepare is to have a conversation with a group of people about how you can best answer questions on elements of your work that you find difficult to articulate, then a mock viva might not be what you need and instead a more supportive peer process or the sharing of ideas between peers and colleagues could have the potential to be more beneficial to your confidence than an actual mock exam.

If you are going to have a mock viva, then give sufficient time between that mock and the actual viva for you to work on any feedback that you received because of your taking part in the mock. There's no point in holding a mock a few days before the actual event if you then receive a lot of feedback that you don't have time to process or work on. That can only increase your nerves and derail your preparations. Remember, staying calm is important and you can't do that if you don't give yourself enough time to reflect on feedback and be able to enact any advice that you were given.

Consider who you would ask to be your mock examiners too. This will depend on what you want out of the experience. For example, if you really just want to try out answering questions in a similar environment to that of the actual viva, then you could ask peers or colleagues or even friends or family members to take part. If you're wanting to gain experience of answering challenging questions around your methodology though or you want to test out your ability to answer complex questions in an articulate manner when under pressure, you'll want someone who is an expert or has enough knowledge to put the difficult questions to you and to then ask follow-up questions depending on your response. In that case, you might want a member of your supervisory team or a staff member at your institution who has expertise in your method. Your supervisor is not always the best person to take part in the mock, as they probably know your work too well. They are also familiar with your limitations and your areas of expertise, so might not provide a realistic experience of the viva for you.

Summary

Despite being the final hurdle and the only thing standing between you and your completion of your studies and entry into the world of professional practice, the viva can be a daunting and anxiety provoking event. Use the time you have between submission and viva to prepare for this. Take comfort in getting to this stage of your training and be proud of your accomplishments. Make sure you're familiar with your work, with recent updates in the field and with the published work of your examiners. Choose preparation strategies that will work for you, speak to others about their own experiences, and plan out a timeline of activities to help you make the most of the time available to you. Remember that you are almost there, you are about to enter the world of practitioner psychologists and that staying calm, preparing as much as possible and reflecting on your progress to date will set you in good stead for what's ahead.

19 Jobs, Job Interviews, and CPD in Lifelong Learning

Introduction

While following your training route, your end point for planning might well have been your viva voce or graduation. The focus of your goals would have been on completing your studies and becoming a qualified sport and exercise psychologist. If you are at the point of completion now or if you are only part way through your training route, we recommend you think about jobs, interviews, and continuous professional development (CPD). Create goals for your future that go beyond completing your training. Knowing where you want to be in the future and the area you want to work in will help you tailor your training to that endpoint. It will also help you consider the extracurricular activities that you might want to take on to help build your CV and the skills and knowledge that you will need should you decide to set up your own private practice. Considering where you are now, where you want to be, and how to get there are integral to your future success and can save considerable time after graduation if you plan early.

There is an entire literature on employability and while covering that is outside the aims of this chapter, we would recommend that you engage with that literature and consider your current starting point regarding employability. Definitions of employability encompass aspects such as the ability to get and keep employment; the capability to move within the labour market; and the ability to exhibit attributes perceived as necessary for employers. There are also models of employability that can help you think about your own developmental needs, for example, the understanding, skills, efficacy beliefs, and metacognition (USEM) model (understanding, skills, efficacy beliefs and metacognition) developed by Yorke and Knight (2007) that considers understanding; skill; efficacy beliefs and metacognitive facets of employability. Alternatively, the CareerEDGE model of Dacre Pool and Sewell (2007) suggested the need for combining elements to increase confidence and capital, emphasising experience, specific subject knowledge; understanding and skills, generic skills, and emotional intelligence. The narrative around employability has changed over the course of our working lives and we now have a labour market that values the ability to adapt and individual ownership of your career. To be successful, drive your own career progression and plan effectively for your future career.

CPD and lifelong learning

Before we look in more depth at jobs, interviews, and decisions about and logistics associated with setting up in private practice, we are going to give thought to CPD and lifelong learning. As professional psychologists, we are required to practise ethically and align with professional and regulatory body standards. We want to ensure our practice is current, informed by current high-quality research evidence, and that we are providing the most effective interventions for our

DOI: 10.4324/9781003367208-24

clients. We can only achieve these standards if we systematically engage with CPD and lifelong learning. You will be used to working towards meeting and showing competencies, and these competencies will form a clear guiding principle for your training and development. Having that clear identification of competencies is useful, but you need to think about competence as being a continuum that you will keep moving along even after you complete your training. Meeting the competencies for qualification and chartership (e.g., with the British Psychological Society) is the starting point for your development of competence, not the end point. Without that drive to continue to learn and to recognise the need for additional learning, we will not engage with relevant learning activities that will keep our practice up to date, informed, and competent. For sports psychology practitioners to maintain their practitioner status, CPD is required by the Health and Care Practitioners Council (HCPC) in the UK, for example. They mandate this CPD and outline the requirements along with what you need to do to meet those standards. You need to evidence that you are engaging with various learning activities regularly, that you keep a record of that engagement, and that these activities contribute to the improvement of your practice with a benefit to your service user. The HCPC audit practitioners (2.5% are chosen for audit during each renewal) and if they choose you for audit, you need to complete a CPD profile. Keeping a record of your CPD as you engage with it means that if chosen for an audit, this will not be a difficult or time-consuming process. Both the HCPC, British Psychological Society (BPS), and other bodies (e.g., American Psychological Association, APA) provide information on CPD, templates for keeping your records and information about CPD content, and processes. Make sure you are familiar with the requirements and keep records accordingly. If you are audited, then you will need to provide evidence of your CPD, so keep records and make sure that if you change employer, you can still access your CPD record and associated evidence. There are sample CPD profiles on the HCPC website where you can read about early, mid and senior sport psychology practitioner's CPD, and this can help you plan and keep records of your own CPD activities. The BPS, for example, also offers clear guidance stating that they expect members '[adopt a] structured and self-managed approach to further learning through actively engaging in CPD, maintaining a record of CPD and applying learning to professional practice' (BPS, 2012).

Your CPD and lifelong learning will need to apply to your own individual career progression. Consider any skills gaps you have. Think about development work that will help you improve your current or future practice and then identify CPD opportunities that align with these. CPD is not just about undertaking a course or activity, but it is about then using that course or activity to improve your practice, showing your ability to see the relevance of the course or CPD activity to your current or future practice. CPD is an outcome-based activity; it is not about just undertaking activities that add up to a certain number of hours. There is a huge scope for what you can include in your CPD record, for example, post qualification training courses, professional and peer supervision, attendance at conferences, engagement with research evidence, discussions with clients or employers, delivering or attending webinars, membership of an interest group, journal reading and reflection, data protection training, peer discussions, grant proposal writing, attending research seminars and general employer mandated training. The list is endless. What is key is that you can show how that activity or learning experience affected or informed your professional practice.

One way to add to your CPD record now would be to read the work of Quartiroli et al. (2021) who conducted a Delphi study investigating the future of continuing education and lifelong learning in sport psychology professionals. They provided a wealth of information on sport psychology professionals' views of the conceptualisation and operationalisation of continuing education and lifelong learning from an expert panel of 16 professionals in the field. The modes of delivery are altering rapidly and there is a rise in e-learning opportunities for sport and exercise professionals. Fostering a sense of personal responsibility for continued development during training will hopefully follow practitioners into their professional practice and result in them seeking more opportunities to continue to develop and practice in the most effective way possible.

Private practice or paid employment?

One of the biggest decisions to make as you go through your training is whether you are seeking employment at the end of it or whether you want to establish a private practice. The transition from trainee to qualified practitioner is sometimes difficult to navigate, so it is important to think early on about whether you see yourself working for someone else (a sporting body, a consultancy, an organisation or higher education institution) or whether you see yourself as your own boss with your own private practice.

Life Lived: Reflection on Choosing Private Practice or Self-Employment

Take 5 minutes right now and ponder the question of how you see yourself working once you're qualified. You might consider different elements, thinking about how the pieces of your working life will fit together like pieces of a jigsaw to give you the picture you want. From my (Lindsey's) experience, some elements I considered were how important being independent was to me, how many hours a week I wanted to work, and how those hours would fit around other commitments. For example, I did not want to work every weekend and Monday to Friday; I valued having at least one day a week that was free from work, no matter how much I enjoyed my job. Think about this: would you want to work fixed hours or to be flexible? Would you want to work weekends and evenings? Another important aspect I considered was that I enjoy being part of a team. I like the synergy of working with others and the comfort that can provide for referring clients or discussing any potential challenges of my work. In our post-Covid landscape, you will also need to think about whether you want to work remotely or incorporate remote sessions into your practice.

Other considerations that drew me to balance private practice with an academic role were elements such as paid holidays, sick pay, pension contributions, maternity pay, and security.

For me, many of the considerations that were key to my decision-making processes were around balancing work and home commitments and family life. I'd suggest you consider what the most important considerations are for you and your own individual circumstances and then use that to help you decide about the way you want your career to progress.

It is unlikely that you will get a job for life anymore as the career landscape has changed and of course there is the potential for redundancy in any employed position, but managing your career and having a clear picture of what it looks like is something you need. If you value stability and security above other aspects of working life, then private practice might not be for you because the cons of needing to source clients, advertise, find premises, set fees, and balance your books in combination with the risks of your business going under might easily outweigh the pros of being your own boss and having discretion over what work you take on, how you do it, and when. For others, that ability to set your own time and the flexibility that can come with private practice is very appealing. If private practice is not for you, then skip to the section on jobs and interviews, but if it is a possibility, then read on. Before you think about your own private practice, use some skills you have gained through your training and do some research. You can learn a lot from looking at other practitioners and the services they offer in their private practices. For example, do they have a broad offering or a niche area as a practitioner, and what might that mean to you? How do they advertise themselves and who comes up in the area when you do a general internet search? Take time searching for practitioners in your area and further afield. Consider the information provided on their website and note the elements you think work and those you do not. This type of research can help you think about your own unique selling point and how you want to market yourself as a practitioner to attract the clients that you want to work with. Of course, this is only one small step in establishing your practice and before you go any further, you will need to work on a sound business plan. Having a business plan will help you consider all the different elements of a potential start up and can help guard against some factors that can derail a business early on. There are various elements of a business plan, but you should start with basics like the name of your business, the legal structure, when you think your business will start. You will also need to consider whether your business is online only or will also operate within a physical space. Whichever option you will need an online presence, for example, a website, Twitter handle, Facebook page, and LinkedIn account. You will need to have a clear presence on these and to promote your business through them. Your next consideration would be your general business goals. That is what you aim to do and what services you offer. Your earlier research can help here as you will be required to think about what makes your business different from those that are already out there, what will make people choose your services rather than those of a different practitioner. Your business plan would also need to consider who your clients are going to be and an overview of the current market that you will work in. Using your earlier research, you can also include a competitor analysis in your business planning. Premises, pricing, competitors, potential risks, and how to mitigate against them and planning around how much income you'd need to generate to break even or make a profit are also considerations here. Although a business plan can be complex and will take you time, it will also make you consider all the elements of your potential private practice and the result will be clarity in your mind about where you see yourself and how your business will work. Your business plan should be a live document as it will change as your business grows, as you encounter different personal circumstances, or as it adapts to market changes.

On a positive note, there are many sources of help there for business planning and possibly the most comprehensive is Business Gateway (in the UK, for example). Their site provides a wealth of resources and information on starting a business, including a guide to creating a business plan and a template. They also offer a series of events, podcasts, video tutorials, and webinars to help you with your business start-up, for example, how to build an effective strategy to grow your business or digital marketing strategy. Use these resources that are available to you and learn from that repository of information to help create the business you want. Establishing a private practice requires business skills and you can develop these through engaging with resources available online.

For your business plan, you will need a vision of what you offer and how you want to describe and market that. Make sure that you are clear about what you do and what you are offering, because if you are not clear about that, then potential clients certainly will not be. You will also need clarity about how you work. For example, do you charge a certain amount for a block of sessions? Or do you charge a set hourly rate, or do you offer monthly support sessions to particular client groups? All these things need to be clear in your business planning and in your vision for your business. The way you describe yourself and how you highlight your qualifications, the modality you work in and your fees will also need to be clear in order for clients to consider contacting you to engage your services.

Your marketing strategy must clearly articulate your services, and you need to consider how clients will find you. Networking and word of mouth are excellent sources, but take advantage of other ways to advertise your business too. Offer to give talks, ask friends and colleagues to share your website; write articles or blog about your niche; use social media to spread the word.

List all the aspects that you'll need to consider, for example, your contracting, your intake forms, your fees, supervision, data storage, confidentiality issues, how you store client information, what you do if a client does not attend or cancels, other practitioners to refer to if a client presents who is outside your competency. The list goes on, but the concept is clear – establishing and running your own business is complex and you need to be sure that you are well equipped to manage that complexity before you jump in. If considering all these aspects is making you less sure about whether private practice is for you, then there are other options that are lower risk but still provide the opportunities that come with working as a practitioner for yourself. One option would be to take paid employment for some of your working time and balance that with building a private practice and another option would be setting up a practice with colleagues, perhaps one or two others whose areas of expertise complement your own.

Jobs and interviews

So, whether you feel private practice is not for you or whether you want to combine that with paid employment or just keep up to date with employability skills and preparedness searching for and being able to respond eloquently to questions at interview are key skills. While still training, you need to give thought to the jobs you might want in the future, identify the skills required for those, and ensure you are working towards them, building your CV appropriately. Use your time while training to gain experience on placements relevant to the type of work you want to go into. Speak to other practitioners about how they found employment and request advice on how they managed gaining paid work once they qualified. Do not underestimate the power of networking. Networking can be a vital source of information about upcoming jobs, giving you prior knowledge of what is about to hit the market. If you identify a job that you want to apply for, then you need to tailor your CV and cover letter appropriately. This is not easy, but submitting a generic CV and cover letter will not result in success. You need to show the potential employer that you are the candidate they want and that you have something extra that other candidates do not bring. We have suggested this advice numerous times during this chapter, but here it is again – do your research. Dive deep into any information you can find on the organisation that is advertising the post and look at their social media too. Having that information will help you fill out the application form better than just rushing through it without putting in the groundwork. Another possibility to consider is making a speculative job application to an organisation, even if they aren't currently recruiting. This type of speculative application is common in some sectors and can help you increase your connections and lead to voluntary experience, temporary or even permanent roles. Whether the role is advertised or you are taking a chance on their being something for you, putting time and effort into your CV and cover letter are imperative. These must be specific to the organisation you're applying to and will need to highlight the skills the organisation needs in their employees and showing what you can offer that could complement their existing skills base. Use information readily available online for tips on how to write your CV and cover letter things to avoid and examples of existing ones to provide inspiration.

If you're successful at getting shortlisted for an interview, then you need to prepare further. Some organisations require a presentation plus an interview, some use assessment centre type recruitment strategies and others hold group interviews or require you to submit pre-recorded responses to questions. By far the most common selection technique is the interview, and this is something that you can prepare for. Look through the job advert and identify the essential and desired job criteria. The job description and person specification are not just there to let you decide whether to apply for a job, they will guide the organisation's recruitment process, allowing a transparent selection process that is equitable, and you can use that in your own preparation. An example here would be that if the job specification states that candidates *are required to have the ability to work with accuracy and precision and to prescribed standards*, then think of a time when you have done that and use a competency-based response to demonstrate your ability. The recommended technique to use in your preparation and in the interview itself is the STAR technique. This is a method that you can use to respond to competency-based, behavioural and situational questions and if you follow this method, it will result in you providing clear, concise responses that highlight your abilities and use examples from your own experience. The STAR technique provides a framework for you so that you can respond with a clear narrative that makes it easy for the interviewer(s) to see what you have to offer. In its most basic form, the STAR acronym stands for:

Situation	Where you set the scene and outline the situation
Task	Where you explain the challenge or goal you were working on
Action	Where you explain the steps you took to overcome the challenge or meet the goal
Result	Where you outline the positive effects of your actions

At the interview you are trying to convince the panel that you are the best candidate, that you have more to offer than the other candidates and that you will be a good fit for their organisation. Use the research you did on the organisation and combine that with your responses. This is not the time to undersell yourself or be modest. Your STAR responses should focus on what you did personally, not as part of a group, so be careful with the terminology you use. You should also demonstrate how the actions you took resulted in positive outcomes – the effect of your actions. Wherever possible, you can quantify that using numbers or feedback and also make sure you emphasise the impact that had and why your outcome was important.

Mirroring the approach we recommend for your viva, write a list of potential questions suing examples of generic interview questions and questions that you have produced from the job advert and person specification. You should then prepare a response using the STAR technique. The more you use this technique, the more it will become habit and the easier you will find it. It is always a good idea to think about examples that show your ability to manage difficult situations or people and those that show your strengths.

Following the interview, it is good practice to note down the questions you were asked because these can help you reflect on your interview performance and to learn from it going forward. That means that even if you are unsuccessful, you have gained something from the experience that you can use.

Summary

This chapter has covered several key areas and we hope has provided some food for thought. The need for you to drive your own career, to reflect on your learning needs and seek development opportunities will help you to not only meet regulatory requirements but to become better practitioners. The world of work has changed and we all need to be focusing on ensuring we take the right opportunities at the right time that help us develop and meet our long-term goals. There are many considerations needed when contemplating your future career and how you would like it to unfold but key considerations for right now are the type of environment you see yourself working in, your values and whether you believe these will best be met within paid employment or establishing your own private practice. Both have strengths and challenges, and we encourage you to explore all opportunities available to you.

We have liftoff! If you have come to this stage, you are no longer a trainee!

Welcome to the work of applied psychology. We hope you thrive!

References

Abernethy, A. D., & Lancia, J. J. (1998). Religion and the psychotherapeutic relationship: Transferential and countertransferential dimensions. *The Journal of Psychotherapy Practice and Research*, *7*(4), 281.

Adá Lameiras, A., & Rodríguez-Castro, Y. (2021). The presence of female athletes and non-athletes on sports media Twitter. *Feminist Media Studies*, *21*(6), 941–958.

Amari, N. (2021). Social justice in counseling psychology practice: Actualizing the ethics of compassion. *Journal of Humanistic Psychology*, 00221678211039968. https://doi.org/10.1177/00221678211039968

American Psychological Association (2002). Ethical principles of psychologists and code of conduct. *American Psychologist*, *57*, 1060–1073.

American Psychological Association (2017). Ethical principles of psychologists and code of conduct. https://www.apa.org/ethics/code/ethics-code-2017.pdf

Andersen, M. B. (2000). *Doing sport psychology*. Human Kinetics.

Andersen, M. B. (2005). 'Yeah, I work with Beckham': Issues of confidentiality, privacy and privilege in sport psychology service delivery. *Sport & Exercise Psychology Review*, *1*(2), 3–13.

Andersen, M. B., & Brewer, B. W. (2000). When sport psychology consultants and graduate students are impaired: Ethical and legal issues in training and supervision. *Journal of Applied Sport Psychology*, *12*(2), 134–150. https://doi.org/10.1080/10413200008404219

Anderson, A. G., Knowles, Z., & Gilbourne, D. (2004). Reflective practice for sport psychologists: Concepts, models, practical implications, and thoughts on dissemination. *The Sport Psychologist*, *18*(2), 188–203.

Andersen, M. B., & Speed, H. D. (2011). The practitioner and client as storytellers: Metaphors and folktales in applied sport psychology practice. In D. Gilbourne & M. B. Andersen (Eds.), *Critical essays in applied sport psychology* (pp. 87–104). Human Kinetics.

Appuhamilage, U. (2012). Anti-discriminatory practices in counselling and psychotherapy.

Aravind, R., Gupta, S., & Ghayathri Swetha Kumari, R. A. (2022). A pilot study on emotional intelligence & its impact on pre-competitive anxiety: How does it operate in the non-WEIRD Indian sport context. *International Journal of Physiology, Nutrition and Physical Education*, *7*(1), 8–16.

Aoyagi, M. W., Portenga, S. T., Poczwardowski, A., Cohen, A. B., & Statler, T. (2012). Reflections and directions: The profession of sport psychology past, present, and future. *Professional Psychology: Research and Practice*, *43*(1), 32. https://doi.org/10.1037/a0025676

Ballantine Dykes, F., Postings, T., De Winter, A., & Crouch, A. (2017). *Counselling skills and studies*. SAGE Publications.

Barker, J., McCarthy, P., Jones, M., & Moran, A. (2011). *Single-case research methods in sport and exercise*. Routledge.

Barker, J. B., Mellalieu, S. D., McCarthy, P. J., Jones, M. V., & Moran, A. (2013). A review of single-case research in sport psychology 1997–2012: Research trends and future directions. *Journal of Applied Sport Psychology*, *25*(1), 4–32.

Barney, S. T., & Andersen, M. B. (2014). Mindful supervision in sport and performance psychology. In B. Cropley, & Z. Knowles (Eds.), *Reflective practice in sport and exercise sciences* (pp. 147–160). Routledge.

Bennett, R., & Oliver, J. E. (2019). *Acceptance and commitment therapy: 100 key points and techniques*. Routledge.

Bernard, J. M. (1997). The discrimination model. In C. E. Watkins, Jr. (Ed.), *Handbook of psychotherapy supervision* (pp. 310–327). John Wiley & Sons, Inc.

Bezanson, L. (2003) Career development: Policy, proof and purpose. Careers Education and Guidance.

Blodgett, A. T., Schinke, R. J., McGannon, K. R., & Fisher, L. A. (2015). Cultural sport psychology research: Conceptions, evolutions, and forecasts. *International Review of Sport and Exercise Psychology*, *8*(1), 24–43.

Bolton, G. (2010). *Reflective practice: Writing and professional development*. SAGE Publications.

Bolton, G. E., & Delderfield, R. (2018). *Reflective practice: Writing and professional development*. SAGE Publications.

Booth, W. C, Colomb, G. G.; Williams, J. M, Bizup, J., Fitzgerald, W. T. (2016). *The craft of research* (4th ed.). University of Chicago Press.

Borders, L. D., & Brown, L. L. (2022). *The new handbook of counselling supervision*. Taylor & Francis.

Bor, R., & Watts, M. (2017). *The trainee handbook: A guide for counselling and psychotherapy trainees* (4th ed.). SAGE Publications.

Bond, T. (2017). Guidelines for professional practice. In R. Bor & M. Watts (Eds.), *The trainee handbook: A guide for counselling and psychotherapy trainees* (4th ed.). SAGE Publications.

Bourdieu, P. (1990). *In other words: Essays toward a reflexive sociology*. Stanford University Press.

BPS (2012). CPD Policy. www.bps.org.uk/professional-development. Accessed 13 July 2023.

BPS (2019). Standards for the Accreditation of Masters and Doctoral programmes in sport and exercise psychology. Available at https://www.bps.org.uk/accreditation/education-providers

British Psychological Society (2015). *Guidelines on teaching and assessment of ethical competence in psychological education*. BPS.

BPS (2017). BPS practice guidelines. Available at https://doi.org/10.53841/bpsrep.2017.inf115

Bronfenbrenner, U., & Ceci, S. J. (1994). Nature-nuture reconceptualized in developmental perspective: A bioecological model. *Psychological Review*, *101*(4), 568.

Brown, T. N., Jackson, J. S., Brown, K. T., Sellers, R. M., Keiper, S., & Manuel, W. J. (2003). "There's no race on the playing field" Perceptions of racial discrimination among white and black athletes. *Journal of Sport and Social Issues*, *27*(2), 162–183.

Burgo, J. (2012). *Why do I do that? Psychological defence mechanisms and the hidden ways they shape our lives*. New Rise Press.

Butler, G. (1998). Clinical formulation. In A. S. Bellack & M. H. Bellak (Eds.), *Comprehensive clinical psychology* (pp. 1–24). Pergamon.

Cameron, R. (2020). *Working with difference and diversity in counselling and psychotherapy*. SAGE.

Campbell, D. T. (1963). Social attitudes and other acquired behavioural dispositions. In S. Koch (Ed.), *Psychology: A study of science* (vol. 6). McGraw-Hill.

Caudwell, J. (2017). Everyday sexisms: Exploring the scales of misogyny in sport. In D. Kilvington, & J. Price (Eds.), *Sport and discrimination*. Routledge. https://doi.org/10.4324/9781315638799

Castonguay, L. G., Eubanks, C. F., Goldfried, M. R., Muran, J. C., & Lutz, W. (2015). Research on psychotherapy integration: Building on the past, looking to the future. *Psychotherapy Research*, *25*, 365–382. https://doi.org/10.1080/10503307.2015.1014010

Chao, M. M., Takeuchi, R., & Farh, J. L. (2017). Enhancing cultural intelligence: The roles of implicit culture beliefs and adjustment. *Personnel Psychology*, *70*(1), 257–292.

Chungath, A. F., Sudhesh, N. T., Gupta, S., & Divekar, S. (2022). Efficacy of a video modeling and imagery-controlled trial intervention in a non-western adolescent population: A case study. *Case Studies in Sport and Exercise Psychology*, *6*(S1), S1–S24.

Costello, C. Y. (2005). *Professional identity crisis: Race, class, gender, and success at professional schools*. Vanderbilt University Press.

Cotterill, S. T., Schinke, R. J., & Thelwell, R. (2017). Writing manuscripts for case studies in sport and exercise psychology. *Case Studies in Sport and Exercise Psychology*, *1*(1), 1–3.

Cotterill, S., Weston, N., & Breslin, G. (2017). *Sport and exercise psychology: Practitioner case studies*. Wiley.

Cousins, S. (2019). *Overcoming everyday racism: Building resilience and well-being int eh face of discrimination and microaggressions*. Jessica Kingsley Publishers.

Cozolino, L. J. & Santos, E. N. (2014). Why we need therapy – and why it works: A neuroscientific perspective. *Smith College Studies in Social Work*, *84*(2–3), 157–177. https://doi.org/10.1080/00377317.2014.923630

Creaner, M. (2013). *Getting the best out of supervision in counselling and psychotherapy*. SAGE Publications.

Cropley, B., Knowles, Z., Miles, A., & Huntley, E. (2023). *Reflective practice in the sport and exercise sciences* (pp. 3–13). Routledge.

Dacre Pool, L., & P. Sewell. 2007. The key to employability: Developing a practical model of graduate employability. *Education+ Training*, *49*(4), 277–289. https://doi.org/10.1108/00400910710754435

Davis, D. E., DeBlaere, C., Owen, J., Hook, J. N., Rivera, D. P., Choe, E., ... & Placeres, V. (2018). The multicultural orientation framework: A narrative review. *Psychotherapy*, *55*(1), 89.

Deci, E. L., & Ryan, R. M. (2000). The "what" and "why" of goal pursuits: Human needs and the self-determination of behavior. *Psychological Inquiry*, *11*(4), 227–268. https://doi.org/10.1207/S15327965PLI1104_01

Dewey, J. (1938). *Logic: The theory of inquiry*. Holt, Rinehart and Winston.

Douglas, K., & Carless, D. (2009). Exploring taboo issues in professional sport through a fictional approach. *Reflective Practice*, *10*(3), 311–323. https://doi.org/10.1080/14623940903034630

Driscoll J. (1994). Reflective practice for practise. *Senior Nurse*, *13*, 47–50.

Driscoll, J. J. (2007). *Practising clinical supervision: A reflective approach for healthcare professionals* (2nd ed.). Bailliere Tindall.

Eccles, D. W., & Arsal, G. (2017). The think aloud method: what is it and how do I use it? *Qualitative Research in Sport, Exercise and Health*, *9*(4), 514–531.

Eells, T. D., Kendjelic, E. M., & Lucas, C. P. (1998). What's in a case formulation? Development and use of a content coding manual. *The Journal of Psychotherapy Practice and Research*, *7*(2), 144.

ESRC (2022). Framework for research ethics. https://www.ukri.org/councils/esrc/guidance-for-applicants/research-ethics-guidance/framework-for-research-ethics/

Eubank, M., & Hudson, J. (2013). The future of professional training for professional competence. *The Sport & Exercise Psychology Review*, *9*(1), 61–65.

Eubank, M., Nesti, M., & Cruickshank, A. (2014). Understanding high performance sport environments: Impact for the professional training and supervision of sport psychologists. *Sport and Exercise Psychology Review*, *10*(2), 30–37.

Eubank, M., & Tod, D. (2018). *How to become a sport and exercise psychologist*. Routledge.

Faris, A. & van Ooijen, E. (2012). *Integrative counselling and psychotherapy: A relational approach*. SAGE Publications.

Feltham, C., & Dryden, W. (2006) *Brief counselling: A practice integrative approach* (2nd ed.). Open University Press.

Fernández-Álvarez, H., Consoli, A. J., & Gómez, B. (2016). Integration in psychotherapy: Reasons and challenges. *American Psychologist*, *71*, 820–830. https://doi.org/10.1037/amp0000100

Finlayson, A. (2015). Reflective practice: has it really changed over time? *Reflective Practice*, *16*(6), 717–730. https://doi.org/10.1080/14623943.2015.1095723

Foltz, B. D., Fisher, A. R., Denton, L. K., Campbell, W. L., Speight, Q. L., Steinfeldt, J., & Latorre, C. (2015). Applied sport psychology supervision experience: A qualitative analysis. *Journal of Applied Sport Psychology*, *27*(4), 449–463. https://doi.org/10.1080/10413200.2015.1043162

Gardner, F., & Moore, Z. (2006). *Clinical sport psychology*. Human Kinetics.

Gayman, A. M., & Crossman, J. (2006). Referral practices: Are sport psychology consultants out of their league? *Athletic Insight: The Online Journal of Sport Psychology*, *8*, 1–12.

Gilmore, S., Wagstaff, C., & Smith, J. (2018). Sports psychology in the English Premier League: 'It feels precarious and is precarious.' *Work, Employment and Society*, *32*(2), 426–435. https://doi.org/10.1177/0950017017713933

Greenberg, L. S. (2004). Emotion–focused therapy. *Clinical Psychology & Psychotherapy: An International Journal of Theory & Practice*, *11*(1), 3–16.

Golann, S. E. (1969). Emerging areas of ethical concern. *American Psychologist, 24*(4), 454.

Goldman, A., & Gervis, M. (2021). "Women are cancer, you shouldn't be working in sport": Sport psychologists' lived experiences of sexism in sport. *The Sport Psychologist, 35*(2), 85–96.

Goldman, R. N., & Greenberg, L. S. (2015). *Case formulation in emotion-focused therapy: Co-creating clinical maps for change*. American Psychological Association.

Gupta, S., & Sudhesh, N. T. (2019). Grit, self-regulation and resilience among college football players: a pilot study. *International Journal of Physiology, Nutrition and Physical Education, 4*(1), 843–848.

Gupta, S. (2022). Reflect in and speak out: An autoethnographic study on race and the embedded sport psychology practitioner. *Case Studies in Sport and Exercise Psychology, 6*(S1), S1–S10.

Gupta, S., & Divekar, S. (2022). A symmetry or asymmetry: Reflecting upon realities of cultural practice in sport psychology. *Sport and Exercise Psychology Review, 17*(1), 60–72.

Hankes, D. M. (2012). Sport and performance psychology: Ethical issues. In S. M. Murphy (Ed.), *The Oxford handbook of sport and performance psychology*. Oxford Library of Psychology (2012; online ed., Oxford Academic, 21 November 2012), https://doi.org/10.1093/oxfordhb/9780199731763.013.0003. Accessed 6 June 2023.

Hanley, T., Cutts, L. A., & Scott, A. J. (2012). Where does all the research go? Reflections on supporting trainee-applied psychologists to publish their research. *Counselling Psychology Quarterly, 25*(3), 201–210.

Hartveit, M., Thorsen, O., Biringer, E., Vanhaecht, K., Carlsen, B. and Aslaksen, A. (2013). Recommended content of referral letters from general practitioners to specialised mental health care: A qualitative multi-perspective study. *BMC Health Services Research, 13*(1), 329. doi:10.1186/1472-6963-13-329

Hart, G. M., & Nance, D. (2003). Styles of counselor supervision as perceived by supervisors and supervisees. *Counselor Education and Supervision, 43*(2), 146–158.

Hawkins, P., & McMahon, A. (2020). *Supervision in the helping professions* (5th ed.). McGraw-Hill Education.

Hayes, S. C., Luoma, J. B., Bond, F. W., Masuda, A., & Lillis, J. (2006). Acceptance and commitment therapy: Model, processes and outcomes. *Behaviour Research and Therapy, 44*(1), 1–25.

Hayes, S. C., Strosahl, K. D., & Wilson, K. G. (2012). *Acceptance and commitment therapy: The process and practice of mindful change* (2nd ed.). Guilford Press.

HCPC (2016). Standards of conduct, performance, and ethics. https://www.hcpc-uk.org/globalassets/resources/standards/standards-of-conduct-performance-and-ethics.pdf

Hennink, M. M. (2013). *Focus group discussions*. Oxford University Press.

Henriksen, K., Storm, L. K., Stambulova, N., Pyrdol, N., & Larsen, C. H. (2019). Successful and less successful interventions with youth and senior athletes: Insights from expert sport psychology practitioners. *Journal of Clinical Sport Psychology, 13*(1), 72–94.

Hill, A. P., Mallinson-Howard, S. H., & Jowett, G. E. (2018). Multidimensional perfectionism in sport: A meta-analytical review. *Sport, Exercise, and Performance Psychology, 7*(3), 235.

Holder, T., & Winter, S. (2017). Experienced practitioners' use of observation in applied sport psychology. *Sport, Exercise, and Performance Psychology, 6*(1), 6.

Hope, T. (2004). *Medical ethics: A very short introduction*. OUP.

Horvath, S., & Röthlin, P. (2018). How to improve athletes' return of investment: Shortening questionnaires in the applied sport psychology setting. *Journal of Applied Sport Psychology, 30*(2), 241–248.

Hutter, R. I. V., Oldenhof-Veldman, T., & Oudejans, R. R. D. (2015). What trainee sport psychologists want to learn in supervision. *Psychology of Sport & Exercise, 16*, 101–109. https://doi.org/10.1016/j.psychsport.2014.08.003

Hutter, R. I., & Pijpers, J. R. (2020). Practitioner development: Adopting and adapting service delivery approaches. In D. Tod & M. Eubank (Eds.), *Applied sport, exercise, and performance psychology: Current approaches to help clients*. Routledge.

Hylton, K., & Lawrence, S. (2016). 'For your ears only!'Donald Sterling and backstage racism in sport. *Ethnic and Racial Studies, 39*(15), 2740–2757.

Inskipp, F., & Proctor, B. (2001). *Becoming a supervisor*. Cascade.

Jarvie, G. (2003). Sport, popular struggle and South African culture. In *Sport, racism and ethnicity* (pp. 138–148). Routledge.

Johnstone, L., & Dallos, R. (2013). Introduction to formulation. In *Formulation in psychology and psychotherapy* (pp. 1–17). Routledge.

Jowett, S. (2007). Interdependence analysis and the 3+ 1Cs in the coach-athlete relationship. In S. Jowett & D. Lavallee (Eds.), *Social psychology in sport* (pp. 15–27). Human Kinetics.

Juntunen, C. L., Crepeau-Hobson, F., Riva, M. T., Baker, J., Wan, S., Davis III, C., & Caballero, A. M. (2023). Centering equity, diversity, and inclusion in ethical decision-making. *Professional Psychology: Research and Practice*, *54*(1), 17.

Kamphoff, C. S., Gill, D. L., Araki, K., & Hammond, C. C. (2010). A content analysis of cultural diversity in the Association for Applied Sport Psychology's conference programs. *Journal of Applied Sport Psychology*, *22*(2), 231–245.

Kinsella, E. A. (2009). Professional knowledge and the epistemology of professional practice. *Nursing Philosophy*, *11*, 3–14.

Knowles, Z., & Gilbourne, D. (2010). Aspiration, inspiration, and illustration: Initiating debate on reflective practice writing. *The Sport Psychologist*, *24*, 504–520. https://doi.org/10.1123/tsp.24.4.504

Kolb, D. A. (1984). *Experiential learning: Experience as the source of learning and development* (Vol. 1). Prentice-Hall.

Krane, V. & Baird, S. M. (2005). Using ethnography in applied sport psychology. *Journal of Applied Sport Psychology*, *17*(2), 87–107.

Krathwohl, D. R. (2002). A revision of Bloom's taxonomy: An overview. *Theory into Practice*, *41*(4), 212–218. https://doi.org/10.1207/s15430421tip4104_2

Lago, C., & Smith, B. (2010). Anti-discriminatory practice revisited. In C. Lago & B. Smith (Eds.), *Anti-discriminatory practice in counselling and psychotherapy* (2nd edition). SAGE.

Mack, R. J., Breckon, J. D., O'Halloran, P. D., & Butt, J. (2019). Enhancing athlete engagement in sport psychology interventions using motivational interviewing: A case study. *The Sport Psychologist*, *33*(2), 159–168.

Martin, S. (2021). *The better boundaries workbook*. New Harbinger Publications.

Martin, E. A., Winter, S., & Holder, T. (2020). Land Ahoy! Guidelines for navigating the choppy waters of observation practice. *Journal of Sport Psychology in Action*, *11*(1), 34–44.

McCann, D. (2017). Supervision: Making it work for you. In R. Bor, & M. Watts (Eds.), *The trainee handbook: A guide for counselling and psychotherapy trainees*. SAGE Publications.

McCarthy, P., Gupta, S., & Burns, L. (2023). *Cognitive behaviour therapy in sport and performance: An applied practice guide*. Routledge.

McCarthy, P., & Jones, M. (Eds.). (2013). *Becoming a sport psychologist*. Routledge.

McCarthy, P., & Moffat, Z. (2023). *Counselling skills in applied sport psychology: Learning how to counsel*. Taylor & Francis.

McCarthy, P. J., & Moffat, Z. (2024). *Counselling skills in applied sport psychology: Learning how to counsel*. Routledge.

McDougall, M., Nesti, M., & Richardson, D. (2015). The challenges of sport psychology delivery in elite and professional sport: Reflections from experienced sport psychologists. *The Sport Psychologist*, *29*(3), 265–277.

McEwan, H. E., Tod, D., & Eubank, M. (2019). The rocky road to individuation: Sport psychologists' perspectives on professional development. *Psychology of Sport and Exercise*, *45*, Article e101542. https://doi.org/10.1016/j.psychsport.2019.101542

McIntosh, P. (1990). White privilege: Unpacking the invisible knapsack. *The Legislative Library of the Northwest Territories*.

Mearns, D. & Cooper, C. (2005) *Working at relational depth in counselling and psychotherapy*. SAGE Publications.

Messer, S. B. (1991). The case formulation approach: Issues of reliability and validity. *American Psychologist, 46*(12), 1348–1350. https://doi.org/10.1037/0003-066X.46.12.1348

Millward, L. (2012). Focus groups. *Research Methods in Psychology*, *4*, 411–438.

Milne, D. (2009). *Evidence-based clinical supervision. Principles and practice*. BPS Blackwell.
Mitić, P., Nedeljković, J., Bojanić, Ž., Franceško, M., Milovanović, I., Bianco, A., & Drid, P. (2021). Differences in the psychological profiles of elite and non-elite athletes. *Frontiers in Psychology*, *12*, 635651.
Moffat, Z. L., & McCarthy, P. J. (2023). Process reports in applied sport psychology: A tool for professional development. *Journal of Sport Psychology in Action*, 1–12. https://doi.org/10.1080/21520704.2023.2195813
Monasterio, E., Mei-Dan, O., Hackney, A. C., Lane, A. R., Zwir, I., Rozsa, S., & Cloninger, C. R. (2016). Stress reactivity and personality in extreme sport athletes: The psychobiology of BASE jumpers. *Physiology & Behavior*, *167*, 289–297.
Moran, A. (2013). *Sport and exercise psychology: A critical introduction*. Routledge.
Moore, Z. E. (2007). Critical thinking and the evidence-based practice of sport psychology. *Journal of Clinical Sport Psychology*, *1*(1), 9–22.
Moran, A. P., & Toner, J. (2017). *A critical introduction to sport psychology* (3rd ed.). Routledge.
Muse, K., & McManus, F. (2013). A systematic review of methods for assessing competence in cognitive–behavioural therapy. *Clinical Psychology Review*, *33*(3), 484–499. https://doi.org/10.1016/j.cpr.2013.01.010
Nagy, T. F. (2011). *Essential ethics for psychologists: A primer for understanding and mastering core issues*. American Psychological Association. https://doi.org/10.1037/12345-000
Nelson-Jones, R. (2006). *Human relationship skills: Coaching and self-coaching*. Routledge.
Nigam, T., Cameron, P. M., & Leverette, J. S. (1997). Impasses in the supervisory process: A resident's perspective. *American Journal of Psychotherapy*, *51*(2), 252–272.
Norcross, J. C. (2016). Integrative psychotherapy. In H. Friedman (Ed.), *Encyclopedia of mental health* (2nd ed., pp. 390–394). Academic Press.
Norcross, J. C., & Wampold, B. E. (Eds.). (2019). *Psychotherapy relationships that work. Volume 2: Evidence-based responsiveness* (3rd ed.). Oxford University Press.
O'Donohue, W. T. (2016). Oppression, privilege, bias, prejudice, and stereotyping: Problems in the APA code of ethics. *Ethics & Behavior*, *26*(7), 527–544.
O'Halloran, L., Littlewood, M., Richardson, D., Tod, D., & Nesti, M. (2018). Doing Descriptive phenomenological data collection in sport psychology research. *Sport in Society*, *21*(2), 302–313.
Palmer, M., Larkin, M., De Visser, R., & Fadden, G. (2010). Developing an interpretative phenomenological approach to focus group data. *Qualitative Research in Psychology*, *7*(2), 99–121.
Poczwardowski, A., Sherman, C. P., & Ravizza, K. (2004). Professional philosophy in the sport psychology service delivery: Building on theory and practice. *The Sport Psychologist*, *18*(4), 445–463.
Podlog, L., Heil, J., & Schulte, S. (2014). Psychosocial factors in sports injury rehabilitation and return to play. *Physical Medicine and Rehabilitation Clinics*, *25*(4), 915–930.
Poole, B. (2015). The rather elusive concept of 'doctorateness': A reaction to Wellington. *Studies in Higher Education*, *40*(9), 1507–1522.
Pope-Davis, D. B., Coleman, H. L. K., Liu, W., & Toporek, R. L. (2003). *Handbook of multicultural competencies in counseling and psychology*. SAGE.
Price, L., Deville, J., & Ashmore, F. (2021). A guide to developing a rural digital hub. *Local Economy*, *36*(7–8), 683-694. https://doi.org/10.1177/02690942221077575
Purcell, R., Gwyther, K., & Rice, S. M. (2019). Mental health in elite athletes: increased awareness requires an early intervention framework to respond to athlete needs. *Sports Medicine-Open*, *5*(1), 46.
Quartiroli, A., Etzel, E. F., Knight, S. M., & Zakrajsek, R. A. (2019). Self-care as key to others' care: The perspectives of globally situated experienced senior-level sport psychology practitioners. *Journal of Applied Sport Psychology*, *31*(2), 147–167.
Quartiroli, A., Wagstaff, C. R., Herms, M., & Kemmel, C. (2021). The future of continuing education and lifelong learning in sport psychology professionals: A Delphi study. *Professional Psychology: Research and Practice*, *52*(2), 173.
Quartiroli, A., Vosloo, J., Fisher, L., & Schinke, R. (2020). Culturally competent sport psychology: A survey of sport psychology professionals' perception of cultural competence. *The Sport Psychologist*, *34*(3), 242–253.

Rathod, S., Persaud, A., Naeem, F., Pinninti, N., Tribe, R., Eylem, O., … & Irfan, M. (2020). Culturally adapted interventions in mental health: Global position statement. *World Cultural Psychiatry Research Review*, *14*(1–2), 21–29.

Ratner, H., George, E., & Iveson, C. (2012). *Solution focused brief therapy: 100 key points and techniques*. Routledge.

Reeves, A., & Bond, T. (2021). *Standards and ethics for counselling in action*. SAGE Publications.

Rest, J. (1982). A psychologist looks at the teaching of ethics. *The Hastings Center Report*, *12*(1), 29–36.

Rest, J. & Narvaez, D. (1994). *Moral development in the professions: Psychology and applied ethics*. Psychology Press.

Rogers, C.R. (1957). The necessary and sufficient conditions for therapeutic personality change. *Journal of Consulting Psychology*, *21*(2): 95–103.

Rønnestad, M. H., Orlinsky, D. E., Schröder, T.A., Skovholt, T. M., & Willutzki, U. (2018). The professional development of counsellors and psychotherapists: Implications of empirical studies for supervision, training and practice. *Counselling and Psychotherapy Research*, *19*, 214–230. https://doi.org/10.1002/capr.12198

Rønnestad, M. H. & Skovholt, T. M. (2003). The journey of the counselor and therapist: Research findings and perspectives on professional development. *Journal of Career Development*, *30*, 5–44. https://doi.org/10.1177/089484530303000102

Rønnestad, M. H., & Skovholt, T. (2013). *The developing practitioner: Growth and stagnation of therapists and counselors*. Routledge.

Rosenberg, M. B. (2015). *Nonviolent communication: A language of life*. PuddleDancer Press.

Sarantakis, N. P. (2017). Reflections on an anti-discriminatory stance in psychotherapy. *Journal of Contemporary Psychotherapy*, *47*, 135–140.

Schein, E. H. (1980). Developing your career: Know your career anchors and develop your options.

Schinke, R. J., & Hanrahan, S. J. (2009). *Cultural sport psychology*. Human Kinetics.

Schinke, R. J., & McGannon, K. R. (2015). Cultural sport psychology and intersecting identities: An introduction in the special section.

Schwartz, S. H., & Bardi, A. (2001). Value hierarchies across cultures: Taking a similarities perspective. *Journal of Cross-Cultural Psychology*, *32*(3), 268–290.

Shapiro, E. L., & Ginzberg, R. (2003). To accept or not to accept: Referrals and the maintenance of boundaries. *Professional Psychology: Research and Practice*, *34*(3), 258–263. https://doi.org/10.1037/0735-7028.34.3.258

Sharp, L. A., & Hodge, K. (2011). Sport psychology consulting effectiveness: The sport psychology consultant's perspective. *Journal of Applied Sport Psychology*, *23*(3), 360–376.

Sharp, L. A, Hodge, K., & Danish, S. (2021). "I wouldn't want to operate without it": The ethical challenges faced by experienced sport psychology consultant's and their engagement with supervision. *Journal of Applied Sport Psychology*, *33*(3), 259–279, https://doi.org/10.1080/10413200.2019.1646838

Slater, A., & Tiggemann, M. (2010). "Uncool to do sport": A focus group study of adolescent girls' reasons for withdrawing from physical activity. *Psychology of Sport and Exercise*, *11*(6), 619–626.

Sly, D., Mellalieu, S. D., & Wagstaff, C. R. (2020). "It's psychology Jim, but not as we know it!": The changing face of applied sport psychology. *Sport, Exercise, and Performance Psychology*, *9*(1), 87–101.

Spalding, B., Grove, J., & Rolfe, A. (2019). An exploration of Black, Asian and Minority Ethnic counsellors' experiences of working with White clients. *Counselling and Psychotherapy Research*, *19*(1), 75–82.

Sudhesh, N. T., Sreenath, K., Gupta, S., Nair, D., & Avnit. (2021). Snehagram model of an applied psychosocial intervention approach among adolescents living with HIV/AIDS: A blueprint. *Institutionalised Children Explorations and Beyond*, *8*(1), 98–119.

Sue, D. W., Capodilupo, C. M., Torino, G. C., Bucceri, J. M., Holder, A., Nadal, K. L., & Esquilin, M. (2007). Racial microaggressions in everyday life: implications for clinical practice. *American Psychologist*, *62*(4), 271.

Sugarman, J. (2015). Neoliberalism and psychological ethics. *Journal of Theoretical and Philosophical Psychology*, *35*, 103–116. https://doi.org/10.1037/a0038960

Suiter, A. M., & Sarli, C. C. (2019). Selecting a journal for publication: Criteria to consider. *Missouri Medicine*, *116*(6), 461–465.

Sutton, S. (2007). Transtheoretical model of behaviour change. In S. Ayers, A. Baum, C. McManus, S. Newman, K. Wallston, J. Weinman, et al. (Eds.), *Cambridge handbook of psychology, health and medicine* (pp. 228–232). Cambridge University Press. doi:10.1017/CBO9780511543579.050

Swiller, H. I. (2011). Process groups. *International Journal of Group Psychotherapy*, *61*(2), 262–273.

Taylor, J., & Schneider, B. A. (1992). The sport-clinical intake protocol: A comprehensive interviewing instrument for applied sport psychology. *Professional Psychology: Research and Practice*, *23*(4), 318.

Thompson, A. (1990). *A guide to ethical practice in psychotherapy*. Wiley.

Tod, D. & Eubank, M. (2020). *Applied sport, exercise and performance psychology*. Routledge.

Tod, D., Hardy, J., Lavallee, D., Eubank, M., & Ronkainen, N. (2019). Practitioners' narratives regarding active ingredients in service delivery: Collaboration-based problem solving. *Psychology of Sport and Exercise*, *43*, 350–358. https://doi.org/10.1016/j.psychsport.2019.04.009

Tod, D., & Lafferty, M. E. (2020). Developing an integrated approach. In D. Tod & M. Eubank (Eds.), *Applied sport, exercise and performance psychology: Current approaches to helping clients*. Routledge.

Tolan, J., & Cameron, R. (2017). *Skills in person-centred counselling and psychotherapy* (3rd ed.). SAGE Publications.

Tudor, K. (2017). Person-centred therapy. In C. Feltham, T. Hanley, & L. A. Winter (Eds.), *The SAGE handbook of counselling and psychotherapy* (4th ed.). SAGE Publications.

Turner, M. (2022). *The rational practitioner: The sport and performance psychologist's guide to practicing rational emotive behaviour therapy*. Routledge.

Turner, M. (2023). *The rational practitioner: The sport and performance psychologist's guide to practising rational emotive behaviour therapy*. Routledge.

Turner, M. J., Aspin, G., Didymus, F. F., Mack, R., Olusoga, P., Wood, A. G., & Bennett, R. (2020). One case, four approaches: The application of psychotherapeutic approaches in sport psychology. *The Sport Psychologist*, *34*(1), 71–83.

Turner, M. J., Jones, M. V., & Wood, A. G. (Eds.). (2023). *Applying cognitive behavioural therapeutic approaches in sport*. Routledge.

Uphill, M. A., & Hemmings, B. (2017). Vulnerability: Ripples from reflections on mental toughness. *The Sport Psychologist*, *31*, 299–307. https://doi.org/10.1123/tsp.2016-0034

Uphill, M. A., McCarthy, P. J., & Jones, M. V. (2009). Getting a grip on emotion regulation in sport. *Advances in applied sport psychology: A review*, 162–194.

Valentino, A.L., LeBlanc, L.A. & Sellers, T.P. (2016). The benefits of group supervision and a recommended structure for implementation. *Behavior Analysis in Practice* 9, 320–328. https://doi.org/10.1007/s40617-016-0138-8

van Ooijen, E. (2013). *Clinical supervision made easy* (2nd ed.). PCCS Books.

Van Raalte, J.L., & Andersen, M.B. (2000). Supervision I: From models to doing. In M.B. Andersen (Ed.), *Doing sport psychology* (pp. 153–165). Human Kinetics.

Van Raalte, J. L. (2010). Referring clients to other professionals. In S. J. Hanrahan and M. B. Andersen (Eds.), *Routledge handbook of applied sport psychology: A comprehensive guide for students and practitioners* (pp. 205–213). Routledge.

Vealey, R. S., Cooley, R., Nilsson, E., Block, C., & Galli, N. (2019). Assessment and the use of questionnaires in sport psychology consulting: An analysis of practices and attitudes from 2003 to 2017. *Journal of Clinical Sport Psychology*, *13*(4), 505–523.

Wagstaff, C. R., & Burton-Wylie, S. (2018). Organizational culture in sport: A conceptual, definitional, and methodological review. *Sport & Exercise Psychology Review*, *14*(1), 32–52.

Watson, J. C., Lubker, J. R., & Van Raalte, J. (2011). Problems in reflective practice: Self-bootstrapping versus therapeutic supervision. In D. Gilbourne, & M. B. Andersen (Eds.), *Critical essays in applied sport psychology* (pp. 157–172). Human Kinetics.

Weerasekera, P. (1996). Multiperspective case formulation: A step towards treatment integration. Krieger Publishing Company.

Weick, K. E. (1984). Small wins: Redefining the scale of social problems. *The American Psychologist, 39*(1), 40–49. https://doi.org/10.1037/0003-066X.39.1.40

West, J. (2020). Research ethics in sport and exercise science. In R. Iphofen (Ed.), *Handbook of research ethics and scientific integrity*. Springer.

Wheeler, S., & Richards, K. (2007). The impact of clinical supervision on counsellors and therapists, their practice and their clients. A systematic review of the literature. *Counselling and Psychotherapy Research, 7*(1), 54–65. https://doi.org/10.1080/14733140601185274

Wisker, G., Highman, L., Spronken-Smith, R., & Waghorne, J. (2022). Across time and space: Examiner and candidate experiences of online doctoral vivas. *Innovations in Education and Teaching International, 59*(2), 131–141.

Yalom, I. D., & Leszcz, M. (2020). *The theory and practice of group psychotherapy*. Basic Books.

Yorke, M., & Knight, P. (2007). Evidence-informed pedagogy and the enhancement of student employability. *Teaching in Higher Education, 12*(2), 157–170. https://doi.org/10.1080/13562510701191877

Zarbo, C., Tasca, G. A., Cattafi, F., & Compare, A. (2016). Integrative psychotherapy works. *Frontiers in Psychology, 6*, article 2021. https://doi.org/10.3389/fpsyg.2015.02021

Index

Note: *Italicized* and **bold** page numbers refer to figures and tables.

For Product Safety Concerns and Information please contact our EU representative GPSR@taylorandfrancis.com
Taylor & Francis Verlag GmbH, Kaufingerstraße 24, 80331 München, Germany

www.ingramcontent.com/pod-product-compliance
Ingram Content Group UK Ltd.
Pitfield, Milton Keynes, MK11 3LW, UK
UKHW050233200926
475702UK00020B/3000

* 9 7 8 1 0 3 2 4 3 4 1 7 9 *